THE DISCOURSE OF THE BAVLI
Language, Literature, and Symbolism

SOUTH FLORIDA STUDIES IN THE HISTORY OF JUDAISM

Edited by
Jacob Neusner
William Scott Green, James Strange
Darrell J. Fasching, Sara Mandell

Number 34
The Discourse of the Bavli
Language, Literature, and Symbolism

by
Jacob Neusner

THE DISCOURSE OF THE BAVLI
Language, Literature, and Symbolism

Five Recent Findings

by

Jacob Neusner

Scholars Press
Atlanta, Georgia

THE DISCOURSE OF THE BAVLI
Language, Literature, and Symbolism

©1991
University of South Florida

Publication of this book was made possible by a grant from the Tisch Family Foundation, New York City. The University of South Florida acknowledges with thanks this important support for its scholarly projects.

Library of Congress Cataloging in Publication Data

Neusner, Jacob, 1932-
    The discourse of the Bavli : language, literature, and symbolism :
five recent findings / by Jacob Neusner.
    p.   cm. — (South Florida studies in the history of Judaism ;
no. 34)
    Includes bibliographical references and index.
    ISBN 1-55540-650-5 (acid-free paper)
    1. Talmud—Language, style. 2. Talmud—Sources. 3. Tosefta—
Comparative studies. 4. Talmud—Comparative studies. I. Title.
II. Series: South Florida studies in the history of Judaism ; 34.
BM501.N46 1991
296.1'2506—dc20   91-35151
                                  CIP

Printed in the United States of America
on acid-free paper

Contents

Preface

The Bavli, or Talmud of Babylonia, defines in words – what is said, how things are said – the entire social existence of Israel, the Jewish people. From the time the document was formed until our own day, for the faithful of the Judaism that found in the Bavli the canon of law and theology, all decisions appealed to the authority of the Torah, written and oral, of which the Bavli forms the authoritative representation. What makes that document of the seventh century A.D. of special interest, therefore, is its power to show how, through words, intellectuals defined a world, one that, as a matter of fact, others later on continued through words to recreate.

The framers of the Bavli – as I shall point out in the Epilogue – did not spell out everything, rather, they gave signals of how, if you wanted to spell things out, you could on your own do so. So they opened the doors of learning to make place for all to come, learning serving then as an active and a transitive verb, with discovery the synonym for learning. These notes – signals of how a moving argument would be reconstructed, how reason might be recapitulated – were few, perhaps not the eight notes of our octave, but not an infinite repertoire of replicable sounds either. But the medium – notes to the music – is only secondary. Their primary insight into how civilization as they proposed to frame it should be shaped lay in another matter altogether. It had to do with their insistence upon the urgency of clear and vigorous and rigorous thought, the priority of purpose to argument, the demand for ultimate seriousness about things to be critically examined. Through practical reasoning and applied logic, they formed the chains to link mind to mind, past to future, through a process that anyone could enter – and no one, once in, would leave. Understanding precisely how these writers accomplished so remarkable a goal – to write a book that would define worlds they could not imagine, establish the social order under circumstances they could not envision, define culture amid cultures they could never have grasped – defines a task of considerable interest. And that is especially so for those of us who find insight in the character of writing, the quality of the formation of thought in words and the framing of words in such a way as to change worlds. Using a current word, "discourse," to describe what I mean here to illuminate for the document at hand serves to signal to a broad audience what I conceive to be at stake, in the realm of general intelligibility, in an arcane and recondite piece of writing.

Since few pieces of writing have exercised the power that the Bavli did and does, anyone who wants to know about how language affects the social order will grasp the importance of studies of how discourse takes place in this document. But by its nature, the Bavli is not an easily accessible writing, and my studies on it take the form of rather technical monographs. In these mental experiments, a single, rather simple proposition is set forth through sizable abstracts of the primary document, analyzed in a manner meant to test the proposition at hand. These laboratory reports are addressed to a small circle of others who share the questions that motivate my study, questions of the study of text, context, and matrix, aimed at the accurate description, analysis, and interpretation of writings that stand for and represent a religious system in its social setting. Most of the people who study these same documents bring quite different agenda of questions; they study for different reasons, asking about different matters, and finding out different things. And most of the people who ask the kinds of questions I bring to the Bavli do not study the Bavli. To bridge the gap between the document and the people who, when given access to it, find special interest in it, I recast into brief and I hope readable essays the results of long and (to a fairly sizable audience) not very readable research reports in monographic form.

In the five studies summarized here I have asked some fairly fundamental questions.

First, I begin with a very simple fact that the Bavli is written in two languages, Hebrew and Aramaic. So I ask, when this bilingual document uses one of its two languages, what does the language choice signal about the program and intention of its compilers? The answer to that question bears important implications for the debate on the intertextual or intratextual character of the rabbinic literature, favoring the latter classification.

Second, I have asked how, looking backward, the framers of the Bavli reshaped all of the prior writings that they inherited and transmitted onward to us. I maintain that a variety of "talmuds" – systematic commentaries, formed out of applied reason and practical logic, to received compilations accorded the status of Oral Torah, can have emerged, serving other documents besides the Mishnah, which "the

Talmud(s)" treat as their focus. In this way I show how fundamental choices on the theology and law of Judaism were made by the compilers of the principal document.

To underline that choices were made by the Bavli's framers, and that these choices differed from those made by their predecessors, I proceeded, third, to compare the Tosefta's and the Bavli's authors' theory of Mishnah commentary. I found out that not only are the commentaries to the Mishnah different, which is hardly surprising, but that both commentaries – the Tosefta's, the Bavli's – exhibit fixed differences from one another. What this means is that in each case the commentaries appealed to well-crafted and carefully defined programs of exegesis and interpretation.

The fourth and fifth papers turn from studies of the literary traits of the Bavli to comparative studies. In the fourth paper I address the simple fact that we have evidence about ancient Judaism in two distinct forms: written and iconic. So I undertake the comparison of writing to nonverbal symbols in Judaic settings in antiquity. I pursue a very simple question: Do the symbols given expression in writing and those given expression in graphic form, for example, synagogue art, correspond? The answer raises a variety of new questions, of course, but also settles some old ones as well.

The work of comparison yields the fifth paper as well. In various researches on the philosophical character of the Mishnah, I have shown that the Mishnah's authorship appealed to a form of logic of intelligible discourse that appeals to generally accepted philosophical modes of thought in the ancient world.[1] In my accounts of the various logics of intelligible discourse that govern in the writings of the Judaism of the Dual Torah, furthermore, I have shown that the Mishnah's mode of coherent discourse competes with other modes.[2] Not only so, but I have demonstrated that that mode of thought is reshaped in important ways in the later writings in succession to the Mishnah. So the fifth paper

---

[1]*Rabbinic Political Theory: Religion and Politics in the Mishnah* (Chicago, 1991: University of Chicago Press); *The Economics of the Mishnah* (Chicago, 1989: University of Chicago Press); and *Judaism as Philosophy. The Method and Message of the Mishnah* (Columbia, 1991: University of South Carolina Press). These studies rest on *The Philosophical Mishnah* (Atlanta, 1989: Scholars Press for Brown Judaic Studies, Vols. I-IV). The work reached its conclusion in *The Transformation of Judaism. From Philosophy to Religion* (Champaign, 1991: University of Illinois Press).

[2]These studies were set forth in the following items: *The Making of the Mind of Judaism* (Atlanta, 1987: Scholars Press for Brown Judaic Studies), and *The Formation of the Jewish Intellect. Making Connections and Drawing Conclusions in the Traditional System of Judaism* (Atlanta, 1988: Scholars Press for Brown Judaic Studies).

compares the logic of cogent discourse characteristic of the Mishnah with that paramount in Sifra and shows how the authors of the latter both criticized but also recast and revalidated that of the former. Since, it is clear, the results of these monographs aim at a generally shared and broadly intelligible agenda of problems of the continuity of culture, I undertook to present those results in a more readable form than the original monographs are given.

The epilogue in conclusion is a more philosophical statement of what I think is at stake in the work I do. It was my address at "The Brain Event," presented by the University of South Florida Office of Provost and *The Tampa Tribune* on Monday, March 4, at the USF Art Museum; I am glad to share in my University's program of public service.

So, in all, recognizing that interest in my principal results considerably transcends the limited circles of those with the time and knowledge to read, in detail, the documents on which I have worked, I have engaged in a long-term project of *haute vulgarisation* of my scholarly results for colleagues in other fields. Here I summarize and abbreviate some of the findings of five of my recent monographs and books. In that way I accord access to the propositions relevant to the interests of colleagues in Religious Studies who do not specialize in Judaism, and to those who concentrate on Judaism but not on the Talmudic literature on which I work. I have been working on the Talmud of Babylonia, beginning with its characteristics as writing: its rhetoric, logic, and topical program. These monographs focus upon literary analysis in the inquiry into modes of theological (in this context: normative religious) thinking. The books that I summarize are as follows:

1. *Language as Taxonomy. The Rules for Using Hebrew and Aramaic in the Babylonian Talmud.* Atlanta, 1990: Scholars Press for South Florida Studies in the History of Judaism.
2. *How the Bavli Shaped Rabbinic Discourse.* Atlanta, 1991: Scholars Press for South Florida Studies in the History of Judaism.
3. *The Bavli That Might Have Been: The Tosefta's Theory of Mishnah-Commentary Compared with that of the Babylonian Talmud.* Atlanta, 1990: Scholars Press for South Florida Studies in the History of Judaism.
4. "The Two Vocabularies of Symbolic Discourse in Judaism," summarizing *Theology and Symbol in Formative Judaism.* Minneapolis, 1991: Fortress Press.
5. "Re-presenting the Torah: Sifra's Rehabilitation of Taxonomic Logic and the Judaic Conception of How through the Torah We Enter The Mind of God," summarizing *Uniting the Dual Torah: Sifra and the*

Problem of the Mishnah. Cambridge and New York, 1990: Cambridge University Press.

I enjoy my University's support in providing funds for research expenses and express my thanks for it. I have enormously enjoyed the collegiality of my new situation, the Department of Religious Studies, whom I have found stimulating and engaging, engaged by their own constructive and fecund scholarship, therefore able also to share in mine.

JACOB NEUSNER

Martin Buber Gast
Professor für Judaistik　　　　　　　*Graduate Research Professor*
JOHANN WOLFGANG　　　　　　*of Humanities and Religious Studies*
GOETHE-UNIVERSITÅT　　　　　UNIVERSITY OF SOUTH FLORIDA
FRANKFURT AM MAIN, GERMANY　　　　　　　　　　TAMPA

735 Fourteenth Avenue Northeast
St. Petersburg, Florida 33701 1413 USA

July 28, 1991, my fifty-ninth birthday

1

Language as Taxonomy: The Rules for Using Hebrew and Aramaic in the Babylonian Talmud

A document that utilizes two or more languages but is addressed to a single audience conveys to its readers information not only through what is said but also through the language in which a message is set forth. In the Talmud of Babylonia the choice of language carried in particular a message, one of classification. A reader or listener[1] who read or heard Aramaic immediately knew what kind of discourse was underway, and when Hebrew was used, the reader or listener forthwith understood the status and purpose of the discourse that was then subject to representation. The selection of one language over another gave the signal that sayings, and, more to the point, whole paragraphs and even long and sustained passages, in one language were to be classified in one way, sayings or entire compositions in another, in a different way. And that taxonomic function served by the choice of language bore no relationship to the circumstance of time, place, personality, let alone the original words that were said; the same named speakers are given statements in two languages, depending upon the purpose served by a given statement within the unfolding of discourse.

---

[1]The distinction is a valid one but forms no part of the argument of this essay. It is clear that a great many things were memorized within the process of formulating and transmitting the Bavli; it is equally clear that, at a given point, things were written down. I am not sure where or why what was formulated orally was written down. My impression is that the document was written down very early in the process of its composition, and that people who formulated composites drew upon materials that came to them through the memories of official memorizers. But that problem of the literary history of the Bavli is not under study in these pages.

In the Talmud of Babylonia what is said in Hebrew is represented as authoritative and formulates a normative thought or rule. What is said in Aramaic is analytical and commonly signals an argument and formulates a process of inquiry and criticism. That is how language serves a taxonomic purpose: Hebrew is the language of the result, Aramaic, of the way by which the result is achieved; Hebrew is the formulation of the decision, Aramaic, of the work of deliberation. Each language serves to classify what is said in that language, and we always know where we stand, in a given process of thought and the exposition of thought, by reference to the language that is used at that particular place in the sustained discourse to which we are witness. That fixed rule, utilizing language for the purpose of classifying what is said in that language, characterizes only one document in the canon of Judaism, and that is, the Talmud.[2] All other canonical documents are monolingual, ordinarily in Hebrew,[3] so that, where Aramaic occurs, it is generally a brief allusion to something deemed external to what the author wishes to say in his own behalf, for example, a citation of everyday speech, invariably assumed to be in Aramaic.

While subject to much obfuscation, in fact the Talmud of Babylonia is an accessible document, because its authors followed rules, which we can discern and employ in our reading of this writing. The rule of linguistic preference is that where Hebrew is used, it is ordinarily for the purpose of setting forth facts, deriving from authoritative writings, on the one side, or authoritative figures, on the other. Where Aramaic is used, it is ordinarily for the purpose of analyzing facts, though it may serve, also, to set forth cases that invariably are subordinated to the analytical task. The simple fact that in the pages of the Bavli the same figures "speak" in both Hebrew and Aramaic proves that at stake is not merely "how people said things," let alone *ipsissima verba;* if Yohanan in the Land of Israel or Samuel and Rab in Babylonia are sometimes represented as speaking in Hebrew and other times in Aramaic, the function served by using the two languages, respectively, must form the point of inquiry into how and why these languages are used where and

---

[2]I refer, of course, to the Talmud of Babylonia, but the same utilization of language for classification can be shown to characterize the Talmud of the Land of Israel; but that forms a separate arena for inquiry and has to be dealt with in its its own terms.

[3]Obviously within the canon of the Judaism of the Dual Torah some of the translations of the Hebrew Scriptures into Aramaic, or Targumim, are canonical; others are not. The standing of other Aramaic writings, such as Sefer Harazim or Megillat Taanit, remains to be worked out. But if they are canonical within the Judaism of the Dual Torah, then they, too, are monolingual. That fact makes all the more striking the bilingual character of the Bavli (and Yerushalmi).

when they make their appearance.[4] The choice of language clearly conveys part of the message that the authorship means to set forth, signalling to the reader precisely what is happening at any given point. Along these same lines, a story, told in Aramaic, yields a formulation of a general rule or conclusion, presented in (Middle) Hebrew. Once more, the function of the language that is chosen, within the same sustained unit of thought, clearly is to make one thought in one way, another thought in a different way.

Now to make the matter quite concrete: the Talmud of Babylonia contains passages written in two kinds of Hebrew, biblical and Mishnaic (or Middle), and also Aramaic of various classifications. When someone sat down to produce a composition for inclusion in that document, how did he know which language to use? If that writer had received from earlier generations a piece of writing, such as the Hebrew Scriptures ("Old Testament," "Written Torah") or the Mishnah, or a teaching formulated in the name of a prior authority or school, what rules told that writer which language to use for what purpose? These are the questions that motivate this inductive survey of the languages of Bavli tractate Shebuot.

When I speak of "a language," I mean not word choice or fixed formulations that may flow from one language to another, for example, an Aramaism in a Hebrew sentence or a Hebrew formula in an Aramaic one. By language I mean the governing framework in which words and sentences find cogency and make sense: convey meaning. "Language" – Hebrew or Aramaic – here refers to the basic sentences and paragraphs in which a whole thought is expressed. These invariably obey the rules of syntax and grammar, follow the rhetorical rules, of one language and not some other. If Aramaic is the paramount language, then even though Hebrew occurs, it will always bear marks that it is being quoted for a purpose dictated by the discourse that is in Aramaic: Hebrew will be illustrative, Aramaic, determinative. If the language of a passage is

---

[4]Other approaches to the problem dealt with here have taken at face value the reliability and veracity of the attributions of sayings to specific figures and so have claimed, for example, that Hebrew is used early, Aramaic, later on. The simple fact that to early figures are assigned sayings in both Hebrew and Aramaic makes such a theory implausible, and the further fact that whether or not a given authority really said what is assigned to him forms part of the critical agenda of two hundred years of scholarship makes it possible to dismiss as merely gullible these alternative explanations. If we do not know that a given authority really said what is assigned to him, then no narrowly "historical" explanation is feasible, since such an explanation proves simply uncritical. But, as we shall see, since the same authority may set forth statements in either language, and that is so whether early or late, the "historical" explanations on the face of it may be dismissed.

Hebrew, then the occurrence of an Aramaic phrase, for example, a sentence that is represented as a quotation of what someone says in everyday parlance, will not affect the grammar and syntax (not to mention the word choices) of the whole. Ordinarily, therefore, the smallest rhetorical signals will wholly conform to the conventions of one language, and when the other language occurs, it is by way of quotation, on the one side, or utilization of technical terms, on the other. For example, a sentence wholly written in Aramaic may quote a verse of Scripture in biblical Hebrew, or a sentence of the Mishnah in Middle Hebrew. But the structure of that sentence will be in Aramaic. That is not an example of bi- or multilingual writing at all, any more than using *terminus technicus*, rather than technical term, would have made the penultimate sentence a mixture of Latin and American. It is a sentence in American, using a Latin phrase.

There are very few mysteries, as a matter of fact, in the ways in which discourse is advanced through the choice of one or another of the languages that come into play here. Where we find Hebrew, the language of quotation, it will commonly signal one of three facts, which, through the very choice of language, our author wishes to tell us:

1. A passage is from the Hebrew Scriptures.
2. A passage is from the Mishnah or the Tosefta (or from a corpus of sayings out of which the Tosefta as we have it was selected; for our purposes that is a distinction that makes no difference).
3. A statement is authoritative and forms a normative formulation, a rule to be generalized and obeyed even where not from the Mishnah or Scripture, but from a named or anonymous authority of the time of the document itself.

While biblical Hebrew differs from Middle or Mishnaic Hebrew, the use, in the Bavli, of either kind of Hebrew invariably is the same. It is to set forth a normative statement. The fact that sayings of sages will be (re)formulated into the same Hebrew as the Mishnah's conveys the further claim, of course, that those sayings enjoy the same standing and authority as what is in Scripture or the Mishnah, and that allegation clearly is signaled by the choice of Hebrew for, for example, something said by Samuel, Rab, or Yohanan. That the issue is one of authority and standing of what is said is furthermore demonstrated by a rhetorical signal, which assigns to the authority of a professional memorizer of traditions, or Tannaite master, a given formulation. Whenever we find that signal in any of its variations, all of them formed out of the same Hebrew letters, T and N, with a Y or an A (aleph), what follows invariably is in (Middle) Hebrew.

And that is the fact, whether the authority to whom the saying then is assigned is a figure known, also, in the pages of the Mishnah, or a named figure who flourished long after the closure of the Mishnah, such as Rab, Samuel, or Yohanan. As a matter of fact, authorities of our document generally supposed to have flourished fairly late in the formative history of the writing, such as Ashi or Kahana, will not uncommonly instruct the Tannaite colleague of their own time and place to formulate matters in one way rather than in some other, and when that is done, what follows, once more, always is marked TNY or TNA and always is in Middle Hebrew. The upshot is that Hebrew is used to signal that a thought forms a normative statement.

These remarks have now to be made concrete, and, for that purpose, I give three samples of how a single passage conforms to the simple rules that I have announced. The Mishnah paragraph is given in boldface type, Aramaic in italics, Hebrew in regular type. And the rest follows. The first is the simplest. The point of the composition, towards which the author is aiming, is in Aramaic. The sustaining voice, asking, answering, probing, speaks in Aramaic. The facts that are under discussion are in Hebrew; these facts are identified as to source, for example, Mishnah, Tosefta, Scripture, being set off, as Green insists, from the document's authors' utilization of them; our authors do not allude to a shared corpus of facts or truths, though they obviously take for granted the omnipresence of such a corpus; they explicitly and articulately cite items out of that corpus, and, as we shall now see, when they shift language, it serves the purpose of quotation marks or footnotes (media for signification not available to the authors who either formulated and transmitted their composition or composite orally, or who wrote things down, or who found some intermediary medium for the fixed preservation of their thought, and the distinctions make no difference so far as the taxonomic power of language is concerned). The first example, and the simplest, derives from Bavli Bekhorot 4:1-2:

IV.1   A   **[If] a blemish appeared in it during its first year, it is permitted to keep it for the whole twelve months. [If a blemish appeared in it] after its first year, it is permitted to keep it only for thirty days:**

      B   *The question was raised: What is the sense of this passage? When it says,* **[If] a blemish appeared in it during its first year, it is permitted to keep it for the whole twelve months,** *does it mean,* **and an additional thirty days as well? Or perhaps the sense is, [If] a blemish appeared in it during its first year, it is permitted to keep it for the whole twelve months –** *but no longer, and* **[If a blemish appeared in it] after its first year, it is permitted to keep it only for thirty days?**

      C.   *Come and take note, for it has been taught on Tannaite authority:*

D.   At this time [after the destruction of the Temple] a firstling, so long as it is not fit to show to a sage [that is, before there is a blemish on it, to be shown to the sage for a decision on whether it is transient or permanent], may be kept two or three years. Once it is fit to be shown to a sage, if a blemish appeared on it during the first year, he may keep it the entire twelve months. If it was after its first year, he is not allowed to keep it even a single day, even a single hour, but on grounds of restoring what is lost to the owner, rabbis have said that he is permitted to keep the animal for thirty days [T. Bekh. 3:2A-C].

E.   *And still the question is to be raised: Does this mean,* thirty days after the first year, *or does it mean* thirty days before its first year is over?

F.   *Come and take note:* If a blemish appeared on the beast on the fifteenth day within its first year, we complete it for fifteen days after its first year.

G.   *That proves the matter.*

H.   *It further supports the position of R. Eleazar, for* R. Eleazar has said, "They assign to the animal thirty days from the moment at which the blemish appeared on the beast."

I.   *There are those who say,* said R. Eleazar, "How do we know in the case of a firstling that if a blemish appeared in its first year, we assign to it thirty days after its year? 'You shall eat it before the Lord your God year by year' (Deut. 15:20) [but not in the year in which its blemish has appeared]. Now what is the span of days that is reckoned as a year? You have to say it is thirty days."

J.   *An objection was raised:* If a blemish appeared on the beast on the fifteenth day within its first year, we complete it for fifteen days after its first year. *That indicates, then, that we complete the thirty days, but we do not give it thirty full days after the first year, and that would appear to refute the position of R. Eleazar!*

K.   *It does indeed refute his position.*

The reason the example of how the rule that I have defined does its work is blatant and – at this stage – merely formal. Where a received document is cited, here, the Mishnah, it is in Hebrew. The language of citation is in Aramaic, so A, B, C, D alternate within that fixed, formal rule. A poor framing of the rule that is implicit then is that we quote in Hebrew, but talk in Aramaic.

But of course recourse to such formalities hardly supplies the key. For the question is asked properly only when we inquire, what guidance do we gain – automatically and implicitly – when we find words framed in Aramaic, and what does the use of Hebrew tell us? The answer cannot concern only the pedantry involved in knowing what comes from where. Who (other than a mere scholar) would care? The document as a whole is a sustained labor of applied reason and practical logic; it makes important points not only discretely but through the formation of the whole. Its authorship over and over again pursues a single intellectual program, which means that, at every detail, the intellectuals who produced this remarkable document wished to make the same point(s), just as their predecessors did in the treatment of the myriad of details treated in the Mishnah.[5]

In point of fact, the composition means to pursue a problem, which is formulated at B. And the operative language used in the formulation of the problem is Aramaic, pure and simple. We note at E that fixed formulas in Hebrew are preserved, but Hebrew is not the language of the sentence, any more than, in an American legal brief, the occurrence of a phrase or sentence in Latin signals that the author is writing in Latin; these are conventions of rhetoric or technical terms, nothing more. The continuity and coherence derive from what is said in Aramaic, and that is the case throughout. What we are given in Hebrew then are the facts, the received and established data. When Aramaic appears, it is the voice of the framer of the passage. Since, as a matter of fact, that voice is monotonous and ubiquitous, we realize that it is "the Talmud" that speaks Aramaic, or, in less mythic language, Aramaic is the language of the Talmud, and the use of Hebrew serves a purpose dictated by the document and bears significance within the norms of thought that the framers of the document have defined. My second example is a more complex one, yielding the same result as the first.

2:1

A. (1) He who purchases the unborn offspring of the cow of a gentile,
(2) and he who sells it to him (even though one is not permitted to do so),
(3) and he who is a partner with him,

B. (4) and he who receives [cows] from him
(5) and he who delivers [cows] to him under contract [to rear them and share in the profit]

C. is exempt from the law of the firstling,

D. since it is said, [*All the firstborn*] *in Israel* (Num. 3:13) –

E. but not [the firstborn produced] among others.

F. Priests and Levites are liable.

G. They are not exempted from the law of the firstborn of a clean beast.

[5]*The Philosophical Mishnah.* Volume I. *The Initial Probe* (Atlanta, 1989: Scholars Press for Brown Judaic Studies); *The Philosophical Mishnah.* Volume II. *The Tractates' Agenda. From Abodah Zarah to Moed Qatan* (Atlanta, 1989: Scholars Press for Brown Judaic Studies); *The Philosophical Mishnah.* Volume III. *The Tractates' Agenda. From Nazir to Zebahim* (Atlanta, 1989: Scholars Press for Brown Judaic Studies); *The Philosophical Mishnah.* Volume IV. *The Repertoire* (Atlanta, 1989: Scholars Press for Brown Judaic Studies); and *Judaism as Philosophy. The Method and Message of the Mishnah* (Columbia, 1991: University of South Carolina Press).

H   But they are exempt only from the redemption of the firstborn
      son and from [the law of the firstling in regard to] the firstborn of
      an ass.

I.1   A   *How come the framer of the Mishnah formulates the rule for the embryo of*
            the ass first, and then reverts and considers the matter of the embryo of a
            cow? Why not encompass in the initial chapter the rule for the embryo of
            the cow as well, for it is a matter concerning the consecration of an animal
            as to its body, and then take up the matter of the embryo of an ass, which
            involves the consecration not of the body of the animal itself but only of the
            value of the animal?

      B   *They say in the West, "If you like, I shall explain, it is because he took*
            special pleasure in this matter, along the lines of the view of R. Hanina
            [asses helped the Israelites when they left Egypt, for not a single
            Israelite failed to possess ninety Libyan asses loaded with the silver
            and gold of Egypt]. *And if you like, I shall explain, it is because since*
            the rules governing the unclean animal are sparse, the framer got them out
            of the way first of all."

I.2   A   Said R. Isaac bar Nahmani said R. Simeon b. Laqish in the name of
            R. Oshaia, "An Israelite who handed over money to a gentile for his
            beast – [the matter is adjudicated] in accord with their laws, even
            though he has not made formal acquisition of the beast by drawing
            it, he has acquired possession of it, in consequence of which the
            beast is liable to the law of the firstling; and a gentile who handed
            over money to an Israelite for his beast – [the matter likewise is
            adjudicated] in accord with their laws, even though he has not
            made formal acquisition of the beast by drawing it, he has acquired
            possession of it, in consequence of which the beast is liable to the
            law of the firstling]."

      B   A master has said, "An Israelite who handed over money to a
            gentile for his beast – [the matter is adjudicated] in accord with
            their laws, even though he has not made formal acquisition of the
            beast by drawing it, he has acquired possession of it, in
            consequence of which the beast is liable to the law of the firstling":
            what is the meaning of, "in accord with their laws"? *Shall we say that*
            "according to their laws" means, in respect to the person of the gentile,
            and we draw an argument a fortiori: if the person of the gentile is acquired
            by the Israelite for money alone, as Scripture says, "to hold for
            possession" (Lev. 25:46) – comparing a Canaanite slave with a
            possession, so that, just as a possession is acquired by handing over
            money to a seller, by a bill of sale, and by taking possession [e.g.,
            performing work on the estate], so a Canaanite slave is acquired
            with money – then how much the more so would that be the rule
            with respect to the property of a gentile [which then is acquired by
            handing over the purchase money] – then the gentile's property
            should also be acquired by means of a bill of sale and by taking
            possession! *And furthermore, the purchase of an Israelite from an*
            Israelite will prove the contrary, for while the person of an Israelite is
            acquired with money, the property of an Israelite is acquired only by an act
            of formal acquisition through drawing the property into one's own
            domain.

C. Said Abbayye, "The meaning of 'in accord with their laws' is those that the Torah has set forth to apply to them: 'or buy of your neighbor's hand' (Lev. 25:14) – it is a purchase from your neighbor to which the act of acquisition through drawing pertains, lo, purchase from a gentile is through a mere exchange of money."

D. *But why not deduce from the cited verse that from a gentile there is no valid mode of acquisition?*

E. *Do not let such a proposition come to mind! For there is an argument a fortiori to the contrary:* If one may validly acquire possession of the gentile's body [as a slave], is it not an argument a fortiori that one may acquire possession of his property in some valid way?

F. *But might I say that one may effect a valid acquisition from a gentile only if there are two media for effecting possession [money and drawing, but not money alone]?*

G. *One may reply,* is it not an argument a fortiori: if through a single means of the transfer of ownership one acquires possession of his person, should two be required for his property?

H. *But might I say that it may be done either in this way or in that way?*

I. *It must be done by analogy to the form of acquisition mentioned with reference to your neighbor. Just as is the case with your neighbor a single mode of acquisition suffices, so with the gentile a single mode of acquisition suffices.*

I.3   A. A master has said, "...and a gentile who handed over money to an Israelite for his beast – [the matter likewise is adjudicated] in accord with their laws, even though he has not made formal acquisition of the beast by drawing it, he has acquired possession of it, in consequence of which the beast is liable to the law of the firstling]":

B. *Now what is the meaning of,* "in accord with their laws"? *Shall we say that "according to their laws" means, in respect to the person of the Israelite who is acquired by a gentile with money, and we draw the following argument a fortiori: If the person of an Israelite is acquired by him with money, as it is said,* "Out of the money that he was bought for" *(Lev. 25:51), should it all the more so be the case that an Israelite's property is acquired by a gentile by means of a mere exchange of money?*

C. The purchase of an Israelite from an Israelite will prove to the contrary, *for he acquires possession of his body through money, but it must involve also a formal act of drawing.*

D. Rather, said Abbayye, "'...in accord with their laws' means, in accord with the laws that the Torah has set forth for them: 'And if you sell anything to your neighbor' (Lev. 25:14) – 'to your neighbor' the correct mode of effecting the transfer of ownership is through an act of drawing, but in the case of a gentile, the title is acquired with money."

E. *But why not deduce from the cited verse that from a gentile there is no valid mode of acquisition?*

F. No. *For there is an argument a fortiori to the contrary:* If one may validly acquire possession of the gentile's body [as a slave], is it not an argument a fortiori that one may acquire possession of his property in some valid way?

G.   *But might I say that one may effect a valid acquisition from a gentile only if there are two media for effecting possession [money and drawing, but not money alone]?*

H.   *One may reply,* is it not an argument a fortiori: if through a single means of the transfer of ownership one acquires possession of his person, should two be required for his property?

I.   *But might I say that it may be done either in this way or in that way?*

J.   *It must be done by analogy to the form of acquisition mentioned with reference to your neighbor.* [13B] *Just as is the case with your neighbor a single mode of acquisition suffices, so with the gentile a single mode of acquisition suffices.*

What is important is that **I.1** undertakes Mishnah criticism, explaining why the Mishnah organizes its subject matter in the way that it does. That entire discussion is in Aramaic. No. 2 then reverts to a normative statement. That rule is given in (Middle) Hebrew.[6] At 2.C Abbayye introduces a fact, not a question: in Hebrew. But the analytical exercise that follows, D, E, F, G, H, I, all in the voice of "the Talmud" itself – anonymous, conventional, restricted to a fixed vocabulary of language and of thought, repeating the same intellectual initiatives over and over again – is in Aramaic. No. 3 then reverts to the analysis of a rule, stated in Hebrew, A, then discussed in Aramaic, Bff.

So Hebrew is used for data, Aramaic for deliberation. Hebrew then classifies a statement in one way, Aramaic in the other, with the result that the reader or listener always knows where he or she[7] stands in the unfolding of the document. Let me now conclude with an example strikingly conclusive, because of its simplicity. In what follows, the same authorities speak in both Hebrew and Aramaic. What they say in Hebrew is a simple law, a fact and a given. What they say in Aramaic is the reason behind the fact, the secondary considerations in play.

5:4C-G

C.   Any blemishes which are likely to happen at the hands of man –

D.   Israelite-caste shepherds are believed [to testify that the blemishes came about unintentionally].

E.   But priestly caste shepherds are not believed.

I.1   A.   [In reference to the rule, Israelite-caste shepherds are believed [to testify that the blemishes came about unintentionally]. But

---

[6]As is clear, the distinction between biblical and Mishnaic Hebrew plays no role in my argument, any more than the variations among classifications of Aramaic.

[7]The entire canon of Judaism, and certainly all of the documents of the canon that originate within the Oral Torah, are the work of men, so far as we now know; but in times past some few women formed part of the readership or audience, and nowadays, a great many. Where I refer to an author or authors, it is therefore solely in the masculine gender.

priestly caste shepherds are not believed], R. Yohanan and R. Eleazar –

B.	One said, "'Israelite-caste shepherds in the household of priestly-caste shepherds **are believed [to testify that the blemishes came about unintentionally].**" *We do not take account of the possibility that their testimony is on account of their living.* But priestly caste shepherds in the household of Israelite-caste householders **are not believed.** *The shepherd might say, 'Since I work for him, he will not pass me by and give it to someone else.' And the same applies to a priest employed by another priest, for we take account of the possibility of their favoring one another. And Rabban Simeon b. Gamaliel comes to say,* 'He [a priest] is believed concerning another's [firstling] but is not believed concerning his own.' *And R. Meir comes along to say,* 'He who is suspect in a given matter neither judges nor bears witness in that matter.'"

C.	The other said, "'Shepherds for Israelites, who are themselves priests [35B] are believed [to testify that the blemishes came about unintentionally].' *The shepherd will say, 'My employe will not bypass a priest who is a disciple of rabbis to give the firstling to me.* But priestly caste sheep – meaning, animals belonging to priests, and even if the shepherds are Israelites, **are not believed.'** *We take account of the possibility that they may give testimony under the influence of the need to make a living. And all the more so is this the rule when a shepherd of the priestly caste is working for an employer of the priestly caste, for we take account of the possibility of their favoring one another as well as of the possibility that they are concerned about making a living. And Rabban Simeon b. Gamaliel comes to say,* 'He [a priest] is believed concerning another's [firstling] but is not believed concerning his own.' *And R. Meir comes along to say,* 'He who is suspect in a given matter neither judges nor bears witness in that matter.'"

Of special interest is the shift from Hebrew to Aramaic at I.1B, C, the rule being in Hebrew, the exposition of the reasoning behind it, in Aramaic. What is important here is the clear evidence that the author knows precisely which language to use for what type of statement, even when the same authority says the whole thing. That proves beyond a doubt that what is in play is not the consideration of who says what and when, for example, earlier figures talk in Hebrew because they speak Hebrew, later ones, Aramaic. When the same figure speaks both languages, at issue must be something other than historical (or biographical) considerations.

As I suggested in the setting of my first example, the reader may well argue that using Hebrew in citations of Scripture or the Mishnah or related materials is simply a medium for preserving what is cited in the original, not part of the system of signals that the authors at hand utilized for the purpose of communicating with their readers. Admittedly, since the rabbinic literature in general is highly differentiated, so that what derives from a received, canonical writing such as the Written Torah or Scripture is always differentiated from what is assigned to a later figure, for example, by saying "as it is written" or "as it is said," and what derives from the Mishnah likewise is marked off in a similarly intratextualist and profoundly anti-intertextualist manner,[8] that is hardly a source of surprise. But Hebrew is used, the very same Hebrew of the Mishnah, when a statement is made that is not Mishnaic or derived from an associated source or authority. A master generally assumed to have lived in the fifth or sixth century will instruct the Tannaite memorizer of his household or school or court to state matters in one way rather than in some other. His instructions always will be presented in Hebrew: say "this," not "that," and both "this" and "that" are in Hebrew. The use of Hebrew therefore forms part of the conventional substrate of the document, conveying a claim and a meaning, and what it signals is not merely "quoting from the original source," though that is, as a matter of fact, part of the message of facticity, the classification of a statement as a datum, that the use of Hebrew is meant to convey.

---

[8]I assess the allegation that the rabbinic documents in general, encompassing the Bavli, are to be classified as intertextual and I show that the Bavli is not intertextual but intratextual: always distinguishing its boundaries from the frontiers of other writings, never merely alluding, but always explicitly, differentiatedly, citing or quoting, with the ancient equivalent of footnotes or quotation marks. Elsewhere I have dealt with the claim, which is spurious, that the rabbinic literature forms a fine example of what contemporary literary criticism means by "intertextuality," that rabbinic documents "flow" into one another, that the lines that differentiate between and among writings (whether Midrash compilations or otherwise) are not marked and readily crossed. These characterizations of Midrash compilations ignore the distinctive traits that differentiate each such compilation from all others, traits of rhetoric and the logic of cogent discourse for example. The present book forms yet another component in my argument against the "intertextualist" reading of rabbinic literature. The fact that the Bavli differentiates linguistically as it does, always indicating, for example, where Scripture is quoted verbatim by marking out the verse of Scripture and also by using either Mishnaic Hebrew or Aramaic, and not biblical Hebrew, in discussing the verse of Scripture, shows that these representations of the character of the writing are simply false. The linguistic conventions spelled out here show, once more, that the relationship between the Mishnah (and the Tosefta) and the Talmud cannot be characterized as "intertextual," in that the lines of differentiation between the Mishnah and materials given the standing of statements in the Mishnah and the Talmud always are carefully and boldly marked out. For further discussion I refer the reader to my *Canon and Connection: Intertextuality in Judaism* (Lanham, 1986: University Press of America Studies in Judaism Series); *Midrash as Literature: The Primacy of Documentary Discourse* (Lanham, 1987: University Press of America Studies in Judaism Series); *The Bavli and its Sources: The Question of Tradition in the Case of Tractate Sukkah* (Atlanta, 1987: Scholars Press for Brown Judaic Studies).

What about Aramaic? That, too, signals not where or when a saying was formulated but the classification of the saying. Where we find Aramaic, the language of sustained discourse, of continuity, cogency, and coherence, it will commonly tell us, through the very choice of language:

1. A passage formulates an analytical or critical problem and is engaged in solving it.
2. A passage is particular and episodic, for example, commonly case reports about things decided in courts of the time of the document are set forth in Aramaic, or stories about things authorities have done, will be told in Aramaic; these invariably are asked to exemplify a point beyond themselves.

These two purposes for which Aramaic is used on the surface do not entirely cohere. The first is abstract, the second, concrete; the first pursues a problem of theory and calls upon evidence in the service of the sustained process of applied reason and practical logic; the second signals the presence of thought that is singular and concrete. So if we find a passage in Aramaic, we may stand in two quite unrelated points in the unfolding re-presentation of thought.

But, in point of fact, the second way in which Aramaic may be used invariably finds its place within the framework of a discussion formulated as a sustained process of critical analysis, so the choice of Aramaic for what is episodic turns out not surprising, when we realize that the episode is presented specifically so as to be transformed from an anecdote into a medium of demonstration and proof. The case forms part of an argument; evidence flows into argument; and all argument then is in the same language, the Aramaic that forms the language of the document when the framers of the document speak for themselves and within the process of their own thought. When they shift to Hebrew, it will signal either the upshot of analysis, or *mutatis mutandis*, the precipitating occasion for analysis.

That, in the Talmud of Babylonia, language serves a taxonomic purpose, should not be taken for granted, since simply choosing a given language in a bi- or multilingual document does not invariably serve the purpose of classification. A variety of signals can be given through the use of one language, as against some other, in a bi- or multilingual writing. For instance, if everybody spoke Aramaic but an ancient text, in Hebrew, is cited, and then some figure from that same period is given further statements, the choice of the Hebrew of that early document may serve to endow with the authority of antiquity the statement given in that language. (That never happens in the Bavli, but it does happen, for instance, in the Dead Sea Scrolls.) Along these same lines, the antiquity of a passage that utilizes a language no longer spoken; the authority of a passage that is written in a language different from the one that predominates; the different choices characteristic of authorities whose words are preserved at hand – all of these represent signals that may be conveyed by shifting from one to another language in writing addressed to a single set of readers or listeners.

The upshot is that if a document forms a conglomerate of diverse sources, originally written in a variety of languages, then the framer who utilizes passages chosen from those sources will tell us, by preserving the sources in their original language, not only that he assumes we can read and understand those other languages, but that he wants us to know that his writing is authentic to those sources. The range of possible interpretations for the use of more than a single language in a piece of writing hardly runs its course with these few proposals. I mean only to point out that the utilization of more than a single language in a piece of writing may bear a variety of messages, and that the possible conventions dictating the choice of language are many.

Among them, two stand out. One possibility of accounting for the presence of more than a single language directs our attention to the sources that have contributed to the writing. If these sources are in several languages, and if the author of our writing has chosen to preserve his sources in the original, then the multilingual character of his writing attests to the diversity of his sources and his theory of how he wanted his writing to be received. But then, we must ask ourselves, why has he used the Hebrew of his principal source when formulating the words of authorities who do not occur in that source, for example, figures of a clearly later period? The issue of preserving what was originally said in the language in which it was said cannot exhaust the repertoire of explanations. A second possibility of account for the use of more than a single language – not ruled out by the first – is that the use of more than a single language formed an integral part of the author's (or authors') medium for communicating their message. Sentences in one language then bore one set of meanings, those in another, a different set; or sentences in one language functioned in one way within the larger framework of discourse, those in another language then fulfilled a quite different function. And that other convention, it is clear, is the one that, in my view, dictated when one language would be used, when the other. One language in general would stand for fact, another, for analysis of fact. Using one language therefore established one frame of reference, the other, a different, and complementary frame of reference.

The reason that this second theory is not eliminated by the first is that a language used for the re-presentation of givens may well derive from a source that supplies those data. But the second theory does eliminate the first, since if rules intrinsic to the mode and intentionality of discourse govern, then these same rules will tell authors how all the materials that they use, whether early or late, are to be set forth: *which language*. And then any appeal to a long process of agglutination and conglomeration, in which the original words were preserved in the original language, will contradict the fact that, at any point in that allegedly long, historical process, precisely the same rules will have dictated precisely the same choices as to the use of one language or another. If the rules for choosing one language for one purpose and another for a different purpose prove to emerge from an inductive study, then, we shall find it difficult to concur that, over a long period, a great variety of writers found themselves bound to these same rules in the formulation of their thoughts into words to be preserved and handed on. The difficulty will derive from the particularity of the rules to the document that yields them: this writing follows these rules, and no other (extant) writing follows those same rules. On the face of it that fact will point away from the first, and toward the second, possibility just now set forth.[9]

Though the explanation and interpretation of the phenomenon given here are entirely original, the phenomenon of the Talmud's bi- or multilingualism has attracted the attention of others. Four prior scholars in the recent past have drawn conclusions from the use of the two languages. Albert Baumgarten, Abba Bendavid, Shamma Friedman, and Eliezer Margaliot.

Baumgarten deals with not the Bavli but sayings in various sources that deal with a single named authority, Judah the Patriarch; he observes that "Judah...speaks Aramaic in all the stories in which he is portrayed negatively, Hebrew in those in which he is portrayed positively; R.

---

[9]Theories that take at face value the veracity of attributions, assuming that a given authority really said what is assigned to him, and that we know exactly when he lived, rest on gullibility and need not be seriously entertained. But a taxonomic theory is required in any event, even within such theories, by the fact that Hebrew serves the same authority who speaks, also, in Aramaic, and hence we want to know how he knew which language to use, if he really said what he is supposed to have said. The conclusions drawn by Albert I. Baumgarten, for example, who is cited below, take at face value all of the attributions in the document and, therefore, may be dismissed as beside the point. He appears never to have seriously considered the problems involved in believing whatever they read, and has not yet mastered the lessons of my *Reading and Believing: Ancient Judaism and Contemporary Gullibility* (Atlanta, 1986: Scholars Press for Brown Judaic Studies). Resting on untenable foundations, his proposed hypotheses must be dismissed, therefore, as mere curiosities of sectarian scholarship.

Judah's preference for Hebrew is well attested."[10] This observation has
no bearing on our problem, and the conclusions Baumgarten wishes to
draw from the fact that he has discovered hardly are compelling.
Bendavid notes that when the languages occur in the same passage, they
are kept apart from one another and Aramaic forms are not imposed on
Hebrew words or vice versa. The differentiation between the two
languages are articulate and conscious: "There was a clear consciousness
of what was Hebrew and what was Aramaic." Bendavid further gives
rules for the use of Hebrew within the context of Aramaic, the sole
relevant item being the use of Hebrew in every legal statement, but not
in the discussion thereof (just as we have noted).[11] His is the one prior
treatment of the subject that seems to me both to the point and also
accessibly framed. Shamma Friedman observes that when Hebrew and
Aramaic serve together, "the principal wording of the saying (memrah)
is in Hebrew, and the Aramaic is the language of the anonymous
Talmud."[12] Since by "saying" or memrah Friedman seems to mean what
I mean here by "normative statement," "datum," fact," and the like, that
sound observation accords with the principal ones set forth here.
Friedman further notes that it is routine for Hebrew to serve as the
language of legal sayings of Babylonian Amoraim, with the analytical
discussion in Aramaic.[13]

Eliezer Margaliot has provided the most sustained and systematic
account of the problem.[14] But his treatment of the problem is confused
and naive. Some of Margaliot's observations are routine, for example,
paraphrases of what he finds in the sacred literature itself, which, he

---

[10]Albert I. Baumgarten, "Rabbi Judah I and His Opponents," *Journal for the Study of Judaism* 12 (1981): 140.

[11]Abba Bendavid, *Lashon miqra velashon hakhamim* (Tel Aviv, 1967: Devir), 134-5.

[12]Shamma Friedman, "Pereq haishah rabbah babbli," in *Mehqarim ummeqorot. Meassef lemadda'i hayyahadut*, ed. H. Z. Dimitrovsky (New York, 1978: Jewish Theological Seminary of America), 301-302. What Friedman means is so obscure that we are not much helped by his statements; Friedman's exegetical work, analyzed in the essays by my students and me in William S. Green, *Law as Literature* (Chico, 1985: Scholars Press/Semeaia) has been shown to be of equally limited intellectual value, partly for the simple reason that he finds it difficult to say with precision and accuracy what is on his mind. When my seminar devoted a semester to reading his "Pereq haishah rabbah babbli," we time and again found the obfuscation so total as to discourage any serious effort at grasping what he wished to say. Alas, when we did understand him, we found his points either trivial or wrong, as the monograph we devoted to his work shows. But his comments here are unexceptionable.

[13]Friedman, op. cit., 301, n. 60.

[14]Eliezer Margaliot, "Ivrit vearamit battalmud ubammidrash." *Leshonenu* 27 (1963-64): 20-33.

maintains, treats Aramaic as less weighty than Hebrew.[15] That seems to me denied by the fact that the Bavli is an Aramaic writing, as Friedman has also observed. Margaliot's survey of references to the two languages is paraphrastic and uninteresting. He notes, as generalizations, that "all formalized and fixed sayings [*memrot*] in the Talmud and Midrash, whether stated by Tannaite or Amoraic authorities, without differentiation between those of the Land of Israel and those of Babylonia, are stated in Hebrew. [Hebrew is the language of the fixed saying because] the saying is Torah, Oral Torah, and the Torah is holy, and Hebrew is the holy language, and that is why these are stated in the holy language and not in Aramaic. But the discussion, the statements that follow the saying, are in Aramaic, because here there was no meticulous concern about the language that would be used."[16] That "because" introduces nonsense. Again he states, "statements meant to serve as a fixed and final ruling, made for generations to come, are in Hebrew."[17] The implicit reason for using Aramaic – that what is said is ephemeral – defies the character and history of the Bavli itself. Some of Margaliot's other generalizations in point of fact contradict what we find in the Bavli, and others are not relevant to it. In general his categories are not wholly of a single sort, and his language is imprecise. But it is clear that Friedman, Bendavid, and Margaliot have observed the same phenomena with which we deal here. But the interpretation of the linguistic preferences offered by them has nothing in common with the meaning of these facts that I set forth.

When we ask ourselves what difference the distinction makes, the answer I provide shows why the prior observations have yielded no valid generalization. What is at stake in the identification of the rules that govern the choice of language for the expression of thought? The reading of the document in its own framework, on the one side, and the identification of the document's place within the larger context of the canon of the Judaism that treats this document as normative, on the other, define the the importance of these results. At stake is whether or not an authorship intervenes in the formation of a composite and marks its own place off from that of others, represented as external to itself: an authorship engaged in a work of thoughtful differentiation we may call intratextuality. If it does, then the authorship plays an active role in the display of the selected items of their composition, and they give us not a mere scrapbook but a carefully crafted text, a book, a document: their writing, with sources carefully labeled as other, external, in this case,

---

[15]Ibid., 20.
[16]Ibid., 21.
[17]Ibid., 23.

authoritative. If it does not, then what we have is not a collage but an accident, a hodgepodge, a junk heap, this-and-that about nothing in particular to no one. At stake is the character of a literature. The appropriate limits of discourse derive from the documents of which a literature is composed: the document, in our terms, the book, as the generative unit of the cogent syllogism, therefore of intelligible discourse. The Bavli – still more than the Midrash compilations – with its protracted and run-on discussions, provides stunning and probative proof of that fact. For how better to mark of one's own, from others', contributions than by a shift in language? The rule that governs where and when to use Hebrew and how and why to use Aramaic therefore marks the Talmud of Babylonia, Judaism's complete and authoritative, systematic statement, as intratextual.

These facts, now established, bear considerable weight in a contemporary debate on whether the rabbinic literature is "intertextual" or, as I maintain, "intratextual." So let me now turn to an explanation of the issues of intertextuality, with special attention to the gross misrepresentation of the character of the rabbinic canon by contemporary Jewish literary critics, typified here by James Kugel and others. Showing how they read Midrash compilations and propose to characterize the whole of the rabbinic canon as "intertextual," within the choice of this or its opposite, which is that, I prove we must choose that. Kugel's and others' errors demonstrate that I am not rehearsing obvious and familiar truths, commonplaces of learning broadly grasped and understood. Rather, they show us there are choices, people opt for the opposite view from the one that I show banal and self-evident. When, therefore, I propose the alternative, the intratextualist reading of the same writings, it is in the context if vigorous (if, in my view, rather one-sided) debate on questions of literature and religion.

That is why I trouble to explain why the results in this monograph and its companion dictate the classification of the Bavli as intratextual – and that within the very definitions of "intertextual" given by Kugel and others. The reason is not that they bear weight in the larger scholarly discourse that is underway, for, sectarian and self-referential, by the criterion of solid, published scholarship they hardly qualify as heavyweights. But they do prove the vitality of the contrary, and wrong, reading of the same writings. Otherwise, after surveying the writings set forth here, readers will find so obvious and routine the rule that I claim to demonstrate as to wonder, who ever would have thought otherwise, and why? Some have proposed other explanations, others have ignored the issue altogether and – out of careless or slovenly or simply thoughtless reading of the documents – thought nothing in particular, and so, out of ignorance, both sides have vastly misrepresented matters.

That is why we now have to work our way through some passages of Bavli tractate Bekhorot, point by point noting where Aramaic is used and what kind of discussion is set forth in that language, where Hebrew is used and what sort of statement is made in Hebrew, and how the discussions and the data interrelate.

Now, it is clear, we see the recurrence of a few fixed forms and formulas, a few rules govern throughout, and, over all, the rather monotonous and even tedious character of the writing at hand attests to its authorship's adherence to a few rules characteristic of this writing and determinative of its traits, beginning to end. The document exhibits remarkable integrity; the limits of the document clearly are delineated, and when other documents are introduced in evidence, they, too, are marked in the manner in which, in this period and within the technical limitations operative then, people were able to cite or place in quotations or footnote materials borrowed from other sources. This is a writing that does not (merely) allude or hint at something found somewhere else, it articulately cites, it explicitly quotes. Within the limits of the Bavli, the document defines its own infrastructure in both rhetoric and logic.

This result, based on the simple rules governing the use of Hebrew and Aramaic, recapitulates my reading of Midrash compilations, which similarly exhibit the traits of intratextuality, what one might call, invoking an Italian cultural and political metaphor in a religious aesthetic discussion, *integralismo*: inner-directedness, autonomy, self-absorption, acute singularity. Along these same lines, in my analysis of Midrash compilations, I have demonstrated that the document, not its constitutive subunits, forms the definitive analytical category. When we describe a document that compiles Midrash exegeses, we know as fact that [1] a given method of exegesis has yielded [3] a given exegetical comment on a verse of Scripture, the result of which is now in [2] *this particular document*. Since we know the wonderfully simple facts of what is found in which document, we can begin the work of describing the traits imparted *by* [2] that document *to* the [3] exegetical result *of* [1] the exegetical method at hand. Traits characteristic of [2] the documentary setting likewise emerge without a trace of speculation. To state matters more concretely, if a document routinely frames matters in accord with one repertoire of formal conventions rather than some other, and if it arranges its formal repertoire of types of units of discourse in one way, rather than some other, and if its compilers repeatedly propose to make one point, rather than some other, we can easily identify those traits of the passage under study that derive from the larger documentary context. For Midrash compilations, therefore, the document is primary, the contents, derivative.

Now we see that the same is so for the Talmud of Babylonia. Here too, the document – that anonymous voice, speaking in Aramaic – forms the definitive and paramount dimension of the writing, to which everything else is subordinated. The document speaks its message, utilizing evidence, in another language, to make possible the formulation of that message. The voice of "the Bavli," or "the Talmud," is the Aramaic voice of applied reason and practical logic – applied to, practiced upon, the Hebrew language writings (or statements orally formulated and orally transmitted) of the Mishnah and comparable sources. Accordingly, the document, the Bavli, forms the pivot. Its authorship's choices present the one solid fact in relationship to which everything else then takes a position relative to that fact. The formulation of documentary discourse is uniform, beginning with the language preference. What then are some of the documentary facts? Here are some: this saying (in Hebrew) or story occurs here (in Hebrew), bears these traits, is used for this larger redactional and programmatic purpose (which is stated in Aramaic), makes this distinct point in its context – always implicit, rarely explicit, in the very choice of the Aramaic language. These facts of linguistic taxonomy therefore define the initial context of interpretation. Now let me answer the simple question: so what? At stake is a variety of issues, one looking backward, the other, forward.

What is in prospect, as a result of this work on the languages of the Bavli, is a study of not so much what it is that that (Aramaic) speaker wishes to say – the foundations for such a study are not yet fully laid – but how the Aramaic speaker chooses to set forth his message: the types of discourse, the forms that repeatedly serve to formulate and signal those types of discourse, and the order in which those types (and forms) of discourse make their appearance. When we can say what is the message of the (linguistic) medium that communicates with us here, then we can control for the particularizations of that ubiquitous, infrastructural message. But what about the backward perspective: how do these results relate to those already set forth on Midrash compilations? What I have shown here for the Bavli, already established elsewhere for the Midrash compilations of the canon of the Judaism of the dual Torah in late antiquity, is that, as between the classifications of literary criticism, intertextuality and intratextuality, the Bavli is to be described as intratextualist. Let me explain.

As between intertextuality and intratextuality, the Talmud of Babylonia is to be classified as an intratextual writing, in that its author or authors carefully delineate their own document from other documents upon which they draw. What they wish to say is in one language, their other, different (prior, authoritative) sources, in Hebrew. That distinction as to languages validates the classification just now proposed. When we understand the alternative, we shall see how and why the results of this study require us to reject the alternative. This term bears a variety of definitions, but in general has been used when literary critics and other scholars of aesthetics wished to claim that a writer conceived of work "not as a creation but rather as the product of a 'vast and uninterrupted dialogue' with other texts."[18] A current definition, provided by Julia Kristeva as cited by Henry M. Sayre,[19] holds that "each text situates itself at the junction of many texts of which it is at once the re-reading, the accentuation, the condensation, the displacement, and the profound extension." Part of a larger reading of literature, which has brought into question "not only the importance of the author, the audience, and the text as document, but tries to undermine all previous scholarship and the very concept of truth,"[20] "intertextuality" ought to present little to attract scholars who describe themselves as Judaic, for example, Orthodox, authentic, committed to the documents they study, and the like. Viewing documents as indeterminate as to both boundaries and truth contradicts the premises of the Judaic canonical writings. Green's statement, cited at the Preface, certainly affords slight support for the allegations of the intertextualist reading of any rabbinic writing, whether compiling Midrash exegeses or Mishnah exegeses: "In rabbinic Judaism the writing and discourse of scripture had to be inherently separable from, and could be neither merged nor confused with, the commentary upon them....The rabbinic tendency to identify antecedent materials is not limited to scripture....The adjectives 'allusive' and 'intertextual' are analytically useless for a critical description of rabbinic hermeneutics....Rabbinic literature displays its sources." In light of Green's descriptive judgment, which our results have fully confirmed, we must find it surprising that a number of scholars of Jewish origin, describing themselves as Orthodox or as authentically Jewish (whatever they mean by that allegation) identify as a literature peculiarly intertextual in character the canonical writings of Judaism.[21]

---

[18]Henry M. Sayre, *The Object of Performance. The American Avant Garde Since 1970* (Chicago, 1989: The University of Chicago Press), 23.

[19]Ibid., 23.

[20]Peter Gaeffke, "The State of Scholarship. A Rock in the Tide of Time: Oriental Studies Then and Now." *Academic Questions* spring (1990): 73.

[21]I assume Daniel Boyarin's violent and contemptuous attacks on Green and me (among so many others) in his *Intertextuality and the Reading of Midrash* may be accounted for by his obvious displeasure with our results, since nothing within the scholarly issues debated here can justify the obviously personal character of his unpleasant references to scholars with whom he disagrees. In point of fact, he

Why introduce the issue of whether the Bavli is "intertextual" or "intratextual" at all? The Jewish literary critics, after all, speak of Midrash compilations, not the Talmud of Babylonia. The reason is not only that the issue is current, though it is. The term "intertextuality," has recently been made to serve for the description of rabbinic Midrash compilations, with special reference to their relationship to Scripture, but, more generally, as the explanation and classification of how the Midrash compilations relate to one another.[22] The reason is that the

---

is not yet able to show in detail how his "intertextualist" reading of Midrash compilations and Midrash exegeses is able to tell us things we did not know without that reading of those writings; and in these pages, as in other studies of mine, I have demonstrated that his characterization of the rabbinic writings, both Midrash exegesis compilations and Mishnah exegesis compilations, is false in every detail. So his work is null. I think the reason he has reached false conclusions is that he has examined only bits and pieces of this-and-that (as he says in his book, only a half dozen passages of Mekhilta, which is itself an anomalous document, probably medieval and therefore hardly evidence of the state of writing a thousand years prior to its own compilation and redaction!). So it would appear somewhat unseemly for a person who has not yet published his studies of the traits of the literature as a whole so demeaningly to address the persons – and not even the results! – of those who have. Still, like those whom he identifies as his co-workers, such as James Kugel, Boyarin has the merit of framing errors in stimulating ways, so providing a worthwhile null hypothesis for the attention of those of us who have actually done the work of characterizing the literature whole, document by document. What is at stake in all this will be spelled out in the following paragraphs.

[22]See most recently Daniel Boyarin, *Intertextuality and the Reading of Midrash*. I have dealt with this term as it has been invoked in the study of Midrash compilations and Midrash exegeses in several books, but particularly in *Canon and Connection: Intertextuality in Judaism* (Lanham, 1986: University Press of America Studies in Judaism Series), which addresses the characterization of Susan Handelman and some lesser figures, and also in *Midrash as Literature: The Primacy of Documentary Discourse* (Lanham, 1987: University Press of America Studies in Judaism Series), where I deal with the position of James Kugel. There I ask about the precipitant of exegesis, namely, whether it is the literary and systemic (theological) context, as I maintain, or principally the verse that is subject to exegesis, as Kugel and his friends hold, and that issue brings us to the crux of the matter. The premise of all that I have said is that Scripture serves diverse purposes and therefore cannot establish a single definitive plane of meaning, the frame of reference against which all other things constitute variables. Scripture constitutes the neutral background, not the variable. Exegetes tell us what verses of Scripture matter and what we should learn from those verses. Scripture dictates nothing but endures all things. What people tell us about the meaning of Scripture represents the outcome of the work of exegetes, not the inexorable result of the character or contents of Scripture.

The issue for debate as I think it should be argued in the context of Midrash compilations is this: 1) Does the character, that is, the wording, of a verse of Scripture dictate the substance of exegesis? As I said, that has been the position of all exegetes of Midrash compilations for a thousand years and remains the premise of the reading of Midrash compilations and Midrash exegeses by Kugel and his colleagues. 2) Or do exegetes bringing to their task the givens of the Judaism of which they form a part dictate the sense they wish to impart to (or locate in) Scripture? That is the position that emerges when we recognize the primacy of documentary discourse in the reading of Midrash compilations and interpretation of Midrash exegeses. If the former, then the ground for comparison finds definition in a verse of Scripture. What X said, without regard to circumstance or even documentary context, compared with what Y said, viewed also with slight attention to canonical context and concrete literary circumstance, matters.

I have already refuted the former of the two possibilities through a single example of what is, in fact, the ubiquitous datum of Western biblical interpretation: people make of Scripture anything they wish, choosing the passage they deem important to prove the proposition they bring to that passage for validation. Claims to the contrary represent theological apologetics, that alone. They derive from an inner-facing reading of the received literature, from the stance of the faith and for the hearing of the faithful. Those judgments have no independent hermeneutical bearing – and those that make them scarcely pretend otherwise. The paramount fact of the history of the Bible (both Testaments) in the West – the amazing diversity of meanings "discovered" by exegetes precisely where they wish to find them in the workings of either divine grace or wonderful serendipity – imparts to the position espoused by Kugel and his friends a certain piquancy. The canon and its components take pride of place, defining the primary arena of discourse and interpretation.

What diverse persons said about a given verse of Scripture defines only a coincidence, unless proved on the basis of circumstance and context to constitute more than mere coincidence. Then, and only then, will the intrinsic traits of the verse come to the fore as candidates for the generative role of precipitating discourse. Scripture contributed much but dictated nothing, system – circumstance and context – dictated everything and selected what Scripture might contribute in Midrash. I have not seen Kugel's response to this sustained critique of his position; I have the impression that there has been none. The one time I met him personally, many years ago, he stated to me that my work is not on the scholarly canon and therefore no one has to read it. To his credit Boyarin does reject Kugel's characterization of "no one" and does propose to reply to *Midrash as Literature*. But, alas, he, too, does not really keep up, and he does not appear to have read *Canon and Connection*, which makes a quite different argument from that of *Midrash and Literature*.

In any event, if some circles of scholarship choose not to read critical assessments of their ideas, most scholars do not share that sectarian conception of learning, and, as is clear, work has now gone far past the position taken by Kugel and his circle. The broad current interest in the character of Midrash interpretation, pursued through the reading of Midrash compilations, each in documentary context, accounts for the widespread acceptance, shown in both reviews and also (happily) continuing, excellent sales, of my several formulations of the matter, in such works as *Invitation to Midrash: The Working of Rabbinic Bible Interpretation. A Teaching Book* (San Francisco, 1988: Harper & Row); *What Is Midrash?* (Philadelphia, 1987: Fortress Press); *Uniting the Dual Torah: Sifra and the Problem of the Mishnah* (Cambridge and New York, 1989: Cambridge University

Bavli has been drawn into the discussion of "the rabbis'" intertextuality, and this is entirely explicit. Not only have the advocates of this

---

Press); *A Midrash Reader* (Minneapolis, 1990: Augsburg-Fortress); *Making the Classics in Judaism: The Three Stages of Literary Formation* (Atlanta, 1990: Scholars Press for Brown Judaic Studies); *The Midrash. An Introduction* (Northvale, 1990: Jason Aronson, Inc.); *The Canonical History of Ideas. The Place of the So-called Tannaite Midrashim, Mekhilta Attributed to R. Ishmael, Sifra, Sifré to Numbers, and Sifré to Deuteronomy* (Atlanta, 1990: Scholars Press for South Florida Studies in the History of Judaism); and *Tradition as Selectivity: Scripture, Mishnah, Tosefta, and Midrash in the Talmud of Babylonia. The Case of Tractate Arakhin* (Atlanta, 1990: Scholars Press for South Florida Studies in the History of Judaism).

Out of the intertextualist circle of scholarship on Midrash compilations, by contrast, has come not a *single* comparable study, introductory or monograph. None of the "intertextualists" in Midrash criticism has succeeded in presenting Midrash compilations and Midrash exegeses in a systematic and encompassing manner, with attention to all of the Midrash compilations of the formative age of Judaism of the Dual Torah, read one by one (as I have done) and also read as though they formed a single undifferentiated corpus (as the intertextualist claim we must do). Whatever they publish consists of some "examples," for example, Boyarin's half-dozen (!). So, in all, the contrary position is represented not in a professional manner, by sustained and orderly research, but only in an amateur way, by presentations of "examples" of this-and-that (cf. Boyarin). That mode of argument through anecdote is generally abandoned in junior high school and rarely survives adolescence.

The collected writings of Judah Goldin form a fine set of examples of how not to (re)present Midrash compilations and Midrash exegesis. Little of consequence for the description, analysis, and interpretation of Midrash and of rabbinic literature overall is to be learned from his rambling and disorderly musings – the compilation of his life's work – in his *Studies in Midrash and Related Literature*, edited by Barry L. Eichler and Jeffrey H. Tigay (Philadelphia, 1988: Jewish Publication Society). Goldin makes various useful observations on this-and-that, but in his *oeuvre* we find no system and no interest in the demonstration of the propositions implicit in the points that he does make: just a lot of guesses, some of them better than others. Goldin takes for granted that sayings really were said by those to whom they are attributed, and if we have a good manuscript tradition and proper philological analysis, then we know what someone really said and meant (cf. Martin S. Jaffee, review of Goldin, in *Religious Studies Review* 16 (1990): 273). Therefore, as Jaffee characterizes Goldin's work, "These essays, while informative and insightful, contribute to contemporary research only obliquely." That somewhat obscure, and therefore kind, way ("...only obliquely") of characterizing Goldin as a rather tragic figure, who has wasted his scholarly effort, still seems to me a more generous – and a merited – evaluation than the one to be accorded to scholars whose entire *oeuvre* consists of a few opinions joined with, on the one side, professions of self-righteous ignorance ("we do not have to read you anyhow"), and, on the other side, anecdotal argument and episodic evidence, Boyarin and Kugel being merely exemplary of a whole school of "scholarship." Goldin in his time was a scholar of learning, and, if he ignored what he did not like, at least he produced an *oeuvre* in the field in which he claimed to be expert. His continuators reproduce his capacity for ignorance but not his erudition.

intertextualist reading characterized in broad strokes the mind and the writing of "the rabbis," with the result that their presentation of the Midrash compilations has encompassed, also, whatever "the rabbis" wrote. They have introduced in evidence of the character of "Midrash" passages that occur not in Midrash compilations but in the Bavli. So we have every reason to ask whether the Bavli is an "intertextualist" or an "intratextualist" writing.

The most current case in point is Professor Daniel Boyarin, who, in his *Intertextuality and the Reading of Midrash,* is quite explicit in treating everything as the same thing and therefore quoting the Bavli when he wishes to describe a Midrash compilation. One of the principal passages that he treats in his proposed reading of Mekhilta is not in the Mekhilta at all, but in the Talmud of Babylonia. So we are introduced to the Mekhilta by a passage in the Bavli. The reason he gives is that the names that occur in one document occur in another – and that's that. For Boyarin that gullibility does not pose a problem: *"The Talmud preserves a story about the very rabbis of the Mekhilta* which contains a nearly explicit commentary on midrashic intertextuality...."* Since the intertextualist camp thereby introduces into evidence materials of the Bavli, we are entirely justified in asking whether the Bavli is an intertextualist writing. Since the principal writing of the Judaism of the dual Torah is the Bavli, we do well to test in that definitive document the characterization of the writings of "the rabbis" as intertextual.

The specific positions of these Jewish "intertextualists" should be cited in their own language. Boyarin's restatement of this notion, in the context of Midrash exegesis, is, "Midrash is best understood as a continuation of the literary activity which engendered the Scriptures themselves." Susan Handelman frames matters in this language: "The rabbinic world is, to use a contemporary term, one of *intertextuality.* Texts echo, interact, and interpenetrate...."[23] That description directly contradicts Green's (not to mention the careful delineation of boundaries between and among types of documents as well as types of discourse, such as I have drawn here). Handelman further states,

> ...all units are so closely interwoven and simultaneously present that none can be considered in separation from any other at any given moment; it is a world of 'intertextuality'....Interpretation is not essentially separate from the text itself – an external act intruded upon it – but rather the extension of the text, the uncovering of the connective network of relations, a part of the continuous revelation of the text itself, at bottom, another aspect of the text.

---

[23]*The Slayers of Moses* (Albany, 1982: State University of New York Press), 47.

But interpretation is always linguistically separate from the text itself, with the text cited in Hebrew (for example, the Mishnah's rule), and the interpretation then given in Aramaic. In light of what we have seen here, Handelman could not be further from the facts of the Bavli.

Since, in the Midrash compilations, biblical Hebrew is reserved for the citations of verses of Scripture, while Middle Hebrew serves for whatever the document's authorship or those the document's authorship cites may wish to say, there, too, language forms the first step in a sustained process of differentiation – and reintegration (a process Handelman will not perceive within her episteme!). When we realize how carefully interpretation is kept separate from the text itself, we have also to reject her characterization of the compilations of Midrash exegesis (and, by extension, Mishnah exegesis) as "the extension of the text," "a part of the continuous revelation of the text itself." In theological terms, she is absolutely right: the generative problematic of the Midrash compilations and of the Talmuds is to establish the place, within the revelation of the Torah, of the Midrash exegeses and of the Mishnah exegeses of "our sages of blessed memory." But turning a theological problem into a literary critical and hermeneutical principle yields confusion when we turn to the traits of the documents that are supposedly described here. As soon as a sage says, "as it is said," or "as it is written," he signals that there is a distance between what he has just said and now wishes to prove by appeal to a prooftext and the prooftext. And the use of such formal signals of separation only confirms what the implicit differentiation effected by language – even the two kinds of Hebrew – establishes ubiquitously.[24]

Since Boyarin places himself within the circle, as to the alleged intertextuality of Midrash compilations, of Professor James Kugel, we turn to Kugel's "Two Introductions to Midrash," with which I have dealt at length elsewhere.[25] Kugel, in describing the Midrash compilations of

---

[24]Boyarin is silly in claiming as probative evidence what he alleges as the fact that there are manuscripts that omit "as it is said" or "as it is written," when other manuscripts, and the earliest printed editions, reproduce those words, since the probative value of singleton manuscripts, in a literary corpus that today rests upon such flimsy manuscript evidence to begin with, is null. The formal signals of attribution to Scripture, a distinct source and text, are routine, as everyone who knows the manuscript-evidence recognizes, and Boyarin's allegations to the contrary are not to be taken seriously.

[25]*Midrash as Literature: The Primacy of Documentary Discourse* (Lanham, 1987: University Press of America, Studies in Judaism Series). Here I summarize some of the main points of my argument against Kugel's propositions; the evidence upon which the argument rests is extensively presented there.

In his book, cited above, Boyarin treats as strange my devoting an entire book to Kugel's misrepresentation of the rabbinic writings of the canon. But I believe that learning is worthwhile only if we confront in a serious and sustained way propositions contrary to our own. The conception that we make our own points stick by ignoring contradictory ones or that we contribute to learning by ignoring other peoples' work, which is a commonplace in scholarship on Judaism in the State of Israel, where Boyarin has worked for decades, and in Judaic rabbinical schools in the USA, derives from the German academic humanities in the age of their degradation, prior to, and within, the Hitler period. Before and during that dreadful age, academic humanists within the tradition of *Geisteswissenschaft* declined, for one example, even to cite the work by scholars of Jewish origin that pertained to their own. It is sad to note how a sectarian scholarship on Judaism, under Israeli and Judaic theological auspices overseas alike, has practiced this same policy of *Todschweigen*.

To give three outstanding examples of scholarly fraud and malpractice, of the complete failure of scholarly integrity and honesty, I point to Louis Finkelstein, who in his chapter on "the Pharisees" in *Cambridge History of Judaism*, Volume II (Cambridge, 1990: Cambridge University Press), omits all reference to work done on the Pharisees in the past thirty years, not even referring to that work in his bibliography; Judah Goldin, who has pretended that an entire corpus of scholarship on Midrash simply does not exist; and Salo W. Baron, who in his work on religion and history showed how it is possible to write a book on a subject – the place of religion in history – on which the author has read not a single work published in the two decades prior to the appearance of his own. Since allegedly reputable presses, Cambridge University Press for Finkelstein, a variety of presses and journals culminating in the Jewish Publication Society, for Goldin, and Columbia University Press, for Baron, participated in the fraud of *Todschweigen*, we see how the corruption of learning spreads when persons of sufficient political-institutional power practice corruption. Finkelstein, Goldin, and Baron, now having passed from the scene, leaving behind them a legacy of dubious value and no compelling interest, show us how not to conduct scholarly discourse. In their life's work they violated the most elementary canons of academic ethics, misleading their readers into thinking that they had surveyed and responded to evidence, opinion, argument, and analysis, which, in fact, they simply declined to address at all.

Their fate, it already is clear, is to be passed over in silence by subsequent generations of scholars; Finkelstein even now has no hearing at all for his ideas on the Pharisees; Goldin is a cult figure, with no influence beyond a tiny circle of devotees; and Baron's work on the study of religion, like his treatment of Judaism in late antiquity, is utterly ignored. It is from them and the tragic fate of their "scholarship" that I learned how to behave, which is to say, in precisely the opposite way, when addressing opinions or results I think stupid or false: spell out precisely how I understand the other person and specify exactly why I maintain that he or she is wrong as to evidence, argument, or result. Still, in defense of the practice, if not the scholarly integrity, of Finkelstein, Goldin, and Baron, I have to point out that the practice of *Todschweigen* is not merely individual but institutional. For decades my books were not accessible at the Hebrew University Library, but were kept under lock and key. Only very recently were they released from their particular Siberia and placed on the shelves of the reading room where other books in the same area are stored. If

canonical Judaism makes these five points when he invokes the category, "intertextuality":

1. *Midrash stands for Judaic biblical interpretation in general:*

    At bottom midrash is not a genre of interpretation but an interpretative stance, a way of reading the sacred text.... The genres in which this way of reading has found expression include ... translations of the Bible such as the early Aramaic targumim; retellings of biblical passages and books such as the 'Genesis Apocryphon'...; sermons, homilies, exegetical prayers and poems, and other synagogue pieces; and of course the great standard corpora of Jewish exegesis..., in short, almost all of what constitutes classical and much of medieval Jewish writing.... For at heart midrash is nothing less than the foundation stone of rabbinic Judaism and it is as diverse as Jewish creativity itself.[26]

---

two generations of Israeli scholars have proposed to work in complete isolation from the critical perspectives espoused and exemplifed by my books, producing work that was unpublishable in European languages and in critical journals but only in their own house organs, such as Tarbiz and Zion, it is not wholly their fault.

But at fault or otherwise, the Israeli practitioners of "Talmudic history" within the code of Omertà have signally failed to gain a hearing from themselves, and they seem not to want to be heard outside of their own sect in any event. So *Todschweigen* proves reflexive: in the end the practitioners destroy themselves through their own silence on the ideas of others. It is hardly surprising, for *Todschweigen* rapidly yields self-censorship, and the fact that in the field of Talmudic history as defined in Jerusalem, not a single scholar under the age of fifty has published a major book in any language other than Hebrew (and most of them have published no books at all) shows the true cost exacted when scholarly integrity fails, and scholarly ethics are violated. Then utter irrationality takes over, and, as we see with Boyarin, people find amazing the fact that scholars really do argue, in book-length statements, with other scholars. What Boyarin finds bizarre scholarship of integrity treats as routine and ordinary.

When Israeli scholarship in Judaic Studies and sectarian Judaic theological scholarship overseas learn the value of reasoned debate with positions other than those deemed official (that day!), then the results of the scholarly efforts, such as they are, of Israeli specialists and rabbinical school professors will gain a position within the arena of civil and reasonable discourse. At this time, outside of the circles of the believers, those scholarly efforts are treated as curiosities. So, we see, Boyarin's amazement that I took the trouble to write "a whole book" to refute Kugel attests to the mentality of the scholarly world in which he works, which is to say, Israeli Orthodox Judaism. There the old Nazi *Todschweigen* defines the norm, and my practice of writing a book to criticize an idea and to set forth the evidence, argument, and proposition pertaining to the falsification of that idea, elicit the contemptuous surprise that Boyarin expressed.

[26]Op. cit., 91-2.

2. *Midrash is precipitated by the character of the verse subject to exegesis:*

    ...Midrash's precise focus is most often what one might call surface irregularities in the text: a good deal of the time, it is concerned with...*problems.*[27]

3. *Midrash is an exegesis of biblical verses, not of books:*

    ...Midrash is an exegesis of biblical verses, not of books. The basic unit of the Bible for the midrashist is the verse: this is what he seeks to expound, and it might be said that there simply is no boundary encountered beyond that of the verse until one comes to the borders of the canon itself.[28]

4. *The components of midrash compositions are interchangeable:*

    Our midrashic compilations are in this sense potentially deceiving, since they seem to treat the whole text bit by bit; but with the exception of certain patterns, these 'bits' are rather atomistic, and, as any student or rabbinic literature knows, interchangeable, modifiable, combinable – in short, not part of an overall exegesis at all.[29]

5. *Midrash is the way every Jew reads Scripture:*

    Forever after, one cannot think of the verse or hear it recited without also recalling the solution to its problematic irritant – indeed, remembering it in the study house or synagogue, one would certainly pass it along to others present, and together appreciate its cleverness and erudition. And so midrashic explications of individual verses no doubt circulated on their own, independent of any larger exegetical context. Perhaps in this sense it would not be inappropriate to compare their manner of circulating to that of jokes in modern society; indeed, they were a kind of joking, a learned and sophisticated play about the biblical text, and like jokes they were passed on, modified, and improved as they went, until a great many of them eventually entered into the common inheritance of every Jew, passed on in learning with the text of the Bible itself.[30]

Seeing the documents as "intertextual," without boundaries distinguishing one from all the others, Kugel treats documentary lines as null, just as he treats all data, deriving from all times and all places, as equally valid, all writings as wholly undifferentiated evidence for the genre he claims to define. If Kugel is right about the documents before us, then, I am inclined to think, we may generalize as follows.

First, we may reasonably ignore the documentary limits pertaining to the very particular literature at hand. Second, even though the Midrash exegeses were formed into compilations of exegesis in circumstances we may identify, for a social group we may describe in

---

[27]Ibid., 92.
[28]Ibid., 93.
[29]Ibid., 95
[30]Ibid., 95.

detail, in response to issues we may define and describe, we may – so the
argument runs – turn directly to the contents of all the books of Midrash
exegesis, without paying any attention to the context of any one of them.
In the present context, we should anticipate that the Bavli's sages will
obscure the lines that differentiate their writings or statements from the
writings or statements to which they make reference, for example, not
only Scripture but also the Mishnah and other normative statements of
facts or rules. If everything is the same thing, and discourse flows every
which way, without regard to documentary lines, then there should be
no evidence of differentiation as to source and distinction between a
cited source and a comment of an authority for whom the document now
speaks. But, of course, the opposite is the fact.

That is the literary side of the issue. What about the religious
historical aspect? From Kugel's statements, it must follow, second, that
when we read these writings, we address a literature not definitively
circumscribed by time, circumstance, and social setting. So history as the
study of the formation of a complex of ideas – of a religious system, in
relationship to the social order that the framers of that system
contemplated, and in the context of the here-and-now realities that had
to be addressed by that system, proves, within Kugel's premises, not so
much implausible as simply impertinent. That conclusion will then
permit us to maintain as a general principle of hermeneutics an
essentially ahistorical, anti-contextual, and formal reading. In
interpreting all literature we may treat as null those considerations of
society and history, particular sensibility and distinctive circumstance, to
which documents in all their particularity and specificity point. Since, it
is clear, Kugel and those who concur with him identify "intertextuality"
as the paramount trait of Jews in general – in the sense that "Jewish
creativity" encompasses everything any Jew wrote anywhere – it is fair
to ask whether or not the Talmud of Babylonia, universally
acknowledged from its redaction to our own time as the Summa of
Judaism, exhibits the traits of intertextuality.

There are three reasons to reject the intertextualist representation of
the rabbinic canon. The first is extrinsic, the second and third,
evidentiary. The extrinsic consideration is the sheer implausibility of
Kugel's racism. That is to say, Kugel's definition, on the surface, is so
racist as to add up to an unacceptable claim to private discourse
conducted through inherently ethnic or national or religious modes of
sensibility not shared with the generality of humanity. If *midrash* is what
Jews do while *exegesis* is what gentiles do when each party, respectively,
interprets the same verses of the the same Holy Scripture with (in
modern times) essentially the same result as to the meaning of the
passage at hand, then in my mind it follows that *midrash*, a foreign word,

simply refers to the same thing – the same activity or process of thought or intellectual pursuit – as does *exegesis*, an English word. Then the word *midrash* bears no more, or less, meaning than the word *exegesis*. Though much is made of the uniqueness of *midrash* and its definitive power for Judaism, no method or hermeneutic always characteristic of the processes or methods of Jewish *midrash* but never of those of the Christian exegesis is adduced in evidence.

The second reason derives from evidence. When they claim that the authorships of the Bavli ignore the lines that differentiate document from document, for example, Scripture from Midrash, Mishnah from Talmud, Kugel and the other intertextualist readers of canonical Judaism are simply, completely, and totally wrong. When Kugel states (in the context of Midrash), "...there simply is no boundary encountered beyond that of the verse until one comes to the borders of the canon itself," for the Bavli (and the Yerushalmi) he is simply and completely wrong.[31] The very language used for the composition of thought has shown a one-sided and quite regular taxonomic power, and at this point in the argument, I hardly need repeat what we now know to be the fact.

The third point – the second deriving from evidence and not from the character of the intertextualist position itself – follows from the second. What we see in the Bavli is that *context* – this setting, this specific, documentary discourse – in fact is determinative and probative of meaning. The linguistic rules that everywhere are followed will show us how carefully the authors of our document have distinguished between themselves and all other writings, that is, have presented a writing that is intra- and not intertextual at its foundations. That language choice follows rules shows us that the document at hand possesses integrity. That is in three definitive dimensions. First, the Bavli's discrete components follow a cogent outline and an intelligible principle of organization. Second, its discrete components conform, in their large aggregates, to a limited and discernible rhetorical plan. Third, the discrete components also contribute to the demonstration of propositions that recur through the document, indeed that the authorship of the document clearly wishes to make. And fourth, that means that the document takes priority over its details, and that the initial discourse of the document takes place within the documentary setting, viewed whole and within a broad perspective of balance, order, and proportion – there, and not solely, or primarily, within the smallest whole units of discourse of which the document is made up, of which the authorship has made use in proving its broader propositions.

---

[31]In the studies cited earlier, I have shown that he is equally wrong for Midrash compilations as well, so we need not rehearse that error of his.

The specific evidence amassed in these pages has shown us that the framers of the Bavli invariably differentiate their own voice from the voices of those whom they introduce as sources of fact and evidence. Obviously, Scripture is invariably identified as such, and this is in two aspects. First of all, when a verse of Scripture is cited, it is labeled as such with the language of "as it is said...," or "as it is written," or with circumlocutions of various sorts. Second, Scripture's language is always distinct from that of the Mishnah and of the sages in general. So there is no possibility of describing the relationship of the document – the Bavli – and Scripture as "intertextual." It is, to the contrary, intratextual: each document is preserved in all its autonomy. But the intratextuality of the Bavli emerges with still greater clarity in the care with which different languages are utilized for distinct purposes: citation of a source of facts in Mishnaic Hebrew, discussion of the facts for the purposes of proposition and argument in Aramaic. Since that is the case not merely in general but consistently throughout, the taxonomic power of language shows us how our authorship has wished carefully to preserve the distinctions between not only Scripture and the Bavli, but the Mishnah and related authoritative materials of undisputed fact and the Bavli. Authors engaged in a careful process of differentiation of their own words from those of their sources and authorities, defining their role against that of those who have come before, do not fall within the definition of intertextuality that, in general, literary critical scholarship has found accurate.

Once we recognize the rules that tell an author whether to use Hebrew (and which Hebrew) and when to use Aramaic, we see how utterly Kugel's definitions violate the lines of structure, order, and meaning, exhibited by the internal evidence of the documents, inductively construed. To say matters plainly, Kugel and those he represents therefore misrepresent the character of not only the literature they purport to adduce in evidence of their hermeneutic and heuristic program, the Midrash, but also of the religious world and culture they claim to characterize as the Talmud of Babylonia defined that religion and culture. Their misrepresentation affects not merely a minor detail, the spelling or the translation of a phrase, but their fundamental grasp of the literature, midrash. Their picture of midrash does more than beg the question by imposing on the data the theory for demonstration of which the data are adduced. That picture drastically and blatantly misconstrues the data, beginning, middle, and end, by reading only in bits and pieces what originated whole and complete. And the misreading misleads when we turn to the Bavli, with its powerful evidence of a prevailing concern to differentiate one source from another: Scripture, Mishnah, Tannaite formulation, and Talmudic deliberation and debate – all kept distinct and separate through the very medium of expression, language itself.

2

How the Bavli Shaped Rabbinic Discourse

The framers of the Bavli not only defined rabbinic discourse for the future, but they also redefined the discourse of the prior centuries. They were the ones who decided that only the Mishnah would receive a *talmud*, that is, a sustained exercise in applied reason and practical logic, set forth in a moving or dialectical argument aimed at holding together in a single, coherent structure a variety of facts and principles. The Mishnah would have a *talmud*, which then was the *Talmud* (whether of Babylonia or of the Land of Israel) – but not the Sifra, the Tosefta, or other received compositions and composites assigned Tannaite standing along with the Mishnah. Other *talmuds*, for those other Tannaite materials, can have been and were composed. But only one document, the Mishnah, would in the end have a *talmud*, and the other *talmuds* that were under way prior to the closure of the Talmud were either never brought to conclusion and closure or were simply suppressed; I think the former the more likely of the possibilities. So the Talmud, meaning both Talmuds, the Talmud of the Land of Israel and the Talmud of Babylonia, decisively shaped rabbinic discourse not only by what was done but also what was not done but left half-done. That the framers of the Bavli decided to do, and that they did.

The Mishnah is not the sole document of the initial writings of the canon of the Judaism of the Dual Torah – those classified as Tannaite in authority or standing[1] – that was subjected to the sustained application

---

[1] I avoid the word "origin," because it is clear that a saying marked with sigla denoting Tannaite standing is not uncommonly formulated in the context of argument about the meaning of a statement in the Mishnah. Hence, the discussion derives from post-Mishnaic figures, who, by definition, are not Tannaite authorities.

of practical reason and critical analysis that, for the Mishnah, yielded the Talmud of Babylonia. Three other classifications of materials enjoyed that same remarkable reading: the Tosefta, the Sifra, and statements marked as Tannaite (for example, with such sigla as TNY', TN', and the like). Each of these classifications of received statements was read exactly as was the Mishnah, and the results of that reading were expressed in the rhetorical and logical program that characterizes the Talmud to the Mishnah. Not only so, but at a determinate age in the unfolding of the rabbinic writings, defined solely by the point of redaction of various writings, people working on the Mishnah and on these other compilations contemplated a *talmud* not only for the Mishnah, but also for the Tosefta, the Sifra, and some other compositions and even composites bearing Tannaite standing. So – from the perspective of the treatment of those other documents, besides the Mishnah – there can have been a *talmud* to the Tosefta, the Sifra, and other Tannaite formations or conglomerations of sayings. I shall show precisely what those other *talmuds* would have looked like by citing passages, sustained and well executed, of Sifra, Tosefta, and baraita criticism and amplification that are indistinguishable in every detail from passages of Mishnah criticism.

When the reading of the Mishnah that yielded our Talmud was under way, these other documents, or materials of the same status – Tannaite – as the Mishnah, also were being read along the same lines. But those other *talmuds* never reached us, and although the Bavli contains ample indication that such *talmuds* could have come into being, it also contains no evidence that, in any sustained way, they did. Once we realize that ours is not the only Talmud that was under way from the closure of the Mishnah to the conclusion of the Bavli, 200-600 C.E., we then grasp how profoundly the framers of the Talmud of Babylonia reshaped all prior discourse, since they made certain that there would be only one *talmud*, the Talmud, and only one privileged document entitled to such a *talmud*, namely, the Mishnah. The compositors of the Bavli, or the Talmud of Babylonia preserve evidence that, just as the Talmud of Babylonia was worked out as an analysis and critique of the Mishnah, so other documents were subjected to the same kind of critical analysis. These compositors provide us with important samples of the written result of that analysis. When we examine those samples, we see beyond doubt that, just as the Mishnah was studied in a systematic and orderly way so as to yield the Bavli as we have it, so the Sifra and the Tosefta (among numerous documents closed prior to the Bavli) were studied in the same way. Not only so, but certain types of statements, accorded the status of Tannaite, were systematically analyzed in their own terms as well. The bearing of these facts upon the problem of how to find out what passages of the Bavli attest to opinion held prior to the closure of the Bavli is simple. The Mishnah was not the only book produced in the earlier centuries of the Common Era to have been subjected to that sustained analytical criticism that yielded the Bavli (and the Yerushalmi). Other books, and other classifications of statements, also were subjected to that same critical exegetical process. But while the Mishnah's exegesis led to the Bavli, the Sifra's and the Tosefta's did not. A kind of writing that addressed several documents then can have yielded not only the Bavli but an equivalent exegesis, a *talmud* so to speak, for the Sifra and the Tosefta and other materials as well – but we do not have the *talmud* for any other book but the Mishnah. The conclusion I draw from that fact, which I mean to demonstrate in these pages, is that, where we find writing in the Bavli but not pertinent to the requirements of the Bavli's framers, that writing was carried out separate from the work on the Mishnah that led to the Bavli. In the final section of this essay I shall further set forth reasons to conclude that these talmuds that serve documents other than the Mishnah not only are distinct from the Bavli's redactional program but also give evidence of a type of writing that served documents prior to to the Bavli. That is what I mean when I speak of how the Bavli shaped rabbinic discourse.

The upshot is that the framers of the Bavli imposed upon the entirety of rabbinic discourse their own definition of not only what would be said, but also what would not be said: how matters would be organized and categorized, and how they would not be so set forth. The Mishnah would be the only received document that would be accorded a *talmud*, not the Sifra or the Tosefta or the compositions or composites of sayings marked as Tannaite. Not only so, but, still more important, the *talmud* that the Mishnah would receive would be framed by the framers of the Bavli acting on their own, and not as mere heirs and glossators of prior exegesis of the Mishnah. So the Mishnah would have as its *talmud* the only *talmud*, the *Talmud*, the Bavli (in succession after the Yerushalmi). That is precisely how the Talmud shaped rabbinic discourse – not only for time to come, but also for time past. The Bavli reshaped what its authors had received and defined what its heirs would discuss: the Mishnah as they read it, that alone. But that sufficed.

I. The Unrealized Talmud of Sifra:
Cases in Bavli Menahot

What we now shall see is a set of examples of how the analysis, in the Bavli, of a passage in the Sifra follows precisely the same rhetorical and logical rules that govern the analysis in the Bavli of a passage of the Mishnah. That fact by itself shows that the same forms framers of a passage of analysis and criticism of the Mishnah used in the Bavli's commentary to the Mishnah characterized the work of framers of a passage of the Sifra that the Bavli has preserved for us. It would seem to me that the prevalence of the same literary conventions in the reading of two distinct documents, each with its own indicative traits, strongly suggests the work was done more or less within the same period of literary formulation and among people responsive to the same conventions of analysis. Then a further fact will prove exceedingly suggestive. It is that the analysis of the Sifra's passage proceeds wholly in terms required by that passage and ignores the setting, within the composite of the Bavli, in which the Sifra's passage has been preserved. That seems to me to mean that the framers of the commentary on the Sifra's passage had in mind a document that would be devoted to not the Mishnah but Sifra. Then the framers of the critical analysis of the Sifra's materials proposed to produce a commentary to the Sifra, parallel to what was being accomplished for the Mishnah. But that commentary to the Sifra, that is, that *talmud to Sifra*, did not survive, except in bits and pieces in the Bavli itself. In the following example, we see how the Sifra's materials are articulated in relationship to the Mishnah.

6:6

A.	The offering of the first sheaf of barley rendered [the produce of the new crop] permitted in the country, and the two loaves [of Pentecost/Shabuot, Lev. 23:16, rendered new produce permitted for the meal-offering] in the sanctuary.
B.	Before the offering of the first sheaf of barley, they do not bring [from new produce, grain that is to be used for] meal-offerings, first fruits, and the meal-offering which accompanies [drink-] offerings along with beasts.
C.	And if one brought [grain for any of these before the offering of the first sheaf of barley], it is invalid.
D.	[As to bringing grain for any of these items of B] before the two loaves – one should not do so (Lev. 23:16).
E.	And if one brought grain from the new crop for use in preparing them, it is valid.

I.3	A.	*Rami bar Hama raised this question:* "If the two loaves are presented not in the proper order, what is the law on their permitting what is forbidden before that time?" [Cashdan: In the ordinary course grain is sown sometime before the offering of the sheaf of new barley, so that before the grain is permitted for use as meal-offerings, that is, after the offering of the two loaves, the two periods affecting grain have passed in normal sequence; first the offering of the sheaf of barley, second, the offering of the two loaves. What if the grain always permitted for meal-offerings after these two points have passed, without regard to the sequence?]
	B.	*What sort of case is contemplated by this question?*

C.   *For instance, grain was sown in the spell between the offering of the sheaf of first barley and the offering of the two loaves, and then the time for offering the two loaves and the next sheaf of barley passed. Do we say that the two loaves permit use of the new crop only when the offerings follow the usual order but not when they do not follow the usual order, or do they permit the use of the new grain for the meal-offerings even when not in the usual order?*

D.   Said Rabbah, "*Come and take note*":

E.   "If you bring a meal-offering of first fruits to the Lord, [you shall bring new ears parched with fire, grits of the fresh grain, as your meal-offering of first fruits]":

F.   This refers to the meal-offering that is the sheaf of first grain.

G.   And whence does it derive? From barley.

H   You say that it derives from barley. Might one suppose that it derives from wheat?

I.   R. Eliezer says, "Here the word 'new ears' is used here and also with reference to the events in Egypt.

J.   "Just as, with reference to the events in Egypt, the word 'new ears' refers to barley, so here it refers to barley [so we find at Ex. 9:31: 'The flax and the barley were ruined, for the barley was in the ear and the flax was in bud. But the wheat and the spelt were not ruined, for they are late in coming up.']"

K.   R. Aqiba says, "In regard to a communal offering the bringing of first fruits at Passover is noted, and the bringing of first fruits at Pentecost as well. Of the species of grain from which the individual person brings her obligatory offering [that is, the wife accused of adultery], the community brings its offering of first fruits at Passover, and so too, from the species of grain from which the individual brings her obligatory offering, the community likewise should bring its first fruits at Pentecost.

L.   "Now what is the species from which the individual brings his obligatory offering? It is barley [that is, the barley-offering of the wife accused of adultery], and so, too, the community should present its offering from barley.

M   "And do not object by appealing to the analogy to the obligatory offering of the community in connection with the two loaves of bread [which form a meal-offering, and which is obligatory, and which derives from wheat], for the two loaves of bread do not fall into the category of first fruits [and so do not present a relevant analogy]" [Sifra XXVI:III.1-2].

N   *[Rabbah now continues:] "Now if it were the fact that the two loaves permit use of the new crop even when not in the usual order, then how can you claim that the two loaves are not classified as first fruits at all [for the two loaves of bread do not fall into the category of first fruits]? For it can come about that the sheaf of first barley is presented out of the grain that took root before the presentation of the two loaves but after the presentation of the sheaf of first barley for the prior year, and the grain used for the two loaves of the grain that had taken root prior to the presentation of this year's sheaf of first barley but after last year's two loaves."*

O.   *But do you really suppose that* [69A] *we require the two loaves to derive*
      from first fruits of any particular fruit [Cashdan: *and therefore as long as*
      no grain of any particular sowing has been used in the temple, the two
      loaves may serve as first fruits]? *That is not the case. We require them*
      to be first fruits of the altar [that is, first fruits of the year's produce
      to be offered on the altar (Cashdan)], *and in this case the altar has*
      consumed this year's produce [Cashdan: for wheat used for the sheaf
      of barley was of this year's produce, even though of an earlier
      sowing].

What is important is the character of Rabbah's continuation of the
abstract from the Sifra. He spells out the implications of that abstract for
the issue raised at the outset. So we cannot regard N as a comment on
the foregoing; the talmud here focuses upon the question raised by Rami
bar Hami, which is an investigation of how the principles of the law
pertain to interstitial matters. What follows, in context, is a long set of
equivalent theoretical issues, typical of one standard type of Talmudic
amplification of the Mishnah's law. The abstract from Sifra has
contributed only an illustrative fact; the Sifra has not been given a
sustained reading, in its own terms, like that accorded to the Mishnah
and to the issues raised by the Mishnah's principles of law.

Let us now turn to a passage that illustrates my contention that the
Sifra, like the Mishnah, is read in its own terms, and not solely in
relationship to some other, principal document (in the case of the Bavli,
the Mishnah). In my first example, we shall see how the Bavli to M.
Menahot 6:3 reads the Mishnah paragraph. Then Sifra's contribution in
its own terms follows. The important side will be what follows that
passage.

                                    6:3

A.   How did they do it?
B.   Agents of the court go forth on the eve of [the afternoon before]
      the festival [of Passover].
C.   And they make it into sheaves while it is still attached to the
      ground, so that it will be easy to reap.
D.   And all the villagers nearby gather together there [on the night
      after the first day of Passover], so that it will be reaped with
      great pomp.
E.   Once it gets dark [on the night of the sixteenth of Nisan], he says
      to them, "Has the sun set?"
F.   They say, "Yes."
G.   "Has the sun set?"
H.   They say, "Yes."
I.   "[With] this sickle?"
J.   They say, "Yes."
K.   "[With] this sickle?"
L.   They say, "Yes."
M.   "[With] this basket?"

N.   They say, "Yes."

O.   "[With] this basket?"

P.   They say, "Yes."

Q   On the Sabbath, he says to them, "[Shall I reap on] this Sabbath?"

R.   They say, "Yes."

S.   "[Shall I reap on] this Sabbath?"

T.   They say, "Yes."

U.   "Shall I reap?"

V.   They say, "Reap."

W.   "Shall I reap?"

X.   They say, "Reap" –

Y.   three times for each and every matter.

Z.   And they say to him, "Yes, yes, yes."

AA.   All of this [pomp] for what purpose?

BB.   Because of the Boethusians, for they maintain, "The reaping of the [barley for] the offering of the first sheaf of barley is not [done] at the conclusion of the festival."

I.1   A.   *Our rabbis have taught on Tannaite authority:*

B.   *These are the days on which there is to be no fasting, and on some of them also, mourning is forbidden as well:*

C.   *From the first until the eighth day of Nisan, during which the daily whole-offering was set up, mourning is forbidden;*

D.   *From the eighth of Nisan until the close of the festival of Passover, during which time the date for the festival of Pentecost was reestablished, fasting is forbidden.*

The Tannaite complement, when amplified, will tell us the meaning of the references to specific parties or facts that the Mishnah contains. It is now amplified to the point.

I.2   A   *From the first until the eighth day of Nisan, during which the daily whole-offering was set up, mourning is forbidden:*

B.   For the Sadducees said, "A private person may voluntarily present a daily whole-offering."

C.   *What was the exegesis of Scripture that supported their claim?*

D.   "The one lamb you shall offer in the morning and the other lamb you shall offer at dusk" (Num. 28:4) [the "you" is singular, hence an individual may provide the daily whole-offering].

E.   *And what did the other side answer?*

F.   "My food which is presented to me for offerings made by fire, of a sweet savor to me, you shall observe" (Num. 28:2) [and the "you" here is plural].

G.   This indicates that all of them should derive from funds taken up from the public funds in the chamber.

I.3   A   *From the eighth of Nisan until the close of the festival of Passover, during which time the date for the festival of Pentecost was reestablished, fasting is forbidden:*

B.   For the Boethusians say, "The festival of Pentecost must always coincide with a Sunday [seven full weeks after the offering of the first sheaf of barley-grain, which in their view was offered only on a Sunday].

C. Rabban Yohanan ben Zakkai engaged with them and said to them, "You total and complete schmucks! How do you know it?"

D. Not a single one of them could answer, except a doddering old fool, who stumbled and mumbled against him, saying, "Our lord, Moses, loved Israel and knew that Pentecost lasted for only one day, so he therefore made sure to place it on a Sunday, so that Israel would have a two-day vacation."

E. He recited in his regard the following verse: "It is an eleven day journey from Horeb to Kadesh Barnea by way of Mount Seir" (Deut. 1:2).

F. [65B] "Now if our lord, Moses, really loved Israel all that much, why did he delay them in the wilderness for forty years!"

G. He said to him, "My lord, do you think you can get rid of me with that kind of garbage?"

H. He said to him, "You total schmuck! Are you going to treat the complete Torah that is ours like the idle nattering and chattering that is all you can throw up? One verse of Scripture says, 'You shall count for yourself fifty days' (Lev. 23:16), and another verse states, 'Seven weeks shall be complete' (Lev. 23:15). So how about that? The one verse refers to a case in which the festival day coincides with the Sabbath, the other, when a festival day coincides with a week day." [Pentecost may coincide with any day of the week.]

I.4 A. R. Eliezer says, "That proof is not necessary. Lo, Scripture says, 'You shall count for yourself fifty days' (Lev. 23:16) – the counting depends upon the court, [the court fixed the days of the festivals, so they tell the community the time from which to commence counting the days of the waving of the sheaf of barley], and, it follows, the meaning of 'Sabbath' cannot be the Sabbath that commemorates creation, for then the counting would be in the hands of just anybody [and not the court in particular. Everybody could do it]." [Cashdan: If the counting starting on Sunday, after the Sabbath that commemorates creation, everybody could do it just as well.]

I.5 A. R. Joshua says, "The Torah has said, 'count a month of days (Num. 11:20), and [after counting twenty-nine days, the thirtieth day] is to be sanctified as the new moon, and, further, 'sanctify the festival of Pentecost' (Lev. 23:15-16). Just as on the occasion of the new moon, something new takes place at the beginning of the counting" [Cashdan: namely, the new moon, for the twenty-nine days are counted from the first day of the new month], so with Pentecost something new takes place [Cashdan: namely, the festival of Passover. Now if the counting always commenced on Sunday, nothing new would take place].

I.6 A. R. Ishmael says, "The Torah has said, 'Present the sheaf of first barley on Passover and the two loaves on the festival of Pentecost. Just as the latter are offered on the festival, at the start of the festival, so the former is presented on the festival, at the start of the festival [and that is not always on a Sunday]."

I.7   A.   R. Judah b. Betera says, "Here we find a reference to the Sabbath [in regard to Pentecost, 'unto the morrow of the seventh Sabbath, Lev. 23:16] and we find a reference to the Sabbath there as well [with reference to the sheaf of barley, 'on the morrow after the Sabbath,' Lev. 23:11]. Just as in the first instance, the festival day, indeed the commencement thereof, is near the Sabbath [starting as it does immediately after the Sabbath, meaning, the week], so the festival in the latter case must commence near the offering of the barley sheaf, indeed at the beginning of the festival." [Cashdan: Thus the festival of Passover is immediately to precede the offering of the sheaf of barley; Sabbath in context clearly means the festival day.]

Now comes Sifra's treatment of the same theme. The issue is precisely the one that has been treated: proof that "after the Sabbath" refers not to Sunday but to the day following the first festival day of Passover. The proof is worked out in its own terms, but the issue is identical. The purpose of inserting what follows then is clear: further proof of the same proposition, an anthology of such proofs, all of them equally to the point of the amplification of the Mishnah. So Sifra's composition on its own terms has been inserted as an aspect of Mishnah commentary: information required to make sense of what the Mishnah says – not for the purpose of expounding a passage of the Sifra in terms of the requirements of its statements, their logic, their cogency.

I.8   A.   *Our rabbis have taught on Tannaite authority:*
       B.   "And you shall count for yourself" (Lev. 23:15) – the duty of counting is incumbent on every person.
       C.   "On the morrow after the Sabbath" (Lev. 23:16) – that is, on the day after the festival [of Passover].
       D.   But perhaps that refers to the day after the Sabbath that commemorates creation?
       E.   R. Yosé bar Judah says, "Lo, Scripture says, 'You shall count fifty days' (Lev. 23:16) – every time you make a count, it shall not be for more than fifty days. Now if you maintain that the cited verse speaks of the day after the Sabbath, meaning, after the Sabbath of creation, then sometimes the count might reach fifty-one, or fifty-two, or fifty-three, or fifty-four, or fifty-five, or fifty-six!"
       F.   R. Judah b. Batera says, "That proof is hardly required. [66A] Lo, Scripture says, 'And you shall count for yourself' (Lev. 23:15) – the duty of counting is incumbent on every person. So the counting depends upon the decision of the court, and the meaning cannot be the Sabbath that commemorates creation, in which case the counting would be in everybody's hands."
       G.   R. Yosé says, "'On the morrow after the Sabbath' (Lev. 23:16) – that is, on the day after the festival [of Passover]. You say that it is on the day after the festival [of Passover]. But perhaps that refers to the day after the Sabbath that commemorates creation?

H.   "Can you really say so? Now does Scripture say, 'from the morrow after the Sabbath with respect to Passover'? And is not 'from the morrow after the Sabbath' stated without further explanation?

I.   "Now is not the entire year filled with Sabbaths? Then go and reckon what Sabbath is under discussion?

J.   "And, furthermore, here we find a reference to 'from the morrow after the Sabbath,' and elsewhere we find the same language ['counting fifty days to the morrow after the seventh Sabbath'].

K.   "Just as 'from the morrow after the Sabbath' refers to a festival day and the beginning of the festival day [specifically, Pentecost, to which reference is made here],

L.   "So 'on the morrow after the Sabbath' used here refers to the festival and the beginning of the festival [hence, the morrow after the Sabbath that is the first day of Passover]."

M.   R. Simeon b. Eleazar says, "One verse of Scripture says, 'Six days you will eat unleavened bread' (Deut. 16:8), and another verse says, 'Seven days you will eat unleavened bread' (Ex. 12:15).

N.   "How are these two verses of Scripture to be sustained despite their contradiction?

O.   "It must be unleavened bread that you cannot prepare and eat from new grain all seven days but only for six days, which is to say, unleavened bread made from grain of the new growing season may be eaten [only from the second day of the festival of Passover onward].

P.   "Then how am I to interpret 'on the morrow of the Sabbath'?

Q.   "'On the morrow' after the festival day."

R.   "From the day that you brought the sheaf of the wave-offering; seven full weeks shall they be, counting":

S.   Might one suppose that one may harvest, bring the sheaf of first grain, and count, whenever one wants to do so?

T.   Scripture says, "You shall count seven weeks; begin to count the seven weeks from the time you first put the sickle to the standing grain then you shall keep the feast of weeks to the Lord your God with the tribute of a freewill-offering from your hand" (Deut. 16:9-10).

U.   If "from the time you first put the sickle to the standing grain," might one suppose that one should indeed reap the sheaf and do the counting, but make the presentation whenever he wants to do so?

V.   Scripture says, "from the day that you brought the sheaf of the wave-offering; seven full weeks shall they be, counting fifty days to the morrow after the seventh Sabbath; then you shall present a cereal-offering of new grain to the Lord."

W.   Might one suppose that one reaps, counts, and makes the presentation by day?

X.   Scripture says, "seven full weeks shall they be."

Y.   When are they full? When one begins in the [prior] evening.

Z.   Then might one suppose one should reap by night, count by night, and make the presentation by night also?

AA.   Scripture says, "from *the day* that you brought...."

BB.   The presentation takes place only by day.

CC.   How so?

DD.   The reaping and the counting are by night, and the presentation by day [Sifra CCXXXII:I.1-6].

I.9   A.   *Said Raba, "All of the proposed proofs are subject to refutation except for the last two named authorities of the first, and the last two named authorities of the second formulation [Yosé's second contribution and Simeon b. Eleazar's], which cannot be refuted.*

B.   *"Now as to the demonstration of Rabban Yohanan ben Zakkai, here is the refutation: perhaps the harmonization of the conflicting verses is in line with what Abbayye said, for said Abbayye, "The religious duty is to count the days and also the weeks"* [Cashdan: One verse speaks of counting days, the other, weeks.]

C.   *"As to the demonstration of R. Eliezer and R. Joshua, "How do you know that when reference is made to the festival day, it is to the first day of the festival? It could speak of the last day of the festival."*

D.   *"As to the proof of R. Ishmael and R. Judah b. Batera, these are beyond refutation. For if it is from R. Yosé bar Judah's reading, there is this refutation: perhaps the fifty days excludes the six days you list. And if from the view of R. Judah b. Batera, here is the refutation: how do we know that reference is made to the first day of the festival, perhaps it is to the last day of the festival. So R. Yosé himself perceived the same problem, which is why he added the second interpretation, 'and furthermore.'"*

No. 9 focuses upon the exposition of the Sifra's proofs. It is a tertiary formation, but it can be classified as a gloss upon a gloss upon the Mishnah. What follows cannot:

I.10   A.   *Reverting to the body of the foregoing:*

B.   *Said Abbayye, "The religious duty is to count the days and also the weeks":*

C.   *The rabbis of the household of R. Ashi counted the days and also the weeks.*

D.   *Amemar counted the days but not the weeks, saying, "This is a memorial to the sanctuary."*

No. 10 serves not the Mishnah, nor yet the gloss upon the gloss of the Mishnah, but only the requirement of expounding the clarification of Sifra's clarification – in its own terms. This is not a stunning example of the besought writing, but it suggests what we may expect: a commentary to the Sifra that is not required for the purposes of Mishnah exegesis or amplification of Mishnah exegesis.

In the following, the Sifra's materials are introduced simply to show that a verse adduced in evidence for one proposition serves some other altogether. Any discussion then of the Sifra's passage is irrelevant to the purpose for which the Bavli requires the passage – a mere probative fact, not a dialectical argument – and in fact is joined to the Sifra, in terms of the Sifra, and only then carried over, entire and complete, into the Bavli, where it serves no coherent purpose at all.

7:1

A. And these are meal-offerings [from which] the handful is taken, and the residue of which belongs to the priests (Lev. 7:7-9):

B. (1) the meal-offering of fine flour (Lev. 2:21),

C. and (2) [the meal-offering prepared in] a baking pan (Lev. 2:9, 7:8),

D. and (3) [the meal-offering prepared in] a frying pan,

E. and (4) the loaves,

F. and (5) the wafers (Lev. 2:9-10),

G. and (6) the meal-offering of gentiles,

H. and (7) the meal-offering of women,

I. and (8) the meal-offering of the offering of the first sheaf of barley (Lev. 2:16),

J. and (9) the meal-offering of a sinner (Lev. 5:12),

K. and (10) the meal-offering of a woman accused of adultery (Num. 5:26).

L. R. Simeon says, "[From] the meal-offering of a priest who was a sinner (Lev. 7:16), the handful is taken [even though the whole of it in any case is offered on the altar], and the handful is offered by itself, and the residue [thereof] is offered by itself."

III.1 A. [And these are meal-offerings [from which] the handful is taken, and the residue of which belongs to the priests (Lev. 7:7-9): and (6) the meal-offering of gentiles:] Said R. Huna, [73B] "Peace-offerings of gentiles are to be classified as burnt-offerings." [Cashdan: No part may be eaten, they are wholly burned; their meal-offerings also must be wholly burned.]

B. "If you wish, I shall prove this on the basis of reasoning, and if you wish, I shall prove it on the basis of a verse of Scripture:

C. "If you wish, I shall prove this on the basis of reasoning: the gentile in his heart has only Heaven in mind [and does not possess the intentionality of planning to eat part of the offering himself or have the priest eat any of it; he does not know that such distinctions are feasible].

D. "And if you wish, I shall prove it on the basis of a verse of Scripture: 'Which they will offer to the Lord for a burnt-offering' (Lev. 22:18) – whatever they present shall be classified as a burnt-offering."

E. Objected R. Hama bar Guria: "A gentile who volunteered to present peace-offerings, if he gave them to an Israelite, the Israelite eats them. If he gave them to a priest, the priest eats them [T. Sheq. 3:11A-C]."

F. *Said Raba, "This is the sense of the statement:* 'If it was on the stipulation that an Israelite might achieve atonement through them, then the Israelite eats them; if it was on the stipulation that a priest may achieve atonement through them, then the priest eats them."

G. Objected R. Shizbi, "And these are meal-offerings [from which] the handful is taken, and the residue of which belongs to the priests (Lev. 7:7-9): and (6) the meal-offering of gentiles." [Cashdan: So it is not entirely burned, and the same is the case with his peace-offerings.]

H. *Said R. Yohanan, "That really is no contradiction, for the one statement represents the position of R. Yosé the Galilean, the other, of R. Aqiba, as has been taught on Tannaite authority":*

I. ["And the Lord said to Moses, Say to Aaron and his sons and all the people of Israel, When anyone of the house of Israel or of the sojourners in Israel presents his offering, whether in payment of a vow or as a freewill-offering which is offered to the Lord as a burnt-offering to be accepted, you shall offer a male without blemish, of the bulls or the sheep or the goats. You shall not offer anything that has a blemish, for it will not be acceptable for you. And when any one offers a sacrifice of peace-offerings to the Lord, to fulfil a vow or as a freewill-offering, from the herd or from the flock, to be accepted it must be perfect; there shall be no blemish in it" (Lev. 22:17-21).]

J. "Israel":

K. These are Israelites.

L. "Sojourners":

M. This refers to proselytes.

N. "The sojourners":

O. This encompasses wives of proselytes.

P. "In Israel":

Q. This includes women and slaves.

R. "Then why does Scripture refer to 'any one'?

S. "That encompasses gentiles who may give sacrifices through making vows or as freewill-offerings ["whether in payment of a vow or as a freewill-offering"] like Israelites.

T. "'Whether in payment of a vow or as a freewill-offering which is offered to the Lord as a burnt-offering':

U. "I know that the law at hand applies only to a burnt-offering. How do I know that peace-offerings also are subject to the same rule?

V. "Scripture says, 'in payment of a vow' [which may be for a peace-offering].

W. "How do I know that the law covers a thanksgiving-offering?

X. "Scripture says, 'or as a freewill-offering.'

Y. "How do I know that the law encompasses birds, meal-offerings, libations, frankincense, and wood for the fire?

Z. "Scripture says, 'in payment of a vow,' covering all the vows that people may make to contribute to the temple, 'or as a freewill-offering,' covering all the things that they may contribute as freewill-offerings.

AA. "If so, why does Scripture make explicit reference to the burnt-offering: 'which is offered to the Lord as a burnt-offering'?

BB. "This excludes offerings brought by Nazirites," the words of R. Yosé the Galilean [Sifra: Aqiba].

CC. Said to him R. Aqiba [Sifra: Yosé], "Even if you spend the whole day adding to the arguments, still, here we have a reference only to burnt-offerings alone. '...Which they will offer to the Lord for a burnt-offering' means that gentiles may present only burnt-offerings" [Sifra CCXXIII:I.1-2].

III.2   A. *But does the rule that a gentile may not present a Nazirite offering derive from the stated source? Surely it derives from the following:*

B. "Speak to the children of Israel and say to them, When either man or woman shall clearly utter a vow, the vow of a Nazirite, to consecrate himself to the Lord" (Num. 6:2) – Israelites take a vow, and gentiles do not take such a vow.

C. *If the proof had derived from that source, I might have concluded that it is an offering that he may not present, but that the Nazirite vow does apply. So the passage before us teaches us that that is not the case.*

III.3   A. *In accord with which authority is the following, which we have learned in the Mishnah:* Said R. Simeon, "Seven rules did the court ordain, and this (1) [foregoing one] is one of them. A gentile who sent his burnt-offering from overseas and sent drink-offerings with it – they are offered from what he has sent. But if not, they are offered from public funds. And so, too, a proselyte who died and left animals designated for sacrifices – if it has drink-offerings, they are offered from his estate. And if not, they are offered from public funds. And it is a condition imposed by the court on a high priest who died, that his meal-offering (Lev. 6:13) should derive from public funds" (M. Sheq. 7:6).

B. *May we then say this rule [which allows gentiles to present drink-offerings] is in accord with the position of R. Yosé the Galilean, not with R. Aqiba?*

C. *You may even maintain that it represents the position of R. Aqiba, for the sense is,* burnt-offerings plus everything that goes along with them.

III.4   A. *In accord with which Tannaite authority is the following, which our rabbis have taught as a Tannaite statement:*

B. "All who are native shall do these things in this way, in offering an offering by fire, a pleasing odor to the Lord" (Num. 15:13) – but then a gentile does not present drink-offerings.

C. Might one suppose that his burnt-offering will not require drink-offerings?

D. Scripture states, "...in this way...."

E. *Now in accord with whom is that formulation? For it cannot be either R. Yosé the Galilean or R. Aqiba!*

F. *It cannot be R. Yosé the Galilean, for lo, he has said, even wine a gentile may not present, nor can it stand for R. Aqiba, for lo, he has said that a gentile may present a burnt-offering but nothing else!*

G. *If you like, I shall tell you that it accords with the position of R. Yosé the Galilean, and if you like, I shall tell you that it accords with the position of R. Aqiba.*

H. *If you like, I shall tell you that it accords with the position of R. Yosé the Galilean: just remove from the formulation reference to wine.*

I. *And if you like, I shall tell you that it accords with the position of R. Aqiba: he holds that the gentile may present not only a burnt-offering, but* burnt-offerings plus everything that goes along with them.

The Sifra's passage is introduced to begin with to show that there are two distinct positions on the issue at hand. All that is needed from the Sifra, therefore, is evidence of that fact. Then No. 2 addresses the claim of the Sifra's passage to show the source for the rule from the cited passage, rather than from some other; here is a fine example of how a passage of the Sifra is subjected to an analysis entirely congruent to analyses of passages of the Mishnah ("what is the source...it is from this verse...but is that the real source? is not the source the following verse...?"). Not only so, but No. 3, again a mode of analysis entirely familiar from the Mishnah, appeals to the Sifra as its focus. We want to know which of the two of Sifra's authorities stands behind the cited passage of the Mishnah, and No. 4 continues this analysis of how the Sifra's statements relate to other Tannaite statements. None of this is required for the purposes of Mishnah exegesis, but all of it is quite natural to a document that wishes to read the Sifra in the way in which the Mishnah is read.

What follows provides a first-class example of how the treatment of the Sifra's passage will highlight what the Sifra wishes to show, not what the Bavli's frame of a Mishnah commentary cites the Sifra's passage to prove; the two propositions are complementary, but they are distinct. Then the further discussion of the passage at hand concerns not what is proved by the Sifra that is relevant to the Mishnah, but what is proved by the Sifra in terms important to its own framers. The distinction here is critical. The one passage wants to know how come "[From] the meal-offering of a priest who was a sinner (Lev. 7:16), the handful is taken [even though the whole of it in any case is offered on the altar], and the handful is offered by itself, and the residue [thereof] is offered by itself." The Sifra's author is going to prove that "the performance of the meal-offering rite of a priest [who has inadvertently sinned] is assigned to that priest [so that he may perform his own rite and retain possession of the residue of the meal-offering that he himself has presented]." Now as a matter of fact these propositions are entirely complementary. But the one is not the other. And the appended analysis, Nos. 2ff. below, is formulated wholly in terms of the Sifra's issue. That is, then, a talmud to the Sifra, not to the Mishnah.

IV.1   A.   R. Simeon says, "[From] the meal-offering of a priest who was a sinner (Lev. 7:16), the handful is taken [even though the whole of it in any case is offered on the altar], and the handful is offered by itself, and the residue [thereof] is offered by itself":

        B.   *What is the scriptural basis for this position?*

        C.   *It is in line with that which our rabbis have taught on Tannaite authority:*

        D.   "It shall belong to the priest, like the meal-offering" (Lev. 5:13) –

E.   The meaning is that the performance of the meal-offering rite of a priest [who has inadvertently sinned] is assigned to that priest [so that he may perform his own rite and retain possession of the residue of the meal-offering that he himself has presented].

F.   Or might the intent not be to declare permitted [to the priesthood the residue] of the tenth ephah of fine flour that has been brought by a priest? [Cashdan: The verse then tells us that a priest's obligatory meal-offering is like the meal-offering of an Israelite that is eaten by the priests after the handful has been taken out.]

G.   How then shall I interpret the statement, "Every meal-offering of a priest shall be wholly burned, it shall not be eaten" (Lev. 6:23/Heb. 6:16)?

H.   This then would refer to a meal-offering that the priest has brought as a freewill-offering, and as to the tenth ephah that he has presented, that may be eaten.

I.   But [contrary to that line of argument] Scripture states, "It shall belong to the priest, like the meal-offering":

J.   Lo, it is in the status of the meal-offering that he presents as a freewill-offering, with the result that just as the freewill-offering of meal that he presents does not yield a residue that may be eaten, so the tenth ephah of fine flour that he presents may not be eaten.

K.   Said R. Simeon, "And is it written, 'and it shall be the priest's as his meal-offering'? What it says is, 'It shall belong to the priest, like the meal-offering':

L.   [73B] "Lo, the tenth ephah of fine flour that a priest has brought is in the classification of the tenth ephah of fine flour that an Israelite presents.

M.   "Just as the tenth ephah of fine flour that an Israelite presents yields a handful, so a handful is taken up from this offering as well.

N.   "But might one then say, just as the handful is taken from the meal-offering presented by the poor sinner who is an Israelite, and the remainder may be eaten, so when the handful is taken from the poor sinner's meal-offering presented by a priest, the residue may be eaten?

O.   "Scripture states, 'the priest's as the meal-offering': In what regards the priest, it is like the meal-offering of a sinner who is of the Israelite caste, but in respect to what concerns the fire on the altar, it is not like that meal-offering.

P.   "The handful that is taken up is presented by itself, and the residue is presented by itself" [Sifra LXII.I.16].

IV.2   A.   *But is the rule that the rites of the priest's meal-offering may be carried out by the priest drawn from that exposition? Surely it derives from the following:*

B.   How on the basis of Scripture do we know that a priest may come to present his offerings at any occasion and at any time that he wants?

C.   Scripture states, "And come with all the desire of his soul...and minister" (Deut. 18:6).

D.   *Had I derived the ruling from that verse, I might have suppose that reference is made to something that is not presented by reason of sin, but as to something that is presented by reason of sin, I might have said that that is not the case.*

IV.3   A.   *But is the rule that the rites of the priest's meal-offering may be carried out by the priest drawn from that exposition? Surely it derives from the following:*

B.   "And the priest shall make atonement for the soul that errs, when he sins through error" (Num. 15:28) – this teaches that a priest may make atonement for himself through his own act of service.

C.   *Had I derived the ruling from that verse, I might have suppose that that rule pertains only to offerings that are presented for a sin committed in error, but not for offerings presented for a sin committed deliberately; so we are informed that that is the case as well.*

D.   *So are there really offerings that are presented for sins committed deliberately?*

E.   *Yup: deliberately taking a false oath (Lev. 5:1).*

As we proceed to **IV.1**, we find ourselves on familiar ground. A passage of the Sifra is introduced to prove a rule set forth in the Mishnah rests on scriptural foundations. But what that passage proves is distinct, though related: not that the handful of the meal-offering of a priest who has sinned is burned on the altar, along with the residue, but that the priest may present his own meal-offering under the specific circumstances. Then No. 2 raises a question pertinent not to the issue that has required the framer of No. 1 to introduce the abstract of the Sifra, but to the passage of the Sifra itself. And No. 3 goes forward along the same lines. That is important, because the now run-on quality of the composite is entirely routine in the Bavli; here we see that precisely the principles of agglutination that govern in the Bavli's exposition of the Mishnah are in place in the exposition of the Sifra's claims.

Sifra's complement to the following Mishnah paragraph amplifies the Mishnah paragraph's own scriptural demonstration. What is important to us will be whether or not the further extension of discussion concerns the Mishnah's or the Sifra's formulations of matters, and, as we shall see, it is with the latter.

8:2D-I

D.   [77B] And from all of them did one take one [loaf of each kind] out of ten as heave-offering, as it is said, "And he shall offer one out of each offering as a heave-offering to the Lord" (Lev. 8:14) –

E.   "one" – that he should not take a broken one;

F.   "out of each offering" – (1) that all the offerings should be equivalent [ten loaves for each kind of animal],

G.   and (2) that he should not take [two loaves] from one offering [and none at all] for its fellow [that is, he should take one loaf of each kind],

H.	"to the priest who tosses the blood of the peace-offerings it shall belong" (Lev. 8:14) –
I.	and the remainder [of the bread] is eaten by the owner.

I.1   A.   *Our rabbis have taught on Tannaite authority:*

B.   "[And of such he shall offer one cake from each offering, as an offering that is raised up to the Lord;] it shall belong to the priest who throws the blood of the peace-offerings":

C.   [The one cake is to be taken] from the mass [of cakes that are] joined together.

D.   "One":

E.   Meaning that one should not take half a loaf [of five], but rather, a whole loaf of ten. [That is, one should not prepare five loaves of each required type and take of the five loaves a half of a loaf, which would then yield the requisite one of ten in proportion. Rather, there must be ten loaves of each type, and one takes one loaf of each type, for the requisite tenth.]

F.   "From each offering":

G.   This teaches that all of the offerings should be equal in size [so that one is not large, another small]. [Or: that all should be treated in one and the same manner.]

H   [Further,] that one should not take a loaf from one offering in behalf of what is owing from its fellow, [that is, four loaves of a single variety in behalf of all of the loaves of the three sorts].

I.   "As an offering that is raised up to the Lord":

J.   I do not know how many are required.

K.   Lo, I reason as follows:

L.   We find here reference to "an offering that is raised up," and we find the same usage with regard to the offering that is raised up out of the tithe. Just as the latter usage involves one-tenth, so here, too, the requirement is one-tenth. [The offering to the Lord is one-tenth of the number of cakes and wafers of various sorts, e.g., four out of forty, and the residue is left for the priesthood.]

M.   Or take this route:

N   We find here reference to "an offering that is raised up," and we find the same usage with regard to the first fruits.

O.   Just as when we find the usage, "an offering that is raised up" in regard to first fruits, there is no fixed volume that is required, so when we find that same usage here, there is no fixed volume that is required.

P.   Let us then determine the correct analogy:

Q   Let us draw an analogy for "an offering that is raised up" in which there is no further offering to be made, [namely, the offering of the cakes and wafers] from a case of "an offering that is raised up" in which there is no further offering to be made [namely, the offering raised up from the tithe itself, from which no further offerings are exacted],

R.   But let not the case of the offering of first fruits serve as the generative analogy, from which a further offering thereafter is raised up [specifically, the great offering that is raised up and also the offering that is raised up out of the tithe].

S.   Or take this route:

T. We draw an analogy for a case of an offering that is raised up and then eaten in the place in which the offering is made [that is, the offering of the loaves] from the case of an offering that is raised up and then eaten in the place in which the offering is made, [namely, the offering of first fruits, both of them being eaten in Jerusalem],

U. But the offering that is raised up from tithe, which is not eaten in the place in which the offering is made, should not give testimony [since it may be eaten even in the provinces, and not only in Jerusalem].

V. Accordingly, Scripture settles the issue when it says, "as an offering that is raised up to the Lord,"

W. For the use of the language, "raised up," serves to establish an analogy [between offerings in which exactly that language is used]:

X. We find here reference to "an offering that is raised up," and we find the same usage with regard to the offering that is raised up out of the tithe. Just as the latter usage involves one-tenth, so here, too, the requirement is one-tenth. [The offering to the Lord is one-tenth of the number of cakes and wafers of various sorts, and the residue is left for the priesthood.]

Y. Now we have learned that in the case of an offering that is raised up, the requisite proportion is one out of ten.

Z. But I do not know how large a loaf is involved.

AA. Lo, I reason in this way:

BB. Here we find a reference to "leavened bread" ["This offering, with cakes of leavened bread added, he shall offer along with his thanksgiving sacrifice of well being" (Lev. 7:13)], and elsewhere, with reference to the two loaves, we find the same ["You shall bake choice flour and bake of it twelve loaves" (Lev. 24:5)].

CC. Just as leavened bread with reference to the two loaves involves a tenth ephah per loaf, so leavened bread here involves a tenth ephah for each loaf.

DD. Or take this route:

EE. We find reference to loaves here and likewise with reference to the show bread.

FF. Just as when we find a reference to loaf in regard to the show bread, two-tenths of an ephah are required per loaf, so here too, two-tenths of an ephah are required for each loaf.

GG. Let us then determine the correct analogy:

HH. Let us derive an appropriate analogy for a meal-offering which is presented leavened and is presented along with a sacrifice from a meal-offering which is offered leavened and is presented with a sacrifice, but let the show bread not serve, for it is not offered leavened [but only as unleavened bread] and it also is not presented with a sacrifice.

II. Or take this route:

JJ. Let us draw an analogy for a meal-offering which derives from grain grown both in the land and abroad, grain that is of the new season along with grain of the old, from a meal-offering the grain of which may derive from the land or from abroad, and from grain grown in the new season or grain of the old.

KK. But let the case of the two loaves not provide an analogy, for these derive only from grain grown in the land, and they are presented only from loaves back from grain grown in the new growing season.

LL. Scripture states [with references to the two loaves], "You shall bring from your settlements two loaves of bread as an elevation offering; [each one made of two-tenths of a measure of choice flour, baked after leavening, as first fruits to the Lord. With the bread you shall present as burnt-offerings to the Lord seven yearling lambs without blemish....The priest shall elevate these – the two lambs – together with the bread of first fruits as an elevation offering before the Lord...]" (Lev. 23:17-18).

MM. Now Scripture's reference to "you shall bring" can only mean that you must bring the offering which is analogous to one that is specified in another passage [hence the analogy is between the show bread and the bread-offering that goes along with a thanksgiving-offering (following the commentary of Rabbenu Hillel)].

NN. Lo, the one is like the other.

OO. Just as the one involves a tenth ephah of fine flour per loaf, so what you bring that is analogous but in another connection involves a single tenth ephah of fine flour per loaf. [That would prove that the two loaves of the show bread are made each of a tenth of a measure of choice flour!]

PP. Or take this route:

QQ. Just as these [namely, the two loaves of Lev. 23:17-18] have to be made of two-tenths of an ephah of fine flour, so those must be two two-tenths of an ephah of fine flour.

RR. [These conflicting results require attention to the language before us.] Scripture states, "will be...," and the use of the plural indicates that two-tenths of an ephah of fine flour are required here.

SS. We have learned in regard to the leavened bread that it is to be ten-tenths [in all, for the required loaves].

TT. How do we know that the unleavened bread also is to be made of ten-tenths of an ephah of fine flour in all?

UU. Scripture states, "This offering, with cakes of leavened bread added, he shall offer along with his thanksgiving sacrifice of well being" (Lev. 7:13).

VV. As a counterpart to the leavened bread, bring unleavened bread.

WW. Just as the leavened bread involves ten-tenths, so the unleavened bread should involve ten-tenths of an ephah.

XX. Might one suppose that the ten-tenths of an ephah of fine flour involved in the unleavened bread should form a single offering?

YY. Scripture states explicitly, "then he shall offer with the thank-offering unleavened cakes mixed with oil, unleavened wafers spread with oil, and cakes of fine flour well mixed with oil."

ZZ. And then: "And of such he shall offer one cake from each offering [as an offering to the Lord]."

AAA. The upshot is a third of a tenth from each species and so three loaves per tenth, and, further, the upshot is that the bread of a thanksgiving-offering is made up of forty loaves. One takes one of them for each species, thus four loaves, and gives them to the priest,

BBB. "It shall belong to the priest who throws the blood of the peace-offerings":

CCC. And the remainder is eaten by the owner [LXXXVI:I.1-7].

I.2 A. A master has said, "'[And of such he shall offer one cake from each offering, as an offering that is raised up to the Lord;] it shall belong to the priest who throws the blood of the peace-offerings': [The one cake is to be taken] from the mass [of cakes that are] joined together":

B. *But what about the following:* "And all the fat thereof shall he take off from it" (Lev. 4:19) – *how here can we carry out the rule of taking the offering from the mass that is joined together?*

C. *The answer accords with what R. Hisda said Abimi said, for said R. Hisda said Abimi, "The meat may not be cut up before the portions that are presented as a sacrifice have been removed"* [Cashdan: when the fat is taken off, the animal therefore is all connected in a mass].

I.3 A. A master has said, "We find here reference to 'an offering that is raised up,' and we find the same usage with regard to the offering that is raised up out of the tithe. Just as the latter usage involves one-tenth, so here, too, the requirement is one-tenth. [The offering to the Lord is one-tenth of the number of cakes and wafers of various sorts, and the residue is left for the priesthood]":

B. *But why not derive the appropriate rule from the analogy of the heave-offering at Midian* [the portion of the spoil at Num. 31:28-29, which was a five-hundredth part given to the priest, Eleazar (Cashdan)]?

C. We adopt as our governing analogy for heave-offering that is given throughout all generations the law applying to heave-offering that is given throughout all generations, but let not the case of heave-offering presented at the episode of Midian decide matters, for it does not apply for all generations to come.

D. *But how about inferring the rule from the analogy of the heave-offering in the matter of dough-offering [Num. 15:19, a twenty-fourth]?*

E. A Tannaite authority of the household of R. Ishmael [stated], "We adopt as our governing analogy for heave-offering concerning which the language 'of it...as heave-offering unto the Lord' (Lev. 7:14), the rule that pertains to heave-offering concerning which the language 'of it...as heave-offering unto the Lord' (Num. 18:26, the heave-offering of the tithe) is used, *and that eliminates the heave-offering of dough, concerning which the language 'of it...as heave-offering unto the Lord' is not used."*

I.4 A. *Raba raised this question:* "As to the heave-offering taken up from the cakes of thank-offering, are people liable on that account [should non-priests eat this offering deliberately] to the death penalty or [if the act was inadvertent] to the sanction of paying the added fifth of the value, or is that not the case? Since an analogy is drawn to heave-offering of tithe, then in this matter, too, the analogy applies, or perhaps the All-Merciful has excluded this type of heave-offering, otherwise analogous to the other, when it uses the language 'therein' (Lev. 22:9) and 'from it' (Lev. 22:14) [which pertain only to heave-offering of produce, not any other kind of heave-offering]?

B. "If it falls into ordinary food, does it impose upon that food the status of heave-offering or not [as would be the case of heave-offering of ordinary food that was mixed with other produce]?"

C. *The questions stand.*

I.5 A. A master has said, "[These conflicting results require attention to the language before us.] Scripture states, 'will be...,' and the use of the plural indicates that two-tenths of an ephah of fine flour are required here":

B. *What is the exegesis that pertains here?*

C. [78A] Said R. Isaac bar Abdimi, "'Will be' in the plural is used here" [and the word is written with two Ys, each bearing the numerical value of ten, so ten-tenths, which can refer not to the two loaves, which are said explicitly to be made up of two-tenths, it can refer only to the leavened cakes of the thank-offering (Cashdan)].

D. *But maybe it means ten qapizas [ten half-qabs]?*

E. Said Raba, "In context, Scripture is speaking of tenth ephahs."

I.6 A. We have learned in regard to the leavened bread that it is to be ten-tenths [in all, for the required loaves]. How do we know that the unleavened bread also is to be made of ten-tenths of an ephah of fine flour in all? Scripture states, "This offering, with cakes of leavened bread added, he shall offer along with his thanksgiving sacrifice of well-being" (Lev. 7:13). As a counterpart to the leavened bread, bring unleavened bread. Just as the leavened bread involves ten-tenths, so the unleavened bread should involve ten-tenths of an ephah:

B. But can a rule that is derived by analogy based on the congruence of other shared traits [but not verbal ones in context] turn around and teach a lesson through an analogy based on on the congruence of other shared traits [but not verbal ones in context]?

C. It is a case in which the original rule was derived on a polythetic basis ["from itself and something else".] [Cashdan: The original inference that the leavened cakes of the Thank-offering shall consist of ten-tenths, a tenth for every cake, was not entirely drawn from the case of the two loaves, in as much as the number of cakes, ten, is deemed to be expressly stated in connection with the leavened cakes of the thank-offering by virtue of the expression "they shall be." Accordingly, the leavened cakes supplied the rule that there must be ten cakes, and the two loaves supplied the rule that there must be a tenth for each cake.] And any case of polythetic congruence is not classified as an argument that is basically one from congruence.

D. *That poses no problem to him who takes the view that it indeed is not classified as an argument from congruence. But from the perspective of*

       him who maintains that it is indeed an argument from congruence, what
       is to be said?

E.   The language "you shall bring" is augmentative [= Scripture
states explicitly, "then he shall offer with the thank-offering
unleavened cakes mixed with oil, unleavened wafers spread
with oil, and cakes of fine flour well mixed with oil." And then:
"And of such he shall offer one cake from each offering [as an
offering to the Lord]." The upshot is a third of a tenth from each
species and so three loaves per tenth, and, further, the upshot is
that the bread of a thanksgiving-offering is made up of forty
loaves].

There can be no doubt that in this enormous and successful dialectical
argument, Sifra's vast complement and restatement is expounded in its
own framework. In context, the Mishnah's brief version looks like a
summary; or Sifra's like a vast expansion. But in actuality, Sifra's
authorship states this matter the way it commonly works matters out, the
modes of argument being routine for that document, the rhetoric being
standard. So there is no settling the question. It is clear that Nos. 2, 3-4,
5, 6 form a *talmud* to the Sifra's text. It was this passage that first alerted
me to the phenomenon which we now see is routine. The next instance
shows that we deal with what is routine and not isolated.

8:2A-C

A.   For the [bread brought with] consecration [offering, Lev. 8:22 -
28] they brought [the offerings] like the unleavened [bread of the
meal-offering] which goes with the thank-offering: (1) loaves
and (2) wafers and (3) [oil-] soaked cakes.

B.   The [wafers of the] Nazirite's [meal-offering] consisted of two-
thirds of the unleavened [cakes] of the thank-offering: [ten
unleavened] loaves and [ten unleavened] wafers. But soaked
cakes are not [brought along] with it.

C.   They [the Nazirite's offering] turn out to be ten Jerusalem qabs
[five for unleavened loaves, five for unleavened wafers] which
are six-tenths [of an ephah]; and something left over [six and
two-thirds tenths].

II.1   A.   They [the Nazirite's offering] turn out to be ten Jerusalem qabs
[five for unleavened loaves, five for unleavened wafers] which
are six-tenths [of an ephah]; and something left over [six and
two-thirds tenths]:

       B.   *Our rabbis have taught on Tannaite authority:*

       C.   "His peace-offerings":

       D.   this serves to encompass the peace-offerings brought by a
Nazirite, indicating that [Sifra lacks:] they [the Nazirite's
offering] turn out to be ten Jerusalem qabs [five for unleavened
loaves, five for unleavened wafers] which are six-tenths [of an
ephah]; and something left over [six and two-thirds tenths].

       E.   Might that involve everything that is stated in the present
context?

F.   Scripture says, "with cakes of unleavened bread," [Bavli lacks:]
          [following Elijah of Vilna's emendation:] and it is not presented
          saturated in oil. How then am I to interpret the meaning of "his
          peace-offerings," so far as that phrase encompasses the peace-
          offerings of a Nazirite? It means that the peace-offerings of the
          Nazirite are subject to the rule requiring ten [cakes made of]
          Jerusalem *qabs* [of flour] for a quarter of a log of oil]
          [LXXXV:I.13].

II.2   A.   *What is the exegesis behind this reading?*
        B.   Said R. Pappa, "['His peace-offerings' encompasses within the
                  Nazirite's offering] only those species that are covered by the
                  language 'unleavened,' *excluding soaked cakes, that are not covered by
                  the term 'unleavened."* [Cashdan: This term describes the cakes and
                  wafers prescribed for the thank-offering, Lev. 7:12, accordingly the
                  unleavened cakes spoken of in the Nazirite offering signify these
                  same cakes.]
        C.   A Tannaite authority of the household of R. Ishmael [stated], "'A
                  basket of unleavened bread' (Num. 5:16) forms an encompassing
                  generalization; 'cakes' and wafers' then represent
                  particularizations of the foregoing. So we have an encompassing
                  generalization followed by a particularization, and whenever we
                  have an encompassing generalization followed by a
                  particularization, then what is covered under the encompassing
                  generalization is only what is explicitly stated in the
                  particularization: *only cakes and wafers, nothing more."*

II.1 provides a routine clarification, borrowed from Sifra, and No. 2
presents an amplification of the foregoing. In the next part we shall see
that the Tosefta's complement to the adjacent Mishnah paragraph, M.
Men. 8:3E-L, is treated in precisely the same manner.

What are we to make of data of this kind (stipulating that I have not
selected the sole candidates for analysis in the whole of the Bavli)? Now
everybody knows that the compilers of the Bavli and even the authors of
some of its compositions will adduce important passages of the Sifra for
their own purposes. What is important for our purpose is how these
abstracts are treated when they have served the Bavli's framers' purpose.
Are they then left unexamined, as inert facts? Yes indeed, in our sample
we found that that was sometimes the case. Are they examined in
relationship to the exegesis of the Mishnah? Yes, that is quite so. But are
the Sifra passages read in terms of their own interests, program, foci,
points of cogency, and coherent discourse? Indeed they are, and for the
present purpose, that is the key. For what I have aimed to show in this
part of the exposition is not that there certainly was a *talmud* to the Sifra
equivalent to the Talmud of Babylonia to the Mishnah. Nor do I mean to
suggest that a sizable proportion of what we find in the Sifra has been
subjected to that program of critical analysis that the Bavli brings to the

Mishnah. Those propositions do not pertain to the thesis I here set forth. All I wish to show is two facts.

[1] The way in which the framers of the Bavli read the Mishnah is the way in which the framers of passages, in the Bavli, on the Sifra read the Sifra.

[2] Passages in the Sifra that are subjected to exegesis may be read not for purposes of Mishnah exegesis but for purposes of Sifra exegesis.

What we have learned is one simple fact. There could have been a *talmud* to the Sifra, and, if there were, it would have looked remarkably like "the Talmud," that is, the Bavli. So the Bavli to the Mishnah ought to have equalled the preserved and recorded composition and set of compositions, the composite of critical analysis to the Sifra. But if there was such a *talmud* to the Sifra, it has not survived. There could have been such a document; we do not have it.

Why not? Maybe there was such a *talmud*, but it did not survive. But what if we can show that materials for a talmud to the Tosefta also were fully in hand? On the one side, that, too, may yield only two accidents of circumstance. After all, our sample for Sifra shows what might have been, for the sample is too much a sequence of brief episodes, and out of such, no *talmud* could have come. But what if we see that, in point of fact, the Talmud that we do have, in fact for large stretches, serves *not* the Mishnah but the Tosefta? Then it would follow that, if there was a talmud to the Tosefta, it has been absorbed into the Talmud to the Mishnah. In that case a very different picture emerges. It is then a fact that will make sense of my question about how the Bavli has shaped rabbinic discourse. So onward to the Tosefta, with a new question: not only whether we find evidences of a talmud to a document other than the Mishnah, but how important such a *talmud* can have been in its own context.

II. The Unrealized Talmud of Tosefta:
The Cases of Bavli and Yerushalmi Berakhot Chapter Eight

Our question concerning the Tosefta is in two parts. First, does the Tosefta enjoy critical analysis of its statements, in the way that the Mishnah and the Sifra do? Second, is it the fact that the Talmud that we do have, in fact for large stretches, serves *not* the Mishnah but the Tosefta? What we now want is a counterpart to what the Bavli does, time and again, in response to a given paragraph of the Mishnah: a large-scale, complete composite, made up of various compositions, in which a sustained reading of the Mishnah paragraph, its foundations in

Scripture, the meaning of its language, the implications of its principles, is fully exposed. A first-class example of exactly that reading of the Tosefta in the manner in which the Mishnah is read will be only suggestive. What we require is something more: a clear instance in which the Tosefta, and not the Mishnah, forms the centerpiece of discourse. In that case, it will be clear, we really do have a talmud to the Tosefta – to the Tosefta and not to the Mishnah. Then, in my judgment, stipulating only that our case is not a singleton, a series of one, it will be proven, for the purpose of setting forth my thesis, that there can have been a talmud to the Tosefta, much like the talmud we now have for the Mishnah. In that case, the fact that no such talmud has survived will validate the question on how the Bavli has shaped rabbinic discourse. We therefore turn to our case in point, Bavli Berakhot Chapter Eight, seeing how the Bavli reads the entirety of the Mishnah to that chapter.

Since the distinction between the Mishnah and the Tosefta is now critical, I mark the Mishnah lines by underlining and italics, and only the Tosefta is in boldface type.

8:1

A.   *These are the things which are between the House of Shammai and the House of Hillel in [regard to] the meal:*

B.   *The House of Shammai say, "One blesses over the day, and afterward one blesses over the wine."*

C.   *And the House of Hillel say, "One blesses over the wine, and afterward one blesses over the day."*

8:2

A.   *The House of Shammai say, "They wash the hands and afterward mix the cup."*

B.   *And the House of Hillel say, "They mix the cup and afterward wash the hands."*

8:3

A.   *The House of Shammai say, "He dries his hands on the cloth and lays it on the table."*

B.   *And the House of Hillel say, "On the pillow."*

8:4

A.   *The House of Shammai say, "They clean the house, and afterward they wash the hands."*

B.   *And the House of Hillel say, "They wash the hands, and afterward they clean the house."*

8:5

A.   *The House of Shammai say, "Light, and food, and spices, and Havdalah."*

B.   *And the House of Hillel say, "Light, and spices, and food, and Havdalah."*

C.   *The House of Shammai say, "Who created the light of the fire."*
D.   *And the House of Hillel say, "Who creates the lights of the fire."*

8:6

A.   *They do not bless over the light or the spices of gentiles, nor the light or the spices of the dead, nor the light or the spices which are before an idol.*
B.   *And they do not bless over the light until they make use of its illumination.*

8:7

A.   *He who ate and forgot and did not bless [say Grace] –*
B.   *The House of Shammai say, "He should go back to his place and bless."*
C.   *And the House of Hillel say, "He should bless in the place in which he remembered."*
D.   *Until when does he bless? Until the food has been digested in his bowels.*

8:8

A.   *Wine came to them after the meal, and there is there only that cup –*
B.   *The House of Shammai say, "He blesses the wine, and afterward he blesses the food."*
C.   *And the House of Hillel say, "He blesses the food, and afterward he blesses the wine."*
D.   *They respond Amen after an Israelite who blesses, and they do not respond Amen after a Samaritan who blesses, until hearing the entire blessing.*

To understand what is to follow, I present the chapter of the pertinent materials of the Tosefta, and then compare the Mishnah and the Tosefta. It is only through that stage of comparison that we shall fully grasp how narrowly focused upon the Tosefta, not the Mishnah, is the Bavli's treatment of the first four Mishnah paragraphs.

Tosefta to Mishnah Berakhot Chapter Eight

5:21 (Lieberman, p. 28, lines. 41-42).

They answer *Amen* after a gentile who says a blessing with the divine name. They do not answer *Amen* after a Samaritan who says a blessing with the divine name until they have heard the entire blessing.

5:25 (Lieberman, p. 29, lines 53-57).

A.   [The] things which are between the House of Shammai and the House of Hillel in [regard to] the meal:
B.   The House of Shammai say, "One blesses over the day, and afterward he blesses over the wine, for the day causes the wine to come, and the day is already sanctified, but the wine has not yet come."

C.   And the House of Hillel say, "One blesses over the wine, and afterward he blesses over the day, for the wine causes the sanctification of the day to be said.
        "Another explanation: The blessing over the wine is regular [= always required when wine is used], and the blessing over the day is not continual [but is said only on certain days]."

D.   And the law is according to the words of the House of Hillel.

5:26 (Lieberman, pp. 29-30, lines 57-61).

A.   The House of Shammai say, "They wash the hands and afterward mix the cup, lest the liquids which are on the outer surface of the cup be made unclean on account of the hands, and in turn make the cup unclean."

B.   The House of Hillel say, "The outer surfaces of the cup are always deemed unclean.
        "Another explanation: The washing of the hands must always take place immediately before the meal.

C.   "They mix the cup and afterward wash the hands."

5:27 (Lieberman, p. 30, lines 61-65).

A.   The House of Shammai say, "He dries his hand on the napkin and leaves it on the table, lest the liquids which are in the napkin be made unclean on account of the cushion, and then go and make the hands unclean."

B.   And the House of Hillel say, "A doubt in regard to the condition of liquids so far as the hands are concerned is resolved as clean."

C.   "Another explanation: Washing the hands does not pertain to unconsecrated food.

D.   "But he dries his hands on the napkin and leaves it on the cushion, lest the liquids which are in the napkin be made unclean on account of the table, and they go and render the food unclean."

5:28 (Lieberman, p. 30, lines 65-68).

A.   The House of Shammai say, "They clean the house, on account of the waste of food, and afterward they wash the hands."

B.   The House of Hillel say, "If the waiter was a disciple of a sage, he gathers the scraps which contain as much as an olive's bulk.

C.   "And they wash the hands and afterward clean the house."

5:29 (Lieberman, p. 30, lines 68-72).

A.   The House of Shammai say, "He holds the cup of wine in his right hand and spiced oil in his left hand."
        He blesses over the wine and afterward blesses over the oil.

B.   And the House of Hillel say, "He holds the sweet oil in his right hand and the cup of wine in his left hand."

C.   He blesses over the oil and smears it on the head of the waiter. If the waiter was a disciple of a sage, he [the diner] smears it on the wall, because it is not praiseworthy for a disciple of a sage to go forth perfumed.

5:30 (Lieberman, pp. 30-31, lines 72-75).

A.   R. Judah said, "The House of Shammai and the House of Hillel did not dispute concerning the blessing of the food, that it is first, or concerning the *Havdalah*, that it is at the end.
"Concerning what did they dispute?
"Concerning the light and the spices, for –
"The House of Shammai say, 'Light and afterward spices.'
"And the House of Hillel say, 'Spices and afterward light.'"

5:30 (Lieberman, p. 31, lines 75-77).

B.   He who enters his home at the end of the Sabbath blesses the wine, the light, the spices, and then says *Havdalah*.

C.   And if he has only one cup [of wine] he leaves it for after the meal and then says all [the liturgies] in order after [reciting the blessing for] it.

5:31 (Lieberman, p. 31, lines 81-85).

A.   If a person has a light covered in the folds of his garment or in a lamp, and sees the flame but does not use its light, or uses its light but does not see its flame, he does not bless [that light]. [He says a blessing over the light only] when he both sees the flame and uses its light.
As to a lantern – even though he had not extinguished it (that is, it has been burning throughout the Sabbath), he recites a blessing over it.

B.   They do not bless over the light of gentiles. One may bless over [the flame of] an Israelite kindled from a gentile, or a gentile who kindled from an Israelite.

5:32 (Lieberman, p. 31, lines 80-81).

In the house of study –
The House of Shammai say, "One [person] blesses for all of them."
And the House of Hillel say, "Each one blesses for himself."

Clearly, the Tosefta has a variety of materials. Some of the materials are freestanding, but some simply cite and gloss the Mishnah. We see in the following comparison just how these things come to the surface. I add in italics the amplificatory language of the Tosefta.

The Tosefta and the Mishnah Compared

Mishnah	Tosefta
M. 8:1. A. These are the things which are between the House of Shammai and the House of Hillel in [regard to] the meal:	Tos. 5:25. [The] things which are between the House of Shammai and the House of Hillel [as regards] the meal:
B. The House of Shammai say, "One blesses the day, and afterward one blesses over the wine."	The House of Shammai say, "One blesses the day, and afterward one blesses over the wine, *for the day causes the wine to come, and the day is already sanctified, but the wine has not yet come.*"
And the House of Hillel say, "One blesses the wine, and afterward one blesses over the day."	And the House of Hillel say, "One blesses over the wine, and afterward one blesses the day, *for the wine causes the sanctification of the day to be said.*" "*Another matter: The blessing of the wine is continual, and the blessing of the day is not continual.*" *And the law is according to the words of the House of Hillel.*
M. 8:2.A. The House of Shammai say, "They wash the hands and afterward mix the cup."	Tos. 5:26. The House of Shammai say, "They wash the hands and afterward mix the cup, *lest the liquids which are on the outer surfaces of the cup may be made unclean on account of the hands, and they may go back and make the cup unclean.*"

And the House of Hillel say, "They mix the cup and afterward wash the hands."

The House of Hillel say, "*The outer surfaces of the cup are perpetually unclean.*

"*Another matter: The washing of the hands is only [done] near [at the outset of] the meal.*"

They mix the cup and afterward wash the hands."

8:3.A. The House of Shammai say, "He dries his hands on the napkin and lays it on the table."

And the House of Hillel say, "On the cushion."

5:27. The House of Shammai say, "He dries his hand on the napkin and lays it on the table, *lest the liquids which are in the napkin may be made unclean on account of the pillow, and they may go and make the hands unclean.*

The House of Hillel say, *A doubt in regard to the condition of liquids so far as the hands are concerned is clean.*

"*Another matter: Washing the hands does not pertain to unconsecrated food. But he dries his hands on the napkin and leaves it on the cushion lest the liquids which are in the pillow may be made unclean on account of the table, and they may go and render the food unclean.*"

M. 8:4.A. The House of Shammai say, "They clean the house and afterward wash the hands."

And the House of Hillel say, "They wash the hands and afterward clean the house."

Tos. 5:28. The House of Shammai say, "They clean the house *on account of the waste of food* and afterward wash the hands."

The House of Hillel say, "*If the waiter was a disciple of a sage, he gathers the scraps which contain as much as on olive's bulk.*"

They wash the hands and afterward clean the house."

8:5.A. The House of Shammai say, "Light, and food and spices, and *Havdalah*."

And the House of Hillel say, "Light, and spices, and food, and *Havdalah*."

5:30. R. Judah said, "*The House of Shammai and the House of Hillel did not dispute concerning the blessing of the food, that it is first, and concerning the* Havdalah *that it is the end. Concerning what did they dispute? Concerning the light and the spices, for* the House of Shammai say, 'Light and *afterward* spices,' and the House of Hillel say, 'Spices and *afterward* light.'"

B. The House of Shammai say, "'Who created the light of the fire.'"

And the House of Hillel say, "'Who creates the lights of the fire.'"

[No equivalent.]

M. 8:8.A. Wine came to them after the meal, and there is there only that cup –

B. The House of Shammai say, "He blesses over the wine and afterward he blesses over the food."

Tos. 5:30 (Lieberman, p. 31, lines 75-77). A. *He who enters his home at the end of the Sabbath blesses over the wine, the light, the spices, and then says* Havdalah.

And the House of Hillel say, "He blesses over the food and afterward he blesses over the wine."

[If wine came to them after the meal and] there is there only that cup House of Shammai say, "He blesses the wine and then the food."

(House of Hillel say, "He blesses the food and then the wine.")

B. *And if he has only one cup* [of wine], *he leaves it for after the meal and then says them all in order after* [blessing] *it.*

If he has only one cup [of wine] [he leaves if for after the meal and then says them all in order, thus:] Wine, then food.

M. 8:6.A. They do not bless the light or the spices of gentiles, nor the light or the spices of the dead, nor the light or the spices which are before an idol.

B. And they do not bless the light until they make use of its illumination.

Tos. 5:31.B. They do not bless the light of gentiles. *An Israelite who kindled* [a flame] *from a gentile, or a gentile who kindled from an Israelite – one may bless* [such a flame].

Tos. 5:31 (Lieberman, p. 31, lines 81-85). A. *If a person has a light covered in the folds of his garment or in a lamp, and he sees the flame but does not use its light, or uses its light but does not see its flame, he does not bless.* [He blesses only] *when he both sees the flame and uses its light.*

M. 8:8.C. They respond *Amen* after an Israelite who blesses, and they do not respond *Amen* after a Samaritan who blesses, until one hears the entire blessing.

Tos. 5:21 (Lieberman, p. 28, lines 41-2). *They answer* "Amen" *after a blessing with the divine name recited by a gentile.*

They do not answer *Amen* after a Samaritan who blesses *with the divine name* until they hear the entire blessing.

The pattern is now clear. We simply cannot understand a line of the Tosefta without turning to the Mishnah. That means that the Tosefta passage before us must have been composed after the Mishnah was in hand, that is, after 200 C.E., and that the authorship of the Tosefta had in mind the clarification of the received document, the Mishnah. So in a very simple sense, the Tosefta is the first talmud, that is to say, it is the first sustained and systematic commentary to the Mishnah. Not only so, but as a talmud, the Tosefta succeeds in ways in which the later Talmuds do not, simply because the Tosefta covers nearly the whole of the Mishnah, nearly all lines of all tractates, while the two Talmuds take up only a selection of the Mishnah tractates, thirty-nine in the Yerushalmi of the Mishnah's sixty-two tractates (excluding tractate Avot, the fathers, which is post-Mishnaic by about a generation or fifty years), and the Bavli thirty-seven of the Mishnah's tractates. Now to the Bavli Berakhot.

I.1　　A.　　Gemara: Our rabbis have taught on Tannaite authority:

　　　　B.　　**The things which are between the House of Shammai and the House of Hillel in [regard to] a meal:**

C.   *The House of Shammai say, "One blesses over the day and afterward*
     blesses over the wine, **for the day causes the wine to come, and the**
     day has already been sanctified, while the wine has not yet
     come."

D.   *And the House of Hillel say, "He blesses over the wine and afterward*
     blesses over the day, **for the wine causes the sanctification to be**
     said.

E.   **"Another matter: The blessing over the wine is perpetual, and**
     the blessing over the day is not perpetual. Between that which is
     perpetual and that which is not perpetual, that which is
     perpetual takes precedence" [T. Ber. 5:25].

F.   **And the law is in accordance with the words of the House of**
     Hillel.

The analytical task is now defined: the analysis of the language of the
Tosefta's formulation. We start with the comparison of the Tosefta's and
the Mishnah's statement, so whatever talmud the Tosefta would have
would take account of the Mishnah. That is hardly a surprise, when we
consider that the Tosefta in large stretches is unintelligible out of
relationship to the Mishnah, and in still larger portions is fully
intelligible only in relationship to the Mishnah.

G.   *What is the purpose of* "another matter"?

H   *If you should say that there [in regard to the opinion of the House of*
     Shammai] two [reasons are given] and here [in regard to the opinion of
     the House of Hillel] one, here, too, [in respect to the House of Hillel,]
     there are two [reasons, the second being]: "The blessing of the wine is
     perpetual and the blessing of the day is not perpetual. That which
     is perpetual takes precedence over that which is not perpetual."

We now turn to the sustained explanation of a statement that occurs only
in the Tosefta; this statement will be worked out in its own terms. Once
more, of course, we observe that the Tosefta itself forms a sustained gloss
to the Mishnah. So the *talmud* to the Tosefta is a *talmud* to a *talmud*. But
less than that none can allege, and if that fact is clear, then the further
claim, that this second *talmud* for its authors was intended as a sustained
program, an alternative *talmud* to the one worked out in the same way
for the Mishnah, is hardly beyond plausibility.

I.2 A.   **And the law is in accord with the opinion of the House of Hillel.**
     B.   *This is obvious [that the law is in accord with the House of Hillel], for the*
          echo has gone forth [and pronounced from heaven the decision that the
          law follows the opinion of the House of Hillel].
     C.   *If you like, I can argue that [this was stated] before the echo.*
     D.   *And if you like, I can argue that it was after the echo, and [the passage*
          was formulated in accord with the] opinion of **[52A]** *R. Joshua, who*
          stated, "They do not pay attention to an echo [from heaven]."

What comes next is a direct consequence of the Tosefta's amplification of the reasoning of the House of Shammai:

I.3   A.   *And is it the reasoning of the House of Shammai that the blessing of the day is more important?*

       B.   *But has a Tanna not taught:* "He who enters his house at the close of the Sabbath blesses over the wine and the light and the spices and afterward he says Havdalah. And if he has only one cup, he leaves it for after the food and then says the other blessings in order after it." [Havdalah is the blessing of the day, yet comes last!]

       C.   *But lo, on what account [do you say] this is the view of the House of Shammai? Perhaps it is the House of Hillel['s opinion]?*

       D.   *Let [such a thought] not enter your mind, for the Tanna teaches:* "Light and afterward spices." *And of whom have you heard who holds this opinion? The House of Shammai, as a Tanna has taught:*

       E.   R. Judah said, "The House of Shammai and the House of Hillel did not differ concerning the [blessing of the] food, that it is first, and the Havdalah, that it is at the end.

       F.   "Concerning what did they dispute? Concerning the light and the spices.

       G.   **"For the House of Shammai say, 'Light and afterward spices.'**

       H   **"And the House of Hillel say, 'Spices and afterward the light'** "[T. Ber. 5:30].

       I.   *And on what account [do you suppose that] it is the House of Shammai as [interpreted by] R. Judah? Perhaps it is [a teaching in accord with] the House of Hillel [as interpreted by] R. Meir?*

       J.   *Do not let such a thing enter your mind, for lo, a Tanna teaches here in our Mishnah:* <u>The House of Shammai say, "Light and food and spices and Havdalah."</u>

       K.   <u>And the House of Hillel say, "Light and spices, food and Havdalah."</u>

       L.   *But there, in the teaching on Tannaite authority, lo, he has taught:* "If he has only one cup, he leaves it for after the food and then says the other blessings in order after it."

       M   *From this it is to be inferred that it is the House of Shammai's teaching, according to the [interpretation] of R. Judah.*

       N   *In any event there is a problem [for the House of Shammai now give precedence to reciting a blessing for the wine over blessing the day].*

       O.   *The House of Shammai suppose that the coming of the holy day is to be distinguished from its leaving. As to the coming of the [holy] day, the earlier one may bring it in, the better. As to the leaving of the festival day, the later one may take leave of it, the better, so that it should not seem to us as a burden.*

       P.   *And do the House of Shammai hold the opinion that Grace requires a cup [of wine]? And lo, we have learned:* <u>[If] wine came to them after the food, and there is there only that cup, the House of Shammai say, "He blesses over the wine and afterward blesses over the food" [M. Ber. 8:8].</u> [So Grace is said without the cup.]

       Q.   *Does this not mean that he blesses it and drinks [it]?*

       R.   *No. He blesses it and leaves it.*

S.   *But has not a master said, "He that blesses must [also] taste [it]."*
T.   *He does taste it.*
U.   *And has not a master said, "Tasting it is spoiling it."*
V.   *He tastes it with his hand [finger].*
W.   *And has not a master said, "The cup of blessing requires a [fixed] measure."* And lo, he diminishes it from its fixed measure.
X.   *[We speak of a situation in which] he has more than the fixed measure.*
Y.   *But lo, has it not been taught:* If there is there only that cup... [so he has no more].
Z.   *There is not enough for two, but more than enough for one.*
AA.   *And has not R. Hiyya taught:* The House of Shammai say, "He blesses over the wine and drinks it, and afterward he says Grace."
BB.   *Then we have two Tannas' [traditions] in respect to the opinion of the House of Shammai.*

This entire discussion depends upon not the Mishnah's statement but the Tosefta's gloss of the Mishnah's statement. All the facts that precipitate sustained inquiry are introduced by the Tosefta; the Mishnah on its own demands little of this discussion, since read by itself, it does not yield the generative propositions that are subjected to analysis. We shall now see that the discussion of the next pericope of the Mishnah is identical: a citation of the Mishnah, an abstract from the Tosefta that supplies the Mishnah's rule's operative consideration, then a sustained and detailed analysis of the Tosefta's account of matters.

II.1   A.   *The House of Shammai say [They wash the hands and afterward mix the cup]... [M. 8:2A].*
        B.   Our rabbis have taught:
        C.   The House of Shammai say, "They wash the hands and afterward mix the cup, for if you say they mix the cup first, [against this view is] a [precautionary] decree to prevent the liquids on the outer sides of the cup, which are unclean by reason of his hands' [touching them], from going back and making the cup unclean" [T. Ber. 5:26].
        D.   *But will not the hands make the cup itself unclean [without reference to the liquids]?*
        E.   *The hands are in the second remove of uncleanness, and the [object unclean in] the second remove of uncleanness cannot [then] render [another object unclean] in the third [remove] in respect to profane foods, [but only to heave-offering]. But [this happens] only by means of liquids [unclean in the first remove].*
        F.   And the House of Hillel say, "They mix the cup and afterward wash the hands, for if you say they wash the hands first, [against this view is] a [precautionary] decree lest the liquids which are [already] on the hands become unclean on account of the cup and go and render the hands unclean."
        G.   *But will not the cup [itself] make the hands unclean?*
        H.   *A vessel cannot render a man unclean.*
        I.   *But will they [the hands] not render the liquids which are in it [the cup] unclean?*

J.   *Here we are dealing with a vessel the outer part of which has been made unclean by liquid. The inner part is clean but the outer part is unclean. Thus we have learned:*

K.   *[If] a vessel is made unclean on the outside by liquid, the outside is unclean, [52B] but its inside and its rim, handle, and haft are clean. If, however, the inside is unclean, the whole [cup] is unclean.*

L.   *What, then, do they [the Houses] dispute?*

M   *The House of Shammai hold that it is prohibited to make use of a vessel whose outer parts are unclean by liquids, as a decree on account of the drippings. [There is] no [reason] to decree lest the liquids on the hands be made unclean by the cup.*

N   *And the House of Hillel reckon that it is permitted to make use of a vessel whose outer part is made unclean by liquids, for drippings are unusual. But there is reason to take care lest the liquids which are on the hands may be made unclean by the cup.*

What is interesting here is that the rhetoric of analysis, given in Aramaic, is not to be distinguished in any way from the rhetoric of analysis of either Mishnah sentences or any other sentences assigned Tannaite status. The language is Aramaic, the analysis is dialectical, moving from point to point. So when I speak of a "talmud" to the Tosefta, I use the word not in a generic sense only, that is, "a sustained critical analysis," but in a denotative sense, "this particular kind of sustained, critical analysis," namely, the kind we find in the Bavli. The pattern of Tosefta citation, followed by talmudic analysis thereof, continues.

II.2   A.   **Another matter: [So that] immediately upon the washing of the hands [may come] the meal [itself].**

B.   *What is the reason for this additional explanation?*

C.   *This is what the House of Hillel said to the House of Shammai: "According to your reasoning, in saying that it is prohibited to make use of a cup whose outer parts are unclean, we decree on account of the drippings. But even so, [our opinion] is better,* for **immediately upon the washing of the hands [should come] the meal."**

II.1   A.   The House of Shammai say, "He dries his hand on the napkin..." [M. 8:3A].

B.   *Our rabbis have taught on Tannaite authority:*

C.   **The House of Shammai say, "He wipes his hands with the napkin and lays it on the table, for if you say, 'on the cushion,' [that view is wrong, for it is a precautionary] decree lest the liquids which are on the napkin become unclean on account of the cushion and go back and render the hands unclean" [T. Ber. 5:27].**

Predictably, the consequent discussion will focus upon what the Tosefta has said the Mishnah means to say.

D.   *And will not the cushion [itself] render the napkin unclean?*

E.   *A vessel cannot make a vessel unclean.*

F.   *And will not the cushion [itself] make the man unclean?*

G.   *A vessel cannot make a man unclean.*

H   And the House of Hillel say, "'On the cushion,' for if you say, 'on the table,' [that opinion is wrong, for it is a] decree lest the liquids become unclean on account of the table and go and render the food unclean" [T. Ber. 5:27].

I.   *But will not the table render the food which is on it unclean?*

J.   *We here deal with a table which is unclean in the second remove, and something unclean in the second remove does not render something unclean in the third remove in respect to unconsecrated food, except by means of liquids [which are always unclean in the first remove].*

K.   *What [principle] do they dispute?*

L.   *The House of Shammai reckon that it is prohibited to make use of a table unclean on the second remove, as a decree on account of those who eat heave-offering [which is rendered unfit by an object unclean in the second remove].*

M   *And the House of Hillel reckon that it is permitted to make use of a table unclean in the second remove, for those who eat heave-offering [the priests] are careful.*

N   Another matter: There is no scriptural requirement to wash the hands before eating unconsecrated food.

O.   *What is the purpose of "another explanation"?*

P.   This is what the House of Hillel said to the House of Shammai: If you ask what is the difference in respect to food, concerning which we take care, and in respect to the hands, concerning which we do not take care – even in this regard [our opinion] is preferable, for there is no scriptural requirement concerning the washing of the hands before eating unconsecrated food.

Q   It is better that the hands should be made unclean, for there is no scriptural basis for [washing] them, and let not the food be made unclean, concerning which there is a scriptural basis [for concern about its uncleanness].

By this point the reader will not be surprised that what is to come follows the precise pattern of the treatment of the opening sentences of the Mishnah chapter.

III.1   A   *The House of Shammai say, "They clean house and afterward wash the hands..." [M. 8:4A].*

B.   *Our rabbis have taught on Tannaite authority:*

C.   The House of Shammai say, "They clean the house and afterward wash the hands, for if you say, 'They wash the hands first,' it turns out that you spoil the food" [T. Ber. 5:28].

D.   *But the House of Shammai do not reckon that one washes the hands first.*

E.   *What is the reason?*

F.   *On account of the crumbs.*

G.   And the House of Hillel say, "If the servant is a disciple of a sage, he takes the crumbs which are as large as an olive [in bulk] and leaves the crumbs which are not so much as an olive [in bulk]."

H   *(This view supports the opinion of R. Yohanan, for* R. Yohanan said, "Crumbs which are not an olive in bulk may be deliberately destroyed.")

> I.   *In what do they differ?*
> J.   The House of Hillel reckon that it is prohibited to employ a servant who is an ignorant man, and the House of Shammai reckon that it is permitted to employ a servant who is an ignorant man.

What follows serves both the Mishnah and the Tosefta, which is hardly surprising; this is a trivial complement to the foregoing.

> III.2   A.   *R. Yosé bar Hanina said in the name of R. Huna, "In our entire chapter the law is in accord with the House of Hillel, excepting this matter, in which the law is in accord with the House of Shammai."*
>   B.   *And R. Oshaia taught the matter contrariwise. And in this matter, too, the law is in accord with the House of Hillel.*

Readers may now wonder whether the entirety of the chapter at hand serves the Tosefta. The answer is negative. Now we have what we should regard as "normal" Bavli, meaning, attention focuses upon the Mishnah in terms of what the Mishnah says, not in terms of what the Tosefta says the Mishnah says.

> IV.1   A.   <u>The House of Shammai say, "Light and food..." [M. 8:5A]</u>.
>   B.   R. Huna bar Judah happened by the house of Rava. He saw that Rava blessed the spices first.
>   C.   He said to him, "Now the House of Shammai and the House of Hillel did not dispute concerning the light, [it should come first].
>   D.   "For it was taught: <u>The House of Shammai say, 'Light, and food, spices, and Havdalah,' and the House of Hillel say, 'Light, and spices, and food, and Havdalah.'</u>"
>   E.   Rava answered him, "This is the opinion [= version] of R. Meir, but R. Judah says, 'The House of Shammai and the House of Hillel did not differ concerning the food, that it comes first, and concerning the Havdalah, that it is at the end.
>   F.   "'Concerning what did they differ?'
>   G.   "'Concerning the light and the spices.'
>   H   "'For the House of Shammai say, 'The light and afterward the spices.'
>   I.   "'And the House of Hillel say, 'The spices and afterward the light.'
>   J.   And R. Yohanan said, "The people were accustomed to act in accord with the House of Hillel as presented by R. Judah."
> V.1   A.   <u>The House of Shammai say, "Who created..." [M. 8:5C]</u>.
>   B.   Rava said, "Concerning the word 'bara' [created] everyone agrees that 'bara' implies [the past tense]. They differ concerning 'boré' [creates]. The House of Shammai reckon that 'boré' means, 'Who will create in the future.' And the House of Hillel reckon that 'boré' also means what was created [in the past]."
>   C.   R. Joseph objected, "'Who forms light and creates darkness' (Isa. 45:7), 'Creates mountains and forms the wind' (Amos 4:13), 'Who creates the heavens and spreads them out'" (Isa. 42:5).
>   D.   "But," R. Joseph said, "Concerning 'bara' and 'boré' everyone agrees that [the words] refer to the past. They differ as to whether one should say 'light' or 'lights.'

E.	"The House of Shammai reckon there is one light in the fire.
F.	"And the House of Hillel reckon that there are many lights in the fire."
G.	We have a Tannaite teaching along the same lines:
	The House of Hillel said to the House of Shammai, "There are many illuminations in the light."

VI.1
A.	*A blessing is not said... [M. 8:6A].*
B.	Certainly, [in the case of] the light [of idolators, one should not say a blessing] because it did not rest on the Sabbath. But what is the reason that for spices [one may not say the blessing]?
C.	R. Judah said in the name of Rav, "We here deal with a banquet held by idolators, because the run-of-the-mill banquet held by idolators is for the sake of idolatry."
D.	But since it has been taught at the end of the clause, "Or over the light or spices of idolatry," we must infer that the beginning of the clause does not deal with idolatry.
E.	R. Hanina from Sura said, "What is the reason is what it explains, namely, what is the reason that they do not bless the light or spices of idolators? Because the run-of-the-mill banquet held by idolators is for the sake of idolatry."

We further note that not all compositions assigned Tannaite authorship and status derive from the Tosefta:

VI.2
A.	*Our rabbis have taught on Tannaite authority:*
B.	One may bless a light which has rested on the Sabbath, but one may not bless a light which has not rested on the Sabbath.
C.	And what is the meaning of "which has not rested on the Sabbath"?
D.	[53A] Shall we say it has not rested on the Sabbath on account of the work [which has been done with it, including] even work which is permitted?
E.	And has it not been taught: They do bless the light [kindled on the Sabbath for] a woman in confinement or a sick person.
F.	R. Nahman bar Isaac said, "What is the meaning of 'which enjoyed Sabbath rest'? Which enjoyed Sabbath rest on account of work, the doing of which is a transgression [on the Sabbath]."
G.	We have learned likewise on Tannaite authority:
H	They may bless a lamp which has been burning throughout the day to the conclusion of the Sabbath.

VI.3
A.	Our rabbis have taught:
B.	They bless [a light] kindled by a gentile from an Israelite, or by an Israelite from a gentile, but they do not bless [a light] kindled by a gentile from a gentile.
C.	What is the reason one does not do so [from a light kindled by] a gentile from a gentile?
D.	Because it did not enjoy Sabbath rest.
E.	If so, lo, [a light kindled by] an Israelite from a gentile also has not enjoyed Sabbath rest.

F. And if you say this prohibited [light] has vanished, and the one [in hand] is another and was born in the hand of the Israelite, [how will you deal] with this teaching?

G. He who brings out a flame to the public way [on the Sabbath] is liable [for violating the Sabbath rule against carrying from private to public property].

H. Now why should he be liable? What he raised up he did not put down, and what he put down he did not raise up.

I. But [we must conclude] that the prohibited [flame] is present, but when he blesses, it is over the additional [flame], which is permitted, that he blesses.

J. If so, a gentile['s flame kindled] from a gentile['s flame] also [should be permitted].

K. That is true, but [it is prohibited by] decree, on account of the original gentile and the original flame [of light kindled on the Sabbath by the gentile].

VI.4 A. Our rabbis have taught:

B. [If] one was walking outside the village and saw a light, if the majority [of the inhabitants of the village] are gentiles, he does not bless it. If the majority are Israelites, he blesses it.

C. Lo, the statement is self-contradictory. You have said, "If the majority are gentiles, he does not bless it." Then if they were evenly divided, he may bless it.

D. But then it teaches, "If the majority are Israelites, he may bless." Then if they are evenly divided, he may not bless it.

E. Strictly speaking, even if they are evenly divided, he may bless. But since in the opening clause [the language is], "The majority are gentiles," in the concluding clause, [the same language is used:] "A majority are Israelites."

VI.5 A. Our rabbis have taught:

B. [If] a man was walking outside of a village and saw a child with a torch in his hand, he makes inquiries about him. If he is an Israelite, he may bless [the light]. If he is a gentile, he may not bless.

C. Why do we speak of a child? Even an adult also [would be subject to the same rule].

D. Rav Judah said in the name of Rav, "In this case we are dealing with [a time] near sunset. As to a gentile, it will be perfectly clear that he certainly is a gentile [for an Israelite would not use the light immediately after sunset]. If it is a child, I might say it is an Israelite child who happened to take up [the torch]."

VI.6 A. Our rabbis have taught:

B. [If] one was walking outside of a village and saw a light, if it was as thick as the opening of a furnace, he may bless it, and if not, he may not bless it.

C. One Tanna [authority] [says], "They may bless the light of a furnace," and another Tanna [says], "They may not bless it."

D. There is no difficulty. The first speaks at the beginning [of the fire], the other at the end.

E. One authority says, "They may bless the light of an oven or a stove," and another authority says, "They may not bless it."

F.   There is no problem. The former speaks of the beginning, the latter of the end.

G.   One authority says, "They may bless the light of the synagogue and the schoolhouse," and another authority says, "They may not bless it."

H   There is no problem. The former speaks [of a case in which] an important man is present, the latter [of a case in which] an important man is not present.

I.   And if you want, I shall explain both teachings as applying to a case in which an important man is present. There still is no difficulty. The former [teaching speaks of a case in which] there is a beadle [who eats in the synagogue], the latter in which there is none.

J.   And if you want, I shall explain both teachings as applying to a case in which a beadle is present. There still is no difficulty. The former teaching [speaks of a case in which] there is moonlight, the latter in which there is no moonlight.

VI.7 A.   Our rabbis have taught:

B.   [If] they were sitting in the schoolhouse, and light was brought before them –

C.   The House of Shammai say, "Each one blesses for himself."

D.   And the House of Hillel say, "One blesses for all of them, as it is said, 'In the multitude of people is the King's glory'" (Prov. 14:28).

E.   Certainly [we can understand the position of the House of Hillel because] the House of Hillel explain their reason.

F.   But what is the reason of the House of Shammai?

G.   They reckon [it as they do] on account of [avoiding] interruption in [Torah study] in the schoolhouse.

H.   We have a further Tannaitic tradition to the same effect:

I.   The members of the house of Rabban Gamaliel did not say [the blessing] "Good health" [after a sneeze] in the schoolhouse on account of the interruption [of study] in the schoolhouse.

VII.1 A.   *They say a blessing neither on the light nor on the spices of the dead... [M. 8:6A].*

B.   What is the reason?

C.   The light is made for the honor [of the deceased], the spices to remove the bad smell.

D.   Rav Judah in the name of Rav said, ["Light made for] whoever [is of such importance that] they take out [a light] before him both by day and by night is not blessed. [And light made for] whoever [is not important, so that] they take out [a light] before him only by night, is blessed."

E.   R. Huna said, "They do not bless spices of the privy and oil made to remove the grease."

F.   Does this saying imply that wherever [spice] is not used for smell, they do not bless over it? It may be objected:

G.   He who enters the stall of a spice dealer and smells the odor, even though he sat there all day long, blesses only one time. He who enters and goes out repeatedly blesses each time.

H   And lo, here is a case in which it is not used for the scent, and still he blesses.

	I.	Yes, but it also is used for the odor – so that people will smell and come and purchase it.
VII.2	A.	Our rabbis have taught:
	B.	If one was walking outside of a village and smelled a scent, if most of the inhabitants are idolators, he does not bless it. If most are Israelites, he blesses it.
	C.	R. Yosé says, "Even if most are Israelites, he still may not bless, because Israelite women use incense for witchcraft."
	D.	But do they "all" burn incense for witchcraft!
	E.	A small part is for witchcraft and a small part is also for scenting garments, which yields a larger part not used for scent, and wherever the majority [of the incense] is not used for scent, one does not bless it.
	F.	R. Hiyya bar Abba said in the name of R. Yohanan, "He who walks on the eve of the Sabbath in Tiberias and at the end of the Sabbath in Sepphoris and smells an odor does not bless it, because it is presumed to have been made only to perfume garments."
	G.	Our rabbis taught: If one was walking in the gentiles' market and was pleased to scent the spices, he is a sinner.
VIII.1	A	[53B] *They do not recite a blessing over the light until it has been used.. [M. 8:6B]:*
	B.	Rav Judah said in the name of Rav, "Not that he has actually used it, but if anyone stood near enough so that he might use the light, even at some distance, [he may say the blessing]."
	C.	So, too, R. Ashi said, "We have learned this teaching even [concerning] those at some distance."
	D.	It was objected [on the basis of the following teaching]: If one had a light hidden in the folds of his cloak or in a lamp, or saw the flame but did not make use of its light, or made use of the light but did not [actually] see the flame, he may not say the blessing. [He may say the blessing only when] he [both] sees the flame and uses its light.
	E.	Certainly one finds cases in which one may use the light and not see the flame. This may be when the light is in a corner.
	F.	But where do you find a case in which one may see the flame and not make use of its light? Is it not when he is at a distance?
	G.	No, it is when the flame keeps on flickering.
VIII.2	A.	Our rabbis have taught:
	B.	They may say a blessing over glowing coals, but not over dying coals ('omemot).
	C.	What is meant by glowing coals?
	D.	R. Hisda said, "If one puts a chip into them and it kindles on its own, [these are] all [glowing coals]."
	E.	It was asked: Is the word 'omemot ['alef] or 'omemot ['ayin]?
	F.	Come and hear, for R. Hisda b. Abdimi said, "'The cedars in the garden of God could not darken ('amamuhu) it'" (Ezek. 31:8).
	G.	And Rava said, "He must make actual use of it."
	H.	And how [near must one be]?
	I.	Ulla said, "So that he may make out the difference between an issar and a pundion [two small coins]."

J.   Hezekiah said, "So that he may make out the difference between a meluzma [a weight] of Tiberias and one of Sepphoris."

K.   Rav Judah would say the blessing [for the light of the] house of Adda the waiter [which was nearby].

L.   Rava would say the blessing [for the light of the] house of Guria bar Hama.

M   Abbayye would say the blessing [for the light of the] house of Bar Abbuha.

N   R. Judah said in the name of Rav, "They do not go looking for the light in the way they go looking for [means to carry out other] commandments."

O.   R. Zera said, "At the outset, I used to go looking [for light]. Now that I have heard this teaching of R. Judah in the name of Rav, I, too, will not go searching, but if one comes my way, I shall say the blessing over it."

IX.1   A.   *He who ate [and did not say Grace]... [M. 8:7A]:*

B.   R. Zevid, and some say, R. Dimi bar Abba, said, "The dispute [between the Houses] applies to a case of forgetfulness, but in a case in which a person deliberately [omitted Grace], all agree that he should return to his place and say the blessing."

C.   This is perfectly obvious. It is [explicitly] taught, "And he forgot."

D.   What might you have said? That is the rule even where it was intentional, but the reason that the Tanna taught, "And he forgot," is to tell you how far the House of Shammai were willing to go [in requiring the man to go back to where he ate. They did so even if a man accidentally forgot]. Thus we are taught [the contrary. Even if one forgot, unintentionally, he must go back].

IX.2   A.   It was taught:

B.   The House of Hillel said to the House of Shammai, "According to your opinion, someone who ate on the top of the Temple Mount and forgot and went down without saying Grace should go back to the top of the Mount and say the blessing."

C.   The House of Shammai said to the House of Hillel, "According to your opinion, someone who forgot a purse on the top of the Temple Mount would not go back and retrieve it.

D.   "For his own sake, he [assuredly] will go back. For the sake of Heaven [should he] not all the more so [go back]?"

E.   There were these two disciples. One did it [forgot Grace] accidentally, and, following the rule of the House of Shammai, [went back to bless], and found a purse of gold. And one did it deliberately [omitted Grace], and following the rule of the House of Hillel [did not go back to say it], and a lion ate him.

F.   Rabbah bar bar Hanna was traveling in a caravan. He ate and was sated but [forgot and] did not say Grace.

G.   He said, "What shall I do? If I tell the men [of the caravan with me] that I forgot to bless, they will say to me, 'Bless here. Wherever you say the blessing, you are saying the blessing to the Merciful [God].' It is better that I tell them I have forgotten a golden dove."

H   So he said to them, "Wait for me, for I have forgotten a golden dove."

I.   He went back and blessed and found a golden dove.

J.   And why was a dove so important?

K.   Because the community of Israel is compared to a dove, as it is written, "The wings of the dove are covered with silver, and her pinions with the shimmer of gold" [Ps. 68:14]. Just as the dove is saved only by her wings, so Israel is saved only by the commandments.

X.1   A.   *Until when can he say the Grace? Until the food is digested in his bowels... [M. 8:7D]:*

B.   How long does it take to digest the food?

C.   R. Yohanan said, "As long as one is no longer hungry."

D.   Resh Laqish said, "As long as one [still] is thirsty on account of his meal."

E.   R. Yemar bar Shelamia said to Mar Zutra – and some say, Rav Yemar bar Shizbi said to Mar Zutra – "Did Resh Laqish really say this? And did not R. Ammi say in the name of Resh Laqish, 'How long does it take to digest a meal? The time it takes to go four miles.'"

F.   There is no problem: Here [we speak of] a big meal, there [we speak of] a small meal.

X.2   A.   *If wine came to them... [M. 8:8A]:*

B.   This implies that in the case of an Israelite['s saying Grace], even though one has not heard the entire blessing, he responds [Amen].

C.   But if he has not heard [the whole Grace], how can he have performed his duty by doing so [assuming he has eaten also]?

D.   Hiyya bar Rav said, "[We speak of a case] in which he did not eat with them."

E.   So, too, did R. Nahman say in the name of Rabbah bar Abbuha, "[We speak of a case] in which he did not eat with them."

F.   Rav said to Hiyya his son, "My son, seize [the cup] and bless."

G.   So did R. Huna say to Rabbah his son, "Seize and bless."

H   This implies that he who says the blessing is better than he who answers Amen. But has it not been taught:

I.   R. Yosé says, "The one who answers Amen is greater than the one who says the blessing."

J.   R. Nehorai said to him, "By heaven! It is so. You should know it, for behold, common soldiers go ahead and open the battle, but the heroes go in and win it."

K.   It is a matter of dispute between Tannaites, as it has been taught:

L.   Both the one who says the blessing and the one who answers Amen are implied [in the Scripture (Neh. 9:5)]. But the one who says the blessing is more quickly [answered] than he who answers Amen.

X.3   A.   Samuel asked Rav, "Should one answer [Amen] after [the blessings of] children in the schoolhouse?"

B.   He said to him, "They answer Amen after everyone except children in the schoolhouse, since they are [saying blessings solely] for the sake of learning."

C.   And this applies when it is not the time for them to say the "Haftarah," but in the time to say "Haftarah," they do respond [Amen].

X.4   A.   Our rabbis have taught:
       B.   "The absence of oil holds up the blessing [Grace]," the words of
             Rabbi Zilai.
       C.   R. Zivai says, "It does not hold it up."
       D.   R. Aha says, "[The absence of] good oil holds it up."
       E.   R. Zuhamai says, "Just as a dirty person [mezuham] is unfit for the
             Temple service, so dirty hands are unfit for the blessing."
       F.   R. Nahman Bar Isaac said, "I know neither Zilai nor Zivai nor
             Zuhamai. But I know a teaching which R. Judah said in the name
             of Rav, and some say it was taught on Tannaite authority:
       G.   "'And be you holy' (Lev. 20:7) – this refers to washing the hands
             before the meal.
       H.   "'And you shall be holy' – this refers to the washing after the meal.
       I.   "'For holy' – this refers to the oil.
       J.   "'Am I the Lord your God' – this refers to the blessing [Grace]."

Two facts are now established. The first is that a sustained set of
composites, made up of important compositions, addresses not the
Mishnah but the Tosefta's amplification of the Mishnah. Viewed in the
context of the Bavli's treatment of the chapter as a whole, units I-III form
a considerable portion of the whole. But there is a second, and more
interesting fact. Once discourse shifts from the Tosefta's reading of the
Mishnah to other matters, the character of the discussion changes rather
strikingly. We move from exceedingly tight exchanges of propositions
and criticism to narrative evidence, deriving from cases, that is, from the
abstract and principled to the concrete and episodic and occasional. That
shift is noteworthy at units IV, V. No. VI does not analyze the law
before us, for example specifying the operative principle at the
foundations of the matter, but compares one law to another. And that is
a different kind of argument altogether. The solution to the problem is
then an interpretation of rhetoric, not an appeal to principle.

Do I then mean to say that merely because the Bavli cites a passage
that occurs in not the Mishnah but the Tosefta, I have a *talmud* made up
within the framework of the Tosefta? Nothing could be further from the
truth. My claim is that there is a talmud to the Tosefta, and that talmud
is purposive, exhibits indicative traits particular to itself, and can be
readily identified and isolated within the framework of the Bavli that
preserves it. My claim rests on a trait of the subsequent units, VI.2, 4, 5,
6, 7; VII.2, IX.2. In all of these units, we find materials accorded Tannaite
status. For none of them is a sustained and ambitious analytical program
devised. So – for the case at hand – where there is a *talmud* other than for
the Mishnah, it will serve what we find in the Tosefta, not materials
accorded Tannaite status but not in the Tosefta; and, further, that other
talmud will exhibit the traits we rightly expect from a well-crafted
composition on a Mishnah sentence or paragraph. What is not given a
talmud but derives from Tannaite authorship is clearly differentiable

from what is given such a *talmud,* and, for the chapter at hand, it is only the Tosefta's materials that enjoy such a striking exposition.

If my contention that people were working on a talmud to the Tosefta in the way in which they were working on a talmud to the Mishnah, then the question arises: when was that counterpart work undertaken? A clear and straightforward answer to that question derives from the Talmud of the Land of Israel (also known as the Yerushalmi), ca. 400 C.E. We shall now see that the discussion of the same chapter of the Mishnah by that other, earlier Talmud drew upon the same Tosefta materials and set forth those materials in much the same way as the framers of the Bavli's Talmud to the Tosefta did. That can only mean one thing. The talmud to the Tosefta was well under way prior to ca. 400, that is, before either of the two Talmuds had reached closure. That proves on narrowly redactional grounds that a talmud to the Tosefta was contemplated very early in the process of the formation of the materials that ultimately flowed into the Bavli. Here is the pertinent part of the Yerushalmi's treatment of the same chapter of the Mishnah.

Yerushalmi to Mishnah Berakhot Chapter Eight

8:1. *The House of Shammai say, "One blesses the day and afterward one blesses over the wine."*
And the House of Hillel say, "One blesses over the wine and afterward one blesses the day."

I.1   A.   *What is the reason of the House of Shammai?*

B.   The sanctification of the day causes the wine to be brought, and the man is already liable for the sanctification of the day before the wine comes.

C.   *What is the reason of the House of Hillel?*

D.   The wine causes the sanctification of the day to be said.

E.   Another matter: wine is perpetual, and the sanctification is not perpetual. [What is always required takes precedence over what is required only occasionally.]

I.2   A.   R. Yosé said, "[It follows] from the opinions of them both that with respect to wine and *Havdalah,* wine comes first."

B.   "*It is not the reason of the House of Shammai* that the sanctification of the day causes the wine to be brought, and here, since *Havdalah* does not cause wine to be brought, the wine takes precedence?"

C.   "*Is it not the reason of the House of Hillel that* the wine is perpetual and the sanctification is not perpetual, and since the wine is perpetual, and the *Havdalah* is not perpetual, the wine comes first?"

D.   R. Mana said, "From the opinions of both of them [it follows] that with respect to wine and Havdalah, *Havdalah* comes first."

E.   "*Is it not the reason of the House of Shammai that* one is already obligated [to say] the sanctification of the day before the wine comes, and here, since he is already obligated for *Havdalah* before the wine comes, *Havdalah* comes first?"

F.   *Is it not the reason of the House of Hillel that* the wine causes the sanctification of the day to be said, and here, since the wine does not cause the *Havdalah* to be said, *Havdalah* comes first?"

G.   R. Zeira said, "From the opinions of both of them [it follows] that they say *Havdalah* without wine, but they say the sanctification only with wine."

H   *This is the opinion of R. Zeira, for* R. Zeira said, they may say *Havdalah* over beer, *but they go from place to place* [in search of wine] *for the sanctification."*

What we see is a sustained analysis of the Tosefta's reading of the Mishnah – and one that is different in its shape and structure from the Bavli's. So the formation of the first of the two Talmuds to the Mishnah comprised, in part, a considerable discussion of not the Mishnah but the Tosefta to the Mishnah – a two-stage talmud. The next discussion is a secondary expansion of the foregoing.

I.3   A.   R. Yosé b. Rabbi said, "They are accustomed there [in Babylonia], where there is no wine, for the prayer leader to go before the ark and say one blessing which is a summary of the seven, and complete it with, 'Who sanctifies Israel and the Sabbath Day.'"

B.   *And thus the following poses a difficulty for the opinion of the House of Shammai: how should one act on the evenings of the Sabbath?*

C.   He *who was sitting and eating on the evening of the Sabbath,* and it grew dark and became Sabbath evening, and there was there only that one cup – [The House of Shammai say, "Wine, then food," and the House of Hillel say, "Food, then wine," so M. 8:8].

D.   Do you say he should leave it for the end of the meal and say all of them [the blessings] on it?

E.   *What do you prefer?*

F.   Should he [first] bless the day? The food takes precedence.

G.   Should he bless the food? The wine takes precedence.

H.   Should he bless the wine? The day takes precedence.

I.   *We may infer* [the answer] *from this:*

J.   If wine came to them after the meal, and there is there only that cup –

K.   Ba said, "Because it [the wine's] is a brief blessing, [he says it first, for] perhaps he may forget and drink [the wine]. But here, since he says them all over the cup, he will not forget [to say a blessing over the wine in the cup]."

L.   What, then, should he do according to the opinion of the House of Shammai?

M   Let him bless the food first, then bless the day, and then bless the wine.

N   *And this poses difficulty for the opinion of the House of Hillel: How should one act at the end of the Sabbath?*

O.   If he was sitting and eating on the Sabbath and it grew dark and the Sabbath came to an end, and there is there only that cup –

P. Do you say he should leave it [the wine] for after the meal and say them all on it?

Q. *What do you prefer?*

R. Should he bless the wine? The food comes first.

S. Should he bless the food? The light comes first.

T. Should be bless the light? The *Havdalah* comes first.

U. *We may infer* [the solution to the impasse] *from this:* R. Judah said, "The House of Shammai and the House of Hillel did not differ concerning the blessing of the food, that it comes first, nor concerning *Havdalah*, that it comes at the end.

V. "Concerning what did they differ?

W. "Concerning the light and the spices, for:

X. "The House of Shammai say, 'The spices and afterward the light.'

Y. "And the House of Hillel say, 'The light and afterward the spices.'"

Z. R. Ba and R. Judah in the name of Rav [said], "The law is according to him who says, 'Spices and afterward light.'"

AA. What should he do according to the opinion of the House of Hillel?

BB. Let him bless the food, afterward bless the wine, and afterward bless the light.

I.4 A. As to [the beginning of the] festival day which coincides with the end of the Sabbath –

B. R. Yohanan said, "[The order of prayer is] Wine, sanctification, light, *Havdalah*."

C. Hanin bar Ba said in the name of Rav, "Wine, sanctification, light, *Havdalah, Sukkah,* and season."

D. *And did not Samuel rule according to this teaching of R. Hanina.*

E. R. Aha said in the name of R. Joshua b. Levi, "When a king goes out and the governor comes in, they accompany the king and afterward bring in the governor."

F. Levi said, "Wine, *Havdalah*, light, sanctification."

I.5 A. R. Zeira asked before R. Yosé, "How shall we do it in practice?"

B. He said to him, "According to Rav, and according to R. Yohanan."

C. And so, too, did the rule come out in practice – according to Rav and according to R. Yohanan.

D. *And when R. Abbahu went south, he would act in accord with R. Hanina, but when he went down to Tiberias, he would act in accord with R. Yohanan, for one does not differ from a man['s ruling] in his own place* [out of courtesy].

E. *According to the opinion of R. Hanina this poses no problem.*

F. *But it poses a problem to the opinion of R. Yohanan:* In the rest of the days of the year does he not bless the light, lest it go out [because of a draft, and he lose the opportunity to say the blessing]? And here, too, he should bless the light before it goes out!

G. *What did R. Yohanan do in this connection?* [How did he explain this difficulty?]

H. Since he has wine [in hand], his light will not go out [for it is protected].

I. Then let him bless the light at the end?

J.   So as not to upset the order [of prayer; lit.: time of the coming Sabbaths], [he does not do so].

8:2.   A   *The House of Shammai say, "They wash the hands and afterward mix the cup." And the House of Hillel say, "They mix the cup first and afterward wash the hands."*

        B.   *What is the reason of the House of Shammai?*

The discussion that follows once more invokes the considerations introduced by the Tosefta:

        C.   So that the liquids which are on the outer side of the cup may not be made unclean by his hands and go and make the cup unclean.

        D.   *What is the reason of the House of Hillel?*

        E.   The outer side of the cup is always unclean [so there is no reason to protect it from the hands' uncleanness].

        F.   Another matter: One should wash the hands immediately before saying the blessing.

        G.   *R. Biban in the name of R. Yohanan [said], "The opinion of the House of Shammai is in accord with R. Yosé and that of the House of Hillel with R. Meir, as we have learned there* [M. Kel. 25:7-8]:

        H   ["In all vessels an outer part and an inner part are distinguished, and also a part by which they are held."]

        I.   R. Meir says, 'For hands which are unclean and clean.'"

        J.   R. Yosé said, 'This applies only to clean hands alone.'"

        K.   R. Yosé in the name of R. Shabbetai, and R. Hiyya in the name of R. Simeon b. Laqish [said], "For *Hallah* [Dough-offering] and for washing the hands, a man goes four miles [to find water]."

        L.   Abbahu in the name of R. Yosé b. R. Hanina said, "This is what he said, '[If the water is] before him [that is, on his way, in his vicinity, or near at hand, he must proceed to it and wash]. But if it is behind him [that is, not on his way], they do not trouble him [to obtain it and wash].'"

        M   Regarding those who guard gardens and orchards [and who cannot leave their posts], what do you do for them as to the insides and the outer sides [of a cup]? [How do we rule in their case? Do we judge them to be in the status of those for whom the water is] on their way, or in the status of those who would have to backtrack?

        N.   Let us infer the answer from this [M. Hal. 2:3]:

        O.   The woman sits and cuts off her Dough-offering *[Hallah]* while she is naked, because she can cover herself up, but a man cannot.

        P.   Now does not a woman sit in the house, yet you say they do not bother her? So, too, here they do not bother him.

I.2   A.   *It has been taught:*

        B.   Washing before the meal is a matter of choice, but afterward it is a matter of obligation.
                But in respect to the first washing, he washes and interrupts, and in the case of the second washing, he washes and does not interrupt.

<table>
<tr><td></td><td>C.</td><td>What is the meaning of "He 'washes and interrupts'?"
R. Jacob b. Aha said, "He washes and then repeats the washing."
R. Samuel bar Isaac said, *"If he is required to repeat the washing,*
how do you claim it is a matter of choice?
["Or if you want, I may point out you require one to go four miles
in search of water], *so how do you claim* it is a matter of choice!"</td></tr>
<tr><td></td><td>D.</td><td>R. Jacob bar Idi said, "On account of the first [washing of hands], a
pig's flesh was eaten; on account of the second [washing of hands],
a woman left her house.
"And some say, three souls were killed on her account. [It is not a
matter of choice at all.]"</td></tr>
</table>

I.3   A.   *Samuel went up to visit Rav. He saw him eating with* [his hands covered by] *a napkin. He said to him, "How so?* [Did you not wash your hands?]"

         B.   *He said to him, "I am sensitive."*

         C.   *When R. Zeira came up here* [to Palestine], *he saw the priests eating with a napkin. He said to them, "Lo, this is in accord with the story of Rav and Samuel."*

         D.   R. Yosé bar Kahana came [and said] *in the name of Samuel,* "One washes the hands for heave-offering, not for unconsecrated food."

         E.   R. Yosé says, "For heave-offering and for unconsecrated food."

         F.   R. Yosah in the name of R. Hiyya bar Ashi, and R. Jonah and R. Hiyya bar Ashi in the name of Rav [said], "They wash the hands for heave-offering up to the wrist, and for unconsecrated food up to he knuckles."

         G.   *Measha the son of the son of R. Joshua b. Levi said, "If one was eating with my grandfather and did not wash his hands up to the wrist, grandfather would not eat with him."*

         H.   R. Huna said, "Washing the hands applies only for bread."

         I.   R. Hoshia taught, "Whatever is unclean on account of liquid [is protected by washing the hands]."

         J.   R. Zeira said, *"Even for cutting beets, he would wash his hands."*

I.4   A.   Rav said, "He who washed his hands in the morning is not required to do so in the afternoon."

         B.   *R. Abina ordered his wine steward, "Whenever you find sufficient water, wash your hands and rely on this washing all day long."*

         C.   *R. Zeira went up to R. Abbahu in Caesarea. He found him saying, "I shall go to eat."*

         D.   *He gave him a chunk of bread to cut. He* [Abbahu] *said to him* [Zeira], *"Begin, bless."*

         E.   *He* [Zeira] *said to him* [Abbahu], *"The host knows the value of his loaf."* [You should bless.]

         F.   *When they had eaten, he* [Abbahu] *said to him* [Zeira], *"Let the elder bless."*

         G.   *He said to him, "Rabbi, does the rabbi* [you] *know R. Huna, a great man, who would say, 'He who opens* [blesses first] *must close* [and say Grace after Meals]'?"

         H.   *A Tannaitic teaching differs from R. Huna, as it has been taught:*

         I.   The order of washing the hands in this: With up to five people present, they begin with the greatest. [If] more than this [are present], they begin with the least. In the middle of the meal, they begin with the eldest. After the meal they begin with the one who blesses.

J.   Is it not [done] so that he may prepare himself for the blessing? [So he did *not* bless at the beginning!

K.   *If you say* the one who opens is the one who closes, he is already prepared [having opened the meal].

L.   *R. Isaac said, "Explain it in regard to those who come in one by one and did not know which one had blessed* [at the outset]."

8:3.   A.   <u>*The House of Shammai say, "He dries his hands on the napkin and puts it on the table." And the House of Hillel say, "On the cushion."*</u>

B.   The Mishnah deals with either a table of marble [which is not susceptible to uncleanness] or a table that can be taken apart and is not susceptible to becoming unclean.

C.   *What is the reason of the House of Shammai?*

D.   So that the liquids which are on the napkin may not become unclean from the cushion and go and render his hands unclean.

E.   *And what is the reason of the House of Hillel?*

F.   The condition of doubt[ful uncleanness] with respect to the hands is always regarded as clean.

G.   Another reason: The [question of the cleanness of] hands does not apply to unconsecrated food [which in any case is not made unclean by unclean hands which are unclean in the second remove].

H.   *And according to the House of Shammai,* does [the question of the cleanness of] hands [indeed] apply to unconsecrated food?

I.   *You may interpret* [the tradition] either in accord with R. Simeon b. Eleazar or in accord with R. Eleazar b. R. Saddoq.

J.   *According to R. Simeon b. Eleazar, as it has been taught:*

K.   R. Simeon b. Eleazar says in the name of R. Meir, "Hands unclean in the first remove of uncleanness can affect [even] unconsecrated food, and in the second remove of uncleanness can affect [only] heave-offering."

L.   *Or according to R. Eleazar b. R. Saddoq, as we have learned there:*

M.   Unconsecrated food which has been prepared along with consecrated [food] is like unconsecrated food [and subject to the same, less strict cleanness rules].

N.   R. Eleazar b. R. Saddoq says, "Lo, it is like heave-offering, capable of becoming unclean from [something unclean in the] second remove of uncleanness and being rendered unfit from [something unclean in] still a further remove of uncleanness."

O.   *There we have learned:*

P.   He who anoints himself with a clean oil and is made unclean and goes down and bathes [in ritual pool] –

Q.   The House of Shammai say, "Even though he drips [with oil], [the oil] is clean."

R.   And the House of Hillel say, "It is unclean [so long as there remains enough to anoint a small member]."

S.   And if the oil was unclean in the first place –

T.   The House of Shammai say, "[It remains unclean, even after he has immersed himself, so long as there remains] sufficient for anointing a small limb."

U.   And the House of Hillel say, "[So long as it remains] a dripping liquid."

V.   R. Judah says in the name of the House of Hillel, "So long as it is dripping so as to moisten something else."

W.   *The principle of the House of Hillel has been turned around.*

X.   *There* [in the just cited law] *they say it is* unclean. *And here* [in our Mishnah] *they say it is* clean.

Y.   *There* it is present. *But here* it is absorbed in the napkin.

8:4.   *The House of Shammai say, "They clean the house and afterward wash the hands." And the House of Hillel say, "They wash the hands and afterward clean the house."*

I.1   A.   *What is the reason of the House of Shammai?*
B.   Because of the waste of food.
C.   *And what is the reason of the House of Hillel?*
D.   If the servant is clever, he removes the crumbs which are less than an olive's bulk, and they wash their hands and afterward they clean the house.

We need not review the remainder of the chapter, since the important point concerns only the passages of the Mishnah in which in the Bavli the Tosefta's talmud to the Mishnah is supplied with a sustained critical analysis and amplification of its own.

Since we see in the Yerushalmi that the same passages are treated in the same way, we may safely conclude that work on the talmud to the Tosefta was well underway between the conclusion of the Tosefta and the closure of the Yerushalmi. Since the Tosefta came to closure only after the Mishnah, citing as it does Mishnah statements and systematically glossing them, we should have to conclude that sometime after 200 and before 400 C.E., the Tosefta took shape as complement to the Mishnah; then that complement itself was subjected to a process of criticism and analysis precisely like the process of criticism and analysis that addressed the Mishnah and Sifra. The results of that process in a sustained document – a talmud to the Tosefta – of course have not survived, but large components thereof did find their place in the two Talmuds. Where the talmud to the Tosefta took its place in the two Talmuds (as exemplified by the passages treated here), that talmud ruled out the inclusion of any other reading of the Mishnah; so a three-stage process predominated: Mishnah, Toseftan complement, critical analytical discussion of the Tosefta. At some point, prior to the formation of the Yerushalmi and its closure, that talmud to the Tosefta that marked the third stage unfolded in a sustained and systematic way. But the result – a talmud to the Tosefta – survived only on the Yerushalmi's and Bavli's terms. And both of these Talmuds were composed so as to serve – in a sustained and systematic way at least – only the Mishnah – that alone.

III. How the Bavli Shaped Rabbinic Discourse

I have shown that we may classify certain passages now preserved in the Bavli as *talmud* to not the Mishnah but Sifra or Tosefta (or baraita compositions and compilations, not presented here). These writings clearly took shape in response to the documentary requirements of a writing other than the Bavli, and I think that they took shape not in the time of the closure of the Bavli but at some prior time. Let me explain why. For two reasons, one general, the other specific, I am inclined to suppose that nondocumentary compositions took shape not only separated from, but in time before, the documentary ones did. The specific reason, for the present study, is the very simple one that the Yerushalmi shows us that the Bavli's treatment of the Tosefta's amplification of the Mishnah's materials in Mishnah-tractate Berakhot Chapter Eight took shape prior to the closure of the Bavli. That is documentary evidence of a very solid order indeed. The more general reason derives from *Making the Classics in Judaism: The Three Stages of Literary Formation*. My "three stages" in ordinal sequence correspond, as a matter of fact, to three types of writing. The first – and last in assumed temporal order – is writing carried out in the context of the making, or compilation, of a classic. That writing responds to the redactional program and plan of the authorship of a classic. The second, penultimate in order, is writing that can appear in a given document but better serves a document other than the one in which it (singularly) occurs. This kind of writing seems to me not to fall within the same period of redaction as the first. For while it is a type of writing under the identical conditions, it also is writing that presupposes redactional programs in no way in play in the ultimate, and definitive, period of the formation of the canon: when people did things this way, and not in some other. That is why I think it is a kind of writing that was done prior to the period in which people limited their redactional work and associated labor of composition to the program that yielded the books we now have.

The upshot is simple: whether the classification of writing be given a temporal or merely taxonomic valence, the issue is the same: Have these writers done their work with documentary considerations in mind? I believe I have shown that they have not. Then where did they expect their work to makes its way? Anywhere it might, because, so they assumed, fitting in no where in particular, it found a suitable locus everywhere it turned up. But I think temporal, not merely taxonomic, considerations pertain. The third kind of writing seems to me to originate in a period prior to the other two. It is carried on in a manner independent of all redactional considerations such as are known to us. Then it should derive from a time when redactional considerations played no paramount role in the making of compositions. A brief essay, rather than a sustained composition, was then the dominant mode of writing. My hypothesis is that people can have written both long and short compositions – compositions and composites, in my language – at one and the same time. But writing that does not presuppose a secondary labor of redaction, for example, in a composite, probably originated when authors or authorships did not anticipate any fate for their writing beyond their labor of composition itself. Along these same lines of argument, this writing may or may not travel from one document to another. What that means is that the author or authorship does not imagine a future for his writing. What fits anywhere is composed to go nowhere in particular. Accordingly, what matters is not whether a writing fits one document or another, but whether, as the author or authorship has composed a piece of writing, that writing meets the requirements of any document we now have or can even imagine. If it does not, then we deal with a literary period in which the main kind of writing was ad hoc and episodic, not sustained and documentary.

Three classifications of writing, all assigned Tannaite standing, all formed after the time of the Mishnah, were read precisely as the Mishnah was read: the Sifra, the Tosefta, and compositions and compositions bearing Tannaite marking known as baraitot. We know that fact because in the pages of the Talmud of Babylonia, substantial passages of all three types are preserved, not solely for the purposes of the compositions concerning the Mishnah or propositions deriving from Mishnah exegesis that the framers of the Bavli formulated. They were preserved along with sustained discussions of their own statements, whether or not those discussions were required for the purposes of the framers of the passages in which they occur. In point of fact, where we find a sustained analysis of a passage of the Sifra or Tosefta, it is clear, that analysis concerns itself with the requirements of the Sifra or the Tosefta and its meanings in its context; we cannot account for the analytical program by appeal to the interests of Mishnah exegesis and its amplification, but only, to the concerns of Sifra or Tosefta or baraita exegesis. That means that the critical analytical reading of passages, sometimes sizable, of the Sifra, the Tosefta, and the baraita corpus, was undertaken in its own terms. This leads to three conclusions.

[1] Because the modes of thought and analysis concerning the Sifra, the Tosefta, and the baraita corpus in no way diverged from

those that guided inquiry into the Mishnah, I claim that the work that was done falls into the category of *talmud*, as defined earlier.

[2]   And because some of these passages are sustained, I allege that, in addition to the Talmud, the one that imposes meaning upon the Mishnah, there not only can have been, but almost certainly were, other talmuds, in progress for the Sifra, the Tosefta, and components of the baraita compositions and even compilations.

[3]   Where a *talmud* was taking shape around the Tosefta, the Talmud to the Mishnah would consist of the Tosefta's talmud, itself amplified and revised in relationship to the Mishnah's statements, thus, Mishnah paragraph, Tosefta amplification through restatement, in the Mishnah's language, of what the Mishnah was supposed to mean, and, third, further analysis of the Tosefta's judgment of the Mishnah's meaning and the Mishnah's unresolved issues.

These facts, set forth here as foundations for a hypothesis to be tested against a variety of other passages of the Talmud of Babylonia, yield a rather unanticipated conclusion, which is that the framers of the Bavli not only set forth a statement of their own, out of a sizable corpus of received materials. That point I have maintained in prior monographs and requires no amplification here.[2] The framers of the Bavli also took control of, and closed off, prior discourse. They not only chose what would form the systemic statement that defined what we should call "Judaism" and what their apologists would call "the one whole Torah of Moses, our rabbi." They also privileged one document of choice, making its exegesis critical, and set in the background other documents that in earlier times, were subjected to exactly the same engaged exegesis as the Mishnah had long enjoyed. Alongside the Talmuds to the Mishnah (the Yerushalmi and the Bavli as we know them), there might have been a variety of *talmuds* – the *talmud* to Sifra, the *talmud* to Tosefta; the Talmud that we do have, had it emerged only as a secondary development of the talmud to Tosefta, might have been a very different document from what

---

[2]*The Bavli and its Sources: The Question of Tradition in the Case of Tractate Sukkah* (Atlanta, 1987: Scholars Press for Brown Judaic Studies); *Tradition as Selectivity: Scripture, Mishnah, Tosefta, and Midrash in the Talmud of Babylonia. The Case of Tractate Arakhin.* (Atlanta, 1990: Scholars Press for South Florida Studies in the History of Judaism); *Language as Taxonomy. The Rules for Using Hebrew and Aramaic in the Babylonian Talmud* (Atlanta, 1990: Scholars Press for South Florida Studies in the History of Judaism); *The Rules of Composition of the Talmud of Babylonia. The Cogency of the Bavli's Composite* (Atlanta, 1991: Scholars Press for South Florida Studies in the History of Judaism); *The Bavli's One Voice: Types and Forms of Analytical Discourse and their Fixed Order of Appearance* (Atlanta, 1991: Scholars Press for South Florida Studies in the History of Judaism).

it is. But that is not what we have. And the extant components of such other *talmuds* as have reached us hardly lead us to suppose that somewhere along the line such *talmuds* existed and then were suppressed, though that judgment must be classed as a merely reasonable guess.

Since, it is clear, a variety of received writings were read in one and the same way and even produced writing of a singularly uniform character as to both rhetoric and logic, we must conclude that the talmud to the Sifra and the *talmud* to the Tosefta as well as the Talmuds to the Mishnah were taking shape among pretty much the same sorts of persons and at the same time. That proposition, ignoring the document's own allegations concerning the names of the authorities cited therein, which in fact are the same names as those who dominate Mishnah exegesis,[3] seems to me a plausible way of explaining the facts in our hands about the uniformity of the exegetical discourse on the variety of documents.[4] It seems to me that at a given point, a variety of writings were read in the same way, so that documentary lines played no important role. But then the other fact, that the results of the exegesis of one document were formed into a massive and authoritative writing, the Talmud (of Babylonia, of the Land of Israel), while the results of the exegesis of the other documents, as well as of received materials not formed into a sustained document at all, comes into play. And that other fact tells me that at some point the received program of exegesis, and the forms that that exegesis was to take for preservation and transmission to the future, were radically redefined. At that point, as I have now suggested, the Mishnah assumed a position of priority; all other (potential) talmuds were moved offstage, and their contents would form a part of the background scenery for the principal drama: the reading of the Mishnah.

---

[3]We cannot verify the attributions, so we cannot use them as historical facts or indicators. That the same names occur in a variety of passages can form a convention of later pseudepigraphic authors, so by themselves, names that recur prove nothing. The next note goes over this same matter.

[4]That is not the sole way in which we may explain the facts I have uncovered. But the proposed supposition depends not on the obvious fact that the same names occur throughout, but on the even more obvious fact that we simply cannot differentiate the *talmuds* that did not survive as complete documents from the one that did. It is possible that authorities living at a later time imitated those living earlier on and even took the same names, for example, Rab, Nahman, Abbayye, worked on the Sifra or the Tosefta, and others, using the names of Rab, Nahman, and Abbayye, worked in exactly the same way later on, on the Mishnah, and suppressed the earlier work. I cannot think of a way definitively to dismiss that possibility, though to me it appears to be implausible.

How then did the Talmud shape rabbinic discourse? The answer to this question is in two parts. The first concerns the first of the two Talmuds, the Yerushalmi. That document clearly found its definition in the work of Mishnah exegesis. The brief passage we examined showed that it defined the program that the Bavli later on would bring to bear upon precisely the same passage of the Mishnah. What the earlier exegetes found important in relationship to that passage derived from the Tosefta, and the later exegetes followed suit; each set of exegetes, to be sure, put forth its own message, the latter in no way depending upon the former for their agendum. So the framers of the Yerushalmi, with their principal interest in the problem of Mishnah exegesis (in relationship to the Tosefta, in our passage, not so in many, many more passages), will not have provoked much astonishment among the framers of the Sifra, or, indeed, of the Tosefta, or of compositions and even composites of exegesis of baraita sayings. We do not know whether the work of forming a talmud to Sifra or the Tosefta or the baraita compositions and composites went forward after the formation of the Yerushalmi. I should be surprised if it ceased with the Yerushalmi, but I cannot think of any compelling reasons to take one position or the other.

But the work of making a *talmud* to the other documents certainly did come to an end prior to the closure of the Bavli, since, it is obvious, nothing like a sustained talmud to them has come down, and that fact brings is to the latter of the two Talmuds, the Bavli. Whether or not systematic work on the Sifra, Tosefta, or baraita compositions went forward, each in its own documentary setting, after the closure of the Yerushalmi, the authorities behind the Bavli clearly had decided that the Mishnah, and the Mishnah alone, would define the structure and order of discourse, and the Mishnah, through the Bavli, did just that. All other writings from the Mishnah forward or assigned the same Tannaite standing as the Mishnah together with received amplifications thereof would be recast into the framework of Mishnah commentary – amplification, complement or thematic supplement – within the pages of the Bavli. Whatever sizable exegeses those materials had already received – once again, amplification, complement or thematic supplement – would follow in the wake of the passages of the primary documents that were selected, and that is why we have them. But there is no grounds for doubting that everything was made to say one thing, which is, the Mishnah is primary, its program paramount, its formation of the Torah authoritative. All other writings, whether the Written Torah or its amplification in the Sifra and parallel compilations, whether the secondary expansion of the Mishnah in its framework, were made to acknowledge this privileged and entitled position accorded to the Mishnah.

If I had to choose a single document, the subordination of which strikes me as remarkable, however, it is not the Sifra but the Tosefta. For the Tosefta can have defined the path that would lead to the talmud to the Mishnah, but in the Talmud as we have it, the Tosefta is merely another source of Tannaite sayings, no more important than any other. I have already set forth, in *The Bavli That Might Have Been: The Tosefta's Theory of Mishnah Commentary Compared with That of the Babylonian Talmud*,[5] a sustained account of what might have been, as against what was. In that work I showed that, while the Tosefta forms a commentary to the Mishnah, and so, too, does the Talmud of Babylonia or the Bavli, the latter document differs from the former in its conception of what is to be done with the Mishnah. By comparing the Tosefta's with the Bavli's treatment of the Mishnah, I demonstrated not only that the Bavli's approach to Mishnah commentary differs from the Tosefta's (which is hardly surprising), *but that the differences in the aggregate are uniform and predictable.* I proved beyond doubt, on the basis of a substantial sample, the fact that the comparison yields a fixed and coherent set of contrasts. So what? In that monograph what I thought important was that, as I had shown to be the case for the Tosefta's authorship in my *The Tosefta: Its Structure and its Sources* (Atlanta, 1986: Scholars Press for Brown Judaic Studies), so, too, the Bavli's authorship referred to a coherent and cogent program of exegetical principles when they turned to the Mishnah. That is why I attach such weight to the fact that the differences between the two documents are fixed and predictable. When we compare one document's reading of the original source to the other document's reading of that same source, therefore, we are able to show by the persistence of a fixed set of differences that the latter document is a well-crafted and thoughtfully composed statement, not a mere compilation of this-and-that: a composition, not a compilation. Since the Bavli is commonly represented as a mere conglomeration of whatever people happened to have received – a sedimentary piece of writing, not a planned and considered one, the result of many centuries of accumulation, not the work of a generation or two of thoughtful writers – these results provide a detailed argument against one proposition and in favor of another.

But here the same results point our attention elsewhere. What is important is not only difference, but a pattern of difference: the Bavli's framers differ in their theory of Mishnah commentary from the Tosefta's framers, and the differences are consistent throughout. Ordinarily, for example, at any given passage of the Bavli, we begin with the clarification of the Mishnah paragraph, turn then to the examination of

[5]Atlanta, 1990: Scholars Press for South Florida Studies in the History of Judaism.

the principles of law implicit in the Mishnah paragraph, and then broaden the discussion to introduce what I called analogies from case to law and law to case. These are the three stages of our discussion. It would be very easy to outline a given Talmudic discussion, beginning to end, and to produce a reasoned account of the position and order of every completed composition and the ordering of the several compositions into a composite. But this tripartite program in no way characterizes the Tosefta's reading of the same passage of the Mishnah. That outline has told the framers of the Bavli's passage what comes first – the simplest matters of language, then the more complex matters of analysis of content, then secondary development of analogous principles and cases. Steinsaltz is wrong: we do move from simple criticism of language to weighty analysis of parallels. True, we invoke facts treated elsewhere; but reference is always verbatim, so, with a modicum of information, we can follow the discussion. True, the Talmud is not an elementary primer of the law, but it does not pretend to be. It claims to discuss the Mishnah paragraph that it cites, and it discusses that Mishnah paragraph. So the Bavli's framers had their own ideas of how to read the Mishnah, and they imposed these ideas upon the entire received corpus. This they did by using what they found pertinent. Their silence on the rest tells the story. They wanted the Mishnah to be read first – and not Scripture, as the Sifra's framers maintained. They wanted the Mishnah to be read in its own terms – and not in terms of the Tosefta, as the framers of the talmud to the Tosefta proposed. And they wanted to read the Mishnah themselves, in their own terms, and not only third in line after the framers of the Tosefta and of other Mishnah exegetes, for example those who worked over the Mishnah in response to Scripture, represented by the Sifra. So in the manner in which they disposed of the received heritage – not only the heritage of exegesis, received from their masters and their masters from theirs, but the heritage of sacred writ, of Torah, encompassing not only the written but also the oral part preserved in the Mishnah and in other statements bearing Tannaite standing – they defined the discourse of Judaism, always precipitated by the Bavli as was the case, from then to now. Discourse in Judaism would commence with the Mishnah, circle around back to Scripture, proceed outward in every possible direction, always ending where it began: with the oral component of the one whole Torah of Moses, our rabbi.

3

The Bavli That Might Have Been

The Tosefta's Theory of Mishnah Commentary Compared with that of the Babylonian Talmud

The Tosefta forms a commentary to the Mishnah, and so, too, does the Talmud of Babylonia or the Bavli. The latter document differs from the former in its conception of what is to be done with the Mishnah. By comparing the Tosefta's with the Bavli's treatment of the Mishnah, we see not only that the Bavli's approach to Mishnah commentary differs from the Tosefta's (which is hardly surprising), *but that the differences in the aggregate are uniform and predictable.* It follows, in my way of thinking, that, as I demonstrated to be the case for the Tosefta's authorship in my *The Tosefta: Its Structure and its Sources* (Atlanta, 1986: Scholars Press for Brown Judaic Studies), so, too, the Bavli's authorship referred to a coherent and cogent program of exegetical principles when they turned to the Mishnah. That is why I attach such weight to the fact that the differences between the two documents are fixed and predictable. When we compare one document's reading of the original source to the other document's reading of that same source, therefore, we are able to show by the persistence of a fixed set of differences that the latter document is a well-crafted and thoughtfully composed statement, not a mere compilation of this-and-that: a composition, not a compilation. Since the Bavli is commonly represented as a mere conglomeration of whatever people happened to have received – a sedimentary piece of writing, not a planned and considered one, the result of many centuries of accumulation, not the work of a generation or two of thoughtful writers

– these results provide a detailed argument against one proposition and in favor of another.

I settle the question, who is it who speaks through the Bavli? Is it the voice of the penultimate and ultimate authorship, or is it the voices of a variety of authors and authorships? I shall show that a severely limited repertoire of formal structures governed the expression of thought by the authors of materials in the Talmud of Babylonia, and an equally limited program told the framers of the document the order in which those materials should be set forth. These results will lay to rest the conception that the Talmud of Babylonia is simply a disorganized mass of whatever happened to find its way into the document's pages. Testing the null hypothesis, of course, yields a very powerful, positive demonstration as well. The positive test, undertaken here, is to show that the framers of the document made choices. That is to say, the people who laid matters out as we now have them did not do their work haphazardly, nor did they simply receive and hand on a hodgepodge of inherited materials. They did things in one way, and not in some other. How do I demonstrate that that is so? The way I have taken here is to compare how the Bavli's framers composed their commentary to the Mishnah with how the authorship of the Tosefta composed its commentary to the Mishnah. In a variety of works, summed up by my *The Tosefta: Its Structure and its Sources* (Atlanta, 1986: Scholars Press for Brown Judaic Studies), I have already shown that rules of structure, order, and intellectual inquiry governed the (earlier) writers who stand behind the Tosefta (or the materials now collected in the Tosefta, the distinction for the present purpose makes no difference). Now, simply ignoring a parallel study for the Bavli, which is *Judaism: The Classical Statement. The Evidence of the Bavli* (Chicago, 1986: University of Chicago Press) where I compared the Bavli's and the Yerushalmi's address to the Mishnah, I reverse course and compare the Bavli's and the Tosefta's responses to the Mishnah.

In this way – comparing one document with another document concerning the same text – I show that the Bavli's framers made choices, followed a program and a plan. It was a different program and plan from that which governed the Tosefta's authors' work. And the established fact that the Bavli's authorship had access to the materials now collected in the Tosefta shows that the difference shows deliberation – not this way, but some other way. Why so? Because, with the Tosefta's systematic response to the Mishnah in hand, the Bavli's authorship chose to utilize what they chose out of the Tosefta, but not to adopt the plan and program of the Tosefta. Rather they chose some other.[1] Let us now examine how the Bavli and the Tosefta read the same chapter of the Mishnah, which is Mishnah-tractate Bekhorot Chapter One.

The opening chapter deals with the redemption of the firstborn of an ass (Ex. 13:11-13), Scripture's first concrete item in its sizable corpus of instructions on firstborn animals. The chapter introduces no important ideas distinctive to its subject, but rather brings to bear upon that topic a fairly standard repertoire of inquiries pertinent to diverse problems. Indeed, I do not see a single idea in the chapter which cannot be applied to the redemption of firstborn of animals other than the ass. For example, the opening point, M. 1:1, is that the firstborn must be wholly owned by an Israelite, not held in common or joint ownership with a gentile, on the one side, or a priest, on the other. This same rule will recur. The exemption of Levites and priests is proved in an argument a fortiori; T. provides an exegetical proof for the same proposition. M. 1:2 adds that the firstling of an ass which resembles a horse is exempt, and the firstling of a cow which resembles an ass is exempt. To this is appended an excellent, but contradictory, unit on eating, making the point that that which comes forth from the unclean is unclean, and that which comes forth from the clean is clean.

M. 1:3-4 present a triplet of problems on matters of doubt in connection with the firstling of an ass. First we have an ass which had not given birth and which bore two males. We do not know which came out first. One of them surely must be redeemed by the presentation of a lamb to a priest. If the animal bore a male and a female, a lamb must be set aside, but if a priest wishes to claim it, he must prove the male came first. The second problem gives us two asses which had not given birth, and the third, two asses, one of which had given birth and one of which had not; in each of these cases, too, we have first two males, then a male and a female, with the appropriate apodosis. Appended at M. 1:4D-K is a unit on the character of the lamb used for the redemption of the firstling of an ass. The exegesis is complicated by its location; some exegetes choose to see the lamb under discussion as the one set aside for, but not given to, the priest. This unitary exegesis certainly is assumed by T. If we see M. 1:4D-K as continuous with M. 1:5, then under discussion is the lamb used for the redemption of *any* firstling of an ass, not only the one subject to the doubts specified at M. 1:3-4C. For M. 1:5 defines what may and may not be used for the redemption of any firstling of an ass.

---

[1]What other plan and program? The answers – as I have said – are in my *The Bavli's One Voice: The Rules of Composition of the Talmud of Babylonia. Types and Forms of Analytical Discourse and their Fixed Order of Appearance.*

M. 1:6 proceeds to another triplet of cases: the disposition of the redemption lamb for a firstborn of an ass, the owner of which dies; the disposition of the redemption lamb which died after being set aside for the firstling of an ass which died; and that of the firstling of an ass which died. At issue is whether the lamb is deemed to belong to the priest. Eliezer and sages participate in the first and third cases, taking entirely consistent positions at both points; a formally distinct pericope of Joshua and Sadoq is intruded at the second point. Eliezer's position is that the firstling belongs to the priest, but, it follows, the redemption lamb does not. Sages maintain that once the redemption lamb is set aside, it belongs to the priest, but then the firstling no longer falls within the priest's domain. M. 1:7 opens with a singleton on the alternative of killing the firstling of an ass instead of redeeming it, and then supplies yet another triplet of rules, on the preferability of one as against another alternative where a person has a choice: redeeming or killing the firstling, espousing or redeeming the Hebrew bondwoman (Ex. 21:8) and executing Levirate marriage or undergoing the ceremony of *halisah*. There are appended some developments of this third item, then a fourth, formally and conceptually relevant but not wholly parallel one.

1:1A-E

A.   (1) He who purchases the unborn offspring of the ass of a gentile, (2) and he who sells it to him (even though one is not permitted to do so), (3) and he who is a partner with him;

B.   (4) and [either] he who receives [asses] from him [under contract to rear them and share in the profit], (5) and [or] he who delivers [asses] to him under contract [to rear them and share in the profit] –

C.   it [the foetus, when born] is exempt from the law of the firstling,

D.   since it is said, [*All the firstborn*] *in Israel* (Num. 3:13) –

E.   but not [the firstborn produced] among others.

The pericope is in two parts, A-E and F-H, both stated in simple declarative sentences. The latter is given below, because the Talmud treats it separately from the opening part. The former is to be divided into A-C, the statement of the rule, and D-E, its appended exegetical proof. The latter follows the same general construction, but G-H of course are not parallel to D-E. The two parts are entirely distinct from one another. The point of A-C is clear as stated. The unborn offspring of the ass of a gentile is not subject to the sanctity of the firstling. That which is purchased by a gentile also is not deemed holy. A 2's gloss alludes to M. A.Z. 1:6's prohibition of selling a large beast to a gentile. The unborn offspring partly owned by a gentile is not subject to the law of the firstling. B makes a separate point. If one undertakes a contract to rear offspring and to share in the profit thereof, whether the Israelite or the gentile does the rearing, the offspring is not consecrated. D-E explain all five rulings. Israelites only are liable to the law.

A.   He who purchases the unborn offspring of the ass of a gentile,
B.   and he who sells it to him (even though he is not permitted to do so),
C.   and he who is a partner with him,
D.   and he who receives [one] from him [under contract to rear and share in the profit],
E.   and he who hands over to him [under contract],
F.   is exempt from the law of the firstling,
G.   since it is said, [All the firstborn] in Israel (Num. 3:13) – and not among others [M. Bekh. 1:1A-E].

T. 1:1 Z p. 534, lines 14-16

So far as I can see, Tosefta has no program for our Mishnah paragraph, which is simply cited verbatim. Now we shall see what might have been – had the Tosefta's framers undertaken a systematic analytical program in Mishnah study, such as the Bavli's authors and compositors set forth.

I.1   A.   *[2A] Why was it necessary to specify all of these cases that are listed by the Mishnah?*
      B.   *All were necessary. For if the Tannaite authority had listed only the matter of the* **purchaser** *of the embryo from a gentile, I might have supposed that that is because an [Israelite] purchaser in any event brings the offspring into a state of consecration, when it is born, but one who sells it [to a gentile] removes the embryo from a state of consecration, so I might have supposed he should be subjected to an extrajudicial sanction [and so forbidden to do so]. So we are informed that that is not the case.*
      C.   *And why did I require the specification of one who is* **a partner with a gentile?**
      D.   *It was necessary so as to exclude the position of R. Judah, for R. Judah said, "A beast held in partnership with a gentile is liable to the law of the firstborn." So we are informed that the beast is exempt from the law of the firstborn.*
      E.   *And why was it necessary to specify he who receives [asses] from him [under contract to rear them and share in the profit]?*
      F.   *It was because the framer of the passage wished to specify,* **and [or] he who delivers [asses] to him under contract [to rear them and share in the profit].**
      G.   *And why was it necessary to specify,* **and [or] he who delivers [asses] to him under contract [to rear them and share in the profit]?**
      H.   *It was necessary to do so. For it might have entered your mind to imagine that since the fundamental ownership of the animal is in the hands of the Israelite, one should apply an extra-judicial sanction, lest the matter come to an exchange with another beast. So we are informed that that is not the rule.*

I.2   A.   *We have learned in the Mishnah there:* [In a place in which they are
             accustomed to sell small cattle to gentiles, they sell them. In a
             place in which they are accustomed not to sell [small cattle] to
             them, they do not sell them. And in every locale they do not sell
             them large cattle, calves, or foals, whether whole or lame.] R.
             Judah permits in the case of lame ones. And Ben Beterah permits
             in the case of a horse [M. A.Z. 1:6A-E].

       B.   *The question was raised: As to selling an embryo to a gentile, what is the
             rule? Is the operative consideration of R. Judah for permitting the sale of
             lame cattle to gentiles because the beast is maimed [and so not going to be
             used for idolatry]? The embryo also is in that classification. Or perhaps
             while the maiming of an animal is uncommon, am embryo is of course
             common and so is not comparable at all to the case of a maimed animal?*

       C.   *Come and take note:* And he who sells to him (even though one is
             not permitted to do so).

       D.   *Now R. Judah does not differ in this matter [so the second alternative is to
             be preferred].*

       E.   *But according to your reasoning, with respect to these other cases,* (3) and
             he who is a partner with him; (4) and [either] he who receives
             [asses] from him [under contract to rear them and share in the
             profit], (5) and [or] he who delivers [asses] to him under contract
             [to rear them and share in the profit], *concerning which, also, R.
             Judah does not take issue, is it the fact that he does not differ?* [Miller &
             Simon: He differs with reference to a partnership with a gentile,
             and he also differs as stated later in the cases where an Israelite
             undertakes to look after a gentile's animal where the gentile looks
             after an Israelite's animal]. *Rather, he does differ but that fact is not
             made explicit here, and with regard to this other case, he does differ but
             that fact is not made explicit [and so the first of the alternative readings is
             the valid one].*

       F.   *Come and take note:* R. Judah says, "He who undertakes in
             partnership to raise a beast in behalf of a gentile and the beast gave
             birth to a firstling – a settlement is made with the gentile partner for
             what it is worth, and half of the value is handed over to a priest
             [but the animal is not consecrated for sacrifice on the altar, since
             half of it belongs to a gentile]. And an Israelite who hands over a
             beast in partnership with a gentile for the latter to raise the beast,
             even though it is not permitted to do so – they impose upon him an
             extrajudicial penalty of redeeming the beast [from the gentile], even
             up to ten times the value, and he gives its whole value to the priest.
             [2B] *Is not reference made here to the embryo [so we can deduce that it is
             forbidden to sell an embryo to a gentile]?*

       G.   No, reference is made to the beast itself.

       H   *But does the passage not make reference to "its value"* [the masculine
             ending then suggesting we speak of the embryo]?

       I.   *Read:* "her value" [the feminine ending referring to the beast].

       J.   *And lo, the passage reads,* and he gives its whole value to the priest!
             *But if "its value" refers to the animal, what has the priest go to do with the
             case [since his claim is only on the firstborn, and not on the animal as a
             whole]?*

K.   *With what sort of a case do we deal here? It is with a case in which the
       Israelite handed over a pregnant beast to fatten it up. Since we impose an
       extrajudicial sanction by means of a fine as to the animal [which should
       not be sold to a gentile], we impose an equivalent sanction on account of
       the embryo.* [Miller & Simon: But elsewhere, Judah may hold that an
       embryo may be sold to a gentile, just as he allows the selling of a
       maimed animal.]

L.   *Said R. Ashi, "Come and take note:* **R. Judah permits in the case of
       lame ones** *because it cannot be healed. But if it could be healed, it
       would be forbidden to do so. Now is not an embryo in the
       classification of a beast that can be cured [since, after it is born, it will be
       fit for work, including work on the Sabbath, which is the operative
       consideration in this context]?"*

M.   *That proves the point [that Judah will forbid selling an embryo to a
       gentile].*

I.3 A.   *And there are those who repeat as a Tannaite version the statement of R.
          Judah in reference to our Mishnah paragraph:* **and he who sells it to
          him (even though one is not permitted to do so):**

     B.   *May we say that our Mishnah paragraph's rule does not accord with the
          position of R. Judah? For we have learned in the Mishnah:* [In a place in
          which they are accustomed to sell small cattle to gentiles, they sell
          them. In a place in which they are accustomed not to sell [small
          cattle] to them, they do not sell them. And in every locale they do
          not sell them large cattle, calves, or foals, whether whole or lame.]
          R. Judah permits in the case of lame ones. [And Ben Beterah
          permits in the case of a horse] [M. A.Z. 1:6A-E].

     C.   *You may even take the view that our Mishnah accords with the position of
          R. Judah. For while the maiming of an animal is uncommon, an embryo is
          of course common and so is not comparable at all to the case of a maimed
          animal.*

     D.   *Come and take note:* R. Judah says, "He who undertakes in
          partnership to raise a beast in behalf of a gentile and the beast gave
          birth to a firstling – a settlement is made with the gentile partner for
          what it is worth, and half of the value is handed over to a priest
          [but the animal is not consecrated for sacrifice on the altar, since
          half of it belongs to a gentile]. And an Israelite who hands over a
          beast in partnership with a gentile for the latter to raise the beast,
          even though it is not permitted to do so – they impose upon him an
          extrajudicial penalty of redeeming the beast [from the gentile], even
          up to ten times the value, and he gives its whole value to the priest.
          *Is not reference made here to the embryo [so we can deduce that it is
          forbidden to sell an embryo to a gentile]?*

     E.   No, reference is made to the beast itself.

     F.   *But does the passage not make reference to* "its value" [the masculine
          ending then suggesting we speak of the embryo]?

     G.   *Read:* "her value" [the feminine ending referring to the beast].

     H.   *And lo, the passage reads,* and he gives its whole value to the priest!
          *But if "its value" refers to the animal, what has the priest go to do with the
          case [since his claim is only on the firstborn, and not on the animal as a
          whole]?*

I. *With what sort of a case do we deal here? It is with a case in which the Israelite handed over a pregnant beast to fatten it up. Since we impose an extrajudicial sanction by means of a fine as to the animal [which should not be sold to a gentile], we impose an equivalent sanction on account of the embryo.* [Miller & Simon: But elsewhere, Judah may hold that an embryo may be sold to a gentile, just as he allows the selling of a maimed animal.]

J. *Said R. Ashi, "Come and take note:* **R. Judah permits in the case of lame ones** *because it cannot be healed. But if it could be healed, it would be forbidden to do so. Now is not an embryo in the classification of a beast that can be cured [since, after it is born, it will be fit for work, including work on the Sabbath, which is the operative consideration in this context]?"*

K. *That proves the point [that Judah will forbid selling an embryo to a gentile].*

I.4 A. *The question was raised:* If one sold a beast to a gentile as to its future offspring [the animal is not sold, only the offspring], what is the rule? *This question may be addressed to both R. Judah and rabbis.*

B. *The question is to be addressed to R. Judah in this way: granted that R. Judah permits doing so in the case of a lame beast, which will never be confused with some other animal, but as to a healthy beast, which he may confuse with some other beast, R. Judah may rule that it is forbidden to do so [since the offspring will also be subject to confusion]. Or perhaps if in the case of the sale of a lame beast, he severs all relationship with the beast [leaving himself no right to the beast after it is sold], all the more so in the case of the sale of a healthy beast, in which case he has not severed all connection to the beast* [Miller & Simon: since the animal itself belongs to the Israelite and is not yet pregnant, and when the beast produces its offspring, it will be in the possession of the gentile, he will have no qualms in permitting the sale].

C. *The question is to be addressed to rabbis in this way: granted that rabbis prohibit in the case of a lame beast, because the Israelite severs all connection with it.* [Miller & Simon: The selling is complete, and therefore there is the fear that one might sell also a whole animal to a gentile], *but in the case of a healthy animal, in which instance he does not wholly sever his connection with the beast, it is permitted; or perhaps we say that, if in the case of a lame beast, where he will not end up confusing the beast with another animal, rabbis forbid the sale to a gentile, how much the more so in the case of a healthy beast, where there can be the consideration of confusion?*

D. *But is the operative consideration in the mind of rabbis the one that has been specified? And has it not been taught on Tannaite authority:*

E. They said to R. Judah, "Is it not going to happen that the farmer will inseminate the lame beast, and it will give birth?"

F. *Therefore the operative consideration is the disposition of the future offspring.* [Miller & Simon: We may therefore solve our query by concluding that according to rabbis it is forbidden to sell an animal to a gentile for the sake of its future offspring, and according to Judah, it is permitted to do so.]

G. *This is the sense of what they said to him: "For us the operative consideration is the possibility that the farmer will end up confusing the* beast with others. *But as to you, what is on your mind in permitting the sale? Is it that the beast cannot be healed, and it is as though he had sold it only for slaughter for the meat? But in that context,* Is it not going to happen that the farmer will inseminate the lame beast, and it will give birth? And since it is the fact that the farmer will inseminate the lame beast, and it will give birth, the purchaser will hold on to the beast [for the offspring] [Miller & Simon: and one who sees it in the house of a gentile at the end of a year or two may conclude that it is permitted to sell an animal not for slaughter to a gentile]. And he said to them, "When it gives birth...," because in fact it cannot be inseminated [because of its disability].

H *Come and take note:* And [or] he who delivers [asses] to him under contract [to rear them and share in the profit] *and it does not state, although one is not permitted to do so.*

I *But according to your reasoning, with respect to these other cases,* **(3) and he who is a partner with him; (4) and [either] he who receives [asses] from him [under contract to rear them and share in the profit], (5) and [or] he who delivers [asses] to him under contract [to rear them and share in the profit],** *concerning which, also,* **even though it is not permitted to do so** *is not specified, is it the fact that one is permitted to do so?* And lo, said the father of Samuel, "A person is forbidden to form a partnership with a gentile, lest he come to be obligated to take an oath to him and so have to take an oath by the other's idol, while the Torah has said, 'And make no mention of the name of other gods, neither let it be heard out of your mouth' (Ex. 23:13)." *Rather, the Tannaite framer of the passage has made mention only of the prohibition as to selling, but that is the law as to partnership. Here, too, he has made mention of the matter of selling, and that is the law as to contracting as well.*

J. *Then why mention the prohibition explicitly only in connection with selling?*

K. *Because the principal prohibition concerns selling.*

L. *Come and take note:* R. Judah says, "He who undertakes in partnership to raise a beast in behalf of a gentile and the beast gave birth to a firstling – a settlement is made with the gentile partner for what it is worth, and half of the value is handed over to a priest [but the animal is not consecrated for sacrifice on the altar, since half of it belongs to a gentile]. And an Israelite who hands over a beast in partnership with a gentile for the latter to raise the beast – even though it is not permitted to do so – they impose upon him an extrajudicial penalty of redeeming the beast [from the gentile], even up to ten times the value, and he gives its whole value to the priest. And sages say, "So long as the gentile's hand is in the middle, the beast is exempt from the law of the firstling altogether." [3A] *Is not reference made here to the beast [so we can deduce that it is forbidden to sell a beast to a gentile for the future offspring; we punish him accord to the opinion of both Judah and rabbis, and the only difference has to do with the firstborn]?*

M *No, reference is made to the embryo. That fact may be ascertained also from the language of the passage:* they impose upon him an extrajudicial penalty of redeeming the beast [from the gentile], even up to ten times the value [which refers to the embryo].

N. That proves it.

I.5 A. *[The imposition of an extrajudicial sanction for selling the beast to a gentile] sustains the view of R. Simeon b. Laqish,* for R. Simeon b. Laqish has said, "He who sells a large beast to a gentile – they impose upon him an extrajudicial penalty of up to ten times its value [to buy the beast back]."

B. *Is the figure, "ten times its value," meant to be precise, or is it simply an estimate?*

C. *Come and take note, for,* said R. Joshua b. Levi, "He who sells his slave to a gentile – they impose upon him an extrajudicial penalty of up to a hundred times his value" [in that the seller may have to spend that amount of money to get the slave back from the gentile]. [So the figure is not a literal one.]

D. *The case of a slave is exceptional, for day by day the gentile removes the slave from the observance of religious duties [but in the case of an animal, the rule is not so strict].*

I.6 A. *There are those who say:*

B. Said R. Simeon b. Laqish, "He who sells a large beast to a gentile – they impose upon him an extrajudicial penalty of up to a hundred times its value [to buy the beast back]."

C. *We have learned in the Mishnah:* **And he who hands over a beast to him on contract, although this is not permitted, we impose the penalty of forcing him to redeem the animal at even ten times its value.**

D. In the case of a sale, the Israelite gives up all connection to the beast, but in the case of a contract to rear the beast, the Israelite has not give up all connection to the beast.

E. *Is the figure, "ten times its value," meant to be precise, or is it simply an estimate?*

F. *Come and take note, for,* said R. Joshua b. Levi, "He who sells his slave to a gentile – they impose upon him an extrajudicial penalty of up to ten times his value" [in that the seller may have to spend that amount of money to get the slave back from the gentile]. [So the figure is not a literal one.]

G. *The case of a slave is exceptional, for he does not go back to his master after he is redeemed.*

H. *And what is the reason that a beast must be redeemed at even a hundred times its value?*

I. *Because it comes back to its master.*

J. *Then why not impose a sanction that he pay one more than ten [eleven times the value, in the theory that since the owner gets the money back, the value of the beast cannot be reckoned as part of the fine]?*

K. *Rather, the operative consideration is that the sale of a slave is uncommon, and for any matter that is uncommon, rabbis imposed no decrees.*

I.7 A. "And sages say, 'So long as the gentile's hand is in the middle, the beast is exempt from the law of the firstling altogether'":

B. Said R. Joshua, "Both authorities expound the same verse of Scripture: 'Sanctify to me all the firstborn, whatever opens the womb in Israel' (Ex. 13:2).

C. "Rabbis take the first to mean that if the firstborn only partially belongs to an Israelite, it falls into the classification of a firstborn. So the All-Merciful has included the word 'all,' to indicate that the law applies only if the whole of the firstborn is the property of the Israelite. And R. Judah takes the view that the word 'firstborn' refers to the whole of the beast, and the All-Merciful has included the word 'all,' so as to indicate that even if a part of the beast belongs to an Israelite, that suffices.

D. "If you prefer, I shall set matters forth in this way:

E. "All parties concur that the word 'firstling' means, the greater part of the beast. One authority maintains that 'all' serves to complement [meaning, any part whatsoever], and the other authority takes the view that it means to limit the matter [so that only if an Israelite owns the whole of the beast is the firstborn subject to the law]."

I.8 A. And [in line with the view of Judah], how much of the beast must be shared in partnership with a gentile so that the beast may be exempt from the law of the firstborn?

B. Said R. Huna, "Even its ear."

C. R. Nahman objected, "Then let the priest say to the gentile, 'Take your portion, the ear, and go along'" [Miller & Simon: for a firstborn, even though blemished by the loss of an ear, is given to the priest, even though it is not fit for sacrifice on the altar].

D. It has been stated:

E. R. Hisda said, "It must be a part of the beast loss of which renders the beast carrion."

F. And Raba said, "It must be a part of the beast the loss of which renders the beast terefah."

G. What is at issue between them?

H. It is whether or not a terefah-beast can live.

I. The one who has said, "It must be a part of the beast the loss of which renders the beast terefah," takes the view that a terefah-beast cannot live, and the one who has said, "It must be a part of the beast loss of which renders the beast carrion" holds that a terefah-beast can live.

J. Our rabbis stated in the presence of R. Pappa, "There really is no conflict among the rulings of R. Huna on the one side and of R. Hisda, and Raba on the other [while Hisda and Raba do differ]. The one [Huna's ruling] speaks to the firstborn [in which case, even if the gentile has a share in the ear of the beast, the law of the firstborn does not apply], and the rulings of Hisda and Raba speak of the mother [and they differ as to whether the blemish must be such as to render it carrion or terefah]."

K. Said to them R. Pappa, "What leads to making this ruling in connection with the firstborn? It is because we require that it be 'all of the firstborn,' and that condition has not been met. In regard to the mother too, we require the condition, 'And of all your cattle you shall sanctify the males' (Ex. 34:19), and that condition has not been met. In fact, there is no difference [Miller & Simon: between the mother and its firstborn, and Huna on the one side and Hisda and Raba on the other do differ]."

L. An objection was raised by Mar b. R. Ashi, "What differentiates the case of a gentile owning a share in an animal, the removal of which share would render the beast either carrion or terefah, from the case of the abortions of animals, which, though not viable, are sacred? For a master has said,

'"...and every firstling that is a male which you have coming from an animal shall be the Lord's" (Ex. 13:12) – this refers to the embryo, which lives in the beast."'

M   *To that case [of a premature firstling], where there is no confusion of an unconsecrated part of the beast, we invoke the language, "in the animal, all the firstborn." In this case, where there is the inclusion of the unconsecrated part of the beast, we do not invoke the language, "all the firstborn."*

I.9 A. *[One day] R. Eleazar did not come to the house of study. He bumped into R. Assi and said to him, "What did rabbis say in the house of study today?"*

B. *He said to him,* [3B] *"This is what R. Yohanan said, 'Even if [a gentile owned in the firstling something that would add up to only] a minor blemish [the law of the firstling does not apply]. And as to that which we have learned in the Mishnah,* **A sheep which gave birth [to an offspring] something like a goat, or a goat which gave birth [to an offspring] something like a sheep – it [the offspring] is exempt from the law of the firstling. But if it bears some of the traits [of the mother], it is liable** [M. Bekh. 2:5A-D], [Yohanan said], 'It is in the classification of a firstling with a permanent blemish, on account of which blemish the beast may be slaughtered [and treated as is any other blemished firstling].'"

C. *Now when R. Yohanan made his ruling with regard to a minor blemish, he informed us that he accords with the position of R. Huna and excludes the rulings of R. Hisda and Raba. But as to his ruling with regard to a permanent blemish, what does he tell us? Is it to indicate that, since the animal is differentiated from others, it is regarded as subject to a permanent blemish? That we have learned on Tannaite authority:* or if the firstling's mouth is like that of a pig, it is a blemish. *And if you maintain that in the passage at hand [concerning the pig], the firstling is in fact classified as a species of animal to which the sanctity of the firstling does not apply, while here the firstling is classified as a species in which the sanctity of the firstling does apply, we have learned this as well on Tannaite authority:* if one of the eyes is large and one is small, it is a blemish, *in which regard a Tannaite authority stated, "large" means, large like a calf's, and "small" means, small like a goose's – so if it is as "small" as a goose's eye, then we have a species to which the sanctity of the firstling does not apply, but if it is as "large" as a calf's eye, then we have a species to which the sanctity of the firstborn does apply. So is it not because the operative consideration is that the animal is abnormal, and that on its own is deemed a blemish?* [Miller & Simon: What new thing consequently does Yohanan tell us in his ruling that a change renders it blemished, since this may be inferred from the Mishnah?]

D. *No, the reason is that it falls into the category of an animal with one limb larger than another* [Miller & Simon: therefore were it not stated in the house of study that a change in the offspring, e.g., where its wool resembles that of a goat, renders it blemished, I should not have been in a position to infer this from the Mishnah, as the classification of sarua, an animal with one limb larger than another, is a permanent blemish explicitly mentioned in Scripture].

E.	*And that really stands to reason, for we have learned in the Mishnah:*
These blemishes, whether permanent or transient, disqualify man
[from serving in the Temple]. In addition to them in the case of
man: [if he has unmatched eyes] [M. 7:1A-B, 7:3F] – if both of
them are large or both of them are small. Now with reference to
human beings it is written, "Whatsoever man of the descendants of
Aaron" (Lev. 22:4) – we require that "a man" belong to the
descendants of Aaron [with normal features]. *But in the case of an
animal, two large or two small eyes are not also classified as a blemish. In
the case of an animal with one large eye or one small eye, why is it a
blemish? It is because it is an abnormality. Then the same rule should
apply because it has two large eyes or two small eyes. So you have to
concede that the operative consideration in the former case is because it
falls into the class of that which has one limb larger than another?*

F.	*No, I maintain that the operative consideration for treating as blemished
an animal with one large eye and one small eye is that it is abnormal. And
as to your question that the same ruling should pertain to an animal with
two large eyes or two small eyes, the answer is that, in the latter case, if the
differentiating trait is because of the animal's extra large size, then the two
eyes are proportionate, and if it is because it is unusually thin, then the
two eyes are proportionately small.* [Miller &Simon: So the two large
or two small eyes do not constitute a differentiating trait. Since we
can deduce from the Mishnah that a change renders the animal
blemished, one can still raise the question, what is new in
Yohanan's ruling?]

I.10	A	*There was a certain convert to Judaism to whom Ahai-gentiles handed over
an animal for fattening. She came before Raba [for a ruling on whether or
not this was a permitted transaction]. He said to her, "You do not have to
pay attention to the ruling of R. Judah, who has said, 'A beast held in
partnership with a gentile is obligated to the law of the firstling.'"*

I.11	A	*R. Mari bar Rahel had a herd of beasts. He would transfer to a gentile the
right of ownership of the ears of firstlings while they were still in the
womb [so as to exempt the beasts from the law of the firstling].
Nonetheless, he would prohibit shearing and working the beasts, and he
gave them over to the priests. The herd of R. Mari bar Rahel died.*

B.	*Now, even though he would prohibit shearing and working the beasts, and
he gave them over to the priests, how come he gave ownership of the ears of
the embryos in the womb to a gentile?*

C.	*It was to avoid committing an offence [in case willy-nilly someone should
shear or work the beast; he rendered the beast exempt by giving part of the
embryo to a gentile].*

D.	*Then how come the herd of R. Mari bar Rahel died?*

E.	*It was because he removed the herd from the status of holiness.*

F.	But did not R. Judah say, "It is permitted for a person to inflict a
blemish on a firstling before it comes forth to the air of the world"?
[So what he did was permitted.]

G.	*In that case, while he removes from the animal the consecration involved
in being sacrificed on the altar, he does not remove the animal from the
consecration of belonging to the priesthood [while here he does].*

H.	*If you prefer, I shall say, R. Mari bar Rahel knew how to transfer complete
ownership to a gentile, but we take account of the possibility that someone*

else may see him do so and go and do the same, in the assumption that R.
Mari did nothing of consequence, and so he, too, will be led to do the same.

The Bavli and Tosefta provide two excellent exercises of Mishnah commentary, but they have nothing in common otherwise. Each authorship has made its own choices. I.1 provides a fine example of Mishnah criticism characteristic overall, showing why each item was necessary in context. No. 2 proceeds to compare our Mishnah's rule with a well-selected counterpart. No. 3 goes over the ground of No. 2. No. 4 continues Nos. 2-3. No. 5 is continuous with No. 4, and No. 6 goes over the ground of No. 5. No. 7 reverts back to 4.O, another mark of the complete unity of the entire composition. No. 8 then provides information required only in consequence of No. 7. No. 9 supplements No. 8, and continues the discussion inaugurated there. Nos. 10, 11 present pertinent cases.

If I had to specify what I conceive to be critical for the Bavli's authorship, it is the position of Judah: "A beast held in partnership with a gentile is liable to the law of the firstborn." That position occurs and recurs throughout. The seamless quality of the discussion of the Bavli contrasts with the composite character of the Tosefta's, though that comparison will not always yield the same result as it does here. A second striking trait of the Bavli is its interest in comparing Mishnah paragraph to Mishnah paragraph, rule to rule; that level of inquiry is simply unimagined in the Tosefta's treatment of the same passage, which remains wholly within the limits of the Mishnah, both as to its language and as to its propositions and even as to its themes. The conception that a given Mishnah paragraph may contain an abstract rule that links that paragraph to some other on a wholly different topic is simply alien to the Tosefta, but commonplace in the Bavli. The upshot is simple. Two sets of authorships reading the same base document have composed quite diverse commentaries, and, just as the one authorship, the Tosefta's, exhibits a clearcut program that guides its work, so the other does the same. The Bavli is different from Tosefta, but it is not on that account to be treated as formless or merely an agglutination of diverse materials. The very difference that the comparison of the two documents' reading of the same Mishnah paragraph reveals shows the purposive character of the Bavli's, as much as of Tosefta's, commentary to the Mishnah.

1:1F-H

F.   Priests and Levites are exempt [from the law of giving a lamb in redemption of the firstborn of an ass],

G.   by an argument a fortiori:

H   If those of Israelites were exempted in the wilderness [by reason of the Levites, Num. 3:45], how much the more so should they exempt their own!

F-H refer to the exemption of priests from two aspects of the law of firstlings, first, the redemption of the firstborn son, second, the redemption of the firstborn of an ass. In the case of the firstborn of a clean beast, however, they *are* liable, since it belongs to the Lord, not to the priest, and the sacrificial parts are offered on the altar. It is not redeemed (Albeck, p. 385; Abbayye, B. Bekh. 4A).

A. And so do you rule in the case of priests and Levites [M. 1:1F].

B. Since priests and Levites are liable to the law of the firstling in the case of a clean beast, one might have supposed that they should be liable to the law of the firstling in the case of an unclean beast.

C. Accordingly, Scripture states, "Both of man and of beast [they shall be mine]" (Num. 3:13).

D. That to which you are subject in the case of man, you are subject in the case of beast. That to which you are not subject in the case of man, you are not subject in the case of beast.

E. Levites are exempt in the case of the firstling of an unclean beast.

F. But they give redemption [money] for the firstborn son, or a redemption [lamb] for the firstborn of an ass only to priests.

T. 1:2 Z p. 534, lines 16-20

A. Among all unclean beasts, you have liable to the law of the firstling only the ass.

B. Among all wild animals you have only the dog which is prohibited because of the price [received therefor].

T. 1:3 Z p. 534, lines 20-21

A. R. Meir did say, "Anyone who carries out the commandment concerning the firstborn of an ass – they accredit it to him as if he carried out the commandment [of redemption of the firstborn] for every unclean beast.

B. "Anyone who does not carry out the commandment concerning the firstborn of an ass – they accredit it to him as if he annulled the commandment for every unclean beast."

T. 1:4 Z p. 534, lines 21-23

After citing M. 1:1, T. supplies its own proof, T. 1:2A-E, for the proposition that priests' and Levites' asses are exempt from the requirement of redemption of the firstborn. The proof is exegetical, rather than logical, as in M. T. 1:2F states what to M. is obvious. T.'s interest in expanding the exegetical foundation has its counterpart in the Bavli, which will underline how different the Bavli really is from the Tosefta in its framing of matters. It is not merely more elaborate, it is engaged in a different exercise altogether. The rest is T.'s usual complementary material. So the Tosefta's treatment of the opening component of M. 1:1 is exegetical, and this is explicit: citation and gloss, amplification. We shall now consider the Bavli's treatment of M. 1:1A-E. The Talmud for the same Mishnah passage now follows.

I.1   A   **[4A]** *Was it they themselves who exempted the firstborn of asses born in the wilderness?* Rather, a Levite man exempted another man, and a Levite's animal exempted an Israelite's ass's firstborn, for it is written, "Take the Levites instead of all the firstborn among the children of Israel, and the cattle of the Levites instead of their cattle" (Num. 3:45).

     B   *Said Abbayye, "This is the sense of the Mishnah passage:* As for priests and Levites, their animals are exempt a fortiori: if the beast [the sheep] of a Levite released the beast of an Israelite in the wilderness [from the requirement of the redemption of the firstborn of an ass], it is a matter of reason that it should release their own [firstborn of their asses; similarly, just as the Levites themselves exempted the firstborn of Israelites in the wilderness, so a fortiori they should exempt their own firstborn (Miller & Simon)]."

     C   *Said to him Raba, "And lo, does it say, they exempt, meaning, the Levites themselves? Further, if it is as you say, they should be exempted even from liability for a clean animal [from the law of the firstling, for the Levites' clean animals exempted the clean animals of Israelites in the wilderness]. Now why have we learned in the Mishnah:* Priests and Levites are liable [to the law of the firstborn]. They are not exempted from the law of the firstborn of a clean beast. But they are exempt only from the redemption of the firstborn son and from [the law of the firstling in regard to] the firstborn of an ass" [M. 2:1].

     D   *Rather, said Raba, "This is the sense of the passage:* Priests and Levites exempt themselves from the law of the firstborn by an argument a fortiori:

     E   "It is, specifically, as follows: If the holiness of the non-firstborn Levites nullified the holiness of the firstborn Israelites in the wilderness, should it not nullify the requirement that their own firstborn be redeemed? So we find that the Levite firstborn son is exempt.

     F   "How do we know that the same rule applies also to an unclean animal [that is, priests and Levites are exempt from the law governing the firstborn of an ass]? Scripture says, 'But the firstborn of man you shall surely redeem, and the firstling of unclean beasts you shall redeem' (Num. 18:15) – whoever is subject to the law covering the firstborn of man is subject to the law of the firstborn of the unclean beast, and whoever is not covered by the law of the firstborn of man is not subject to the law of the firstborn of a beast" [T. Bekh. 1:2D].

     G   *Said R. Safra to Abbayye, "In your view, which maintains that the a fortiori argument also refers to the Levites' animals, a Levite who had a sheep in the wilderness to release the firstborn of an Israelite ass could thereby release his own as well, but he who did not have a sheep of his own to release the firstborn of an Israelite ass could not release his own. And further, according to both your view and that of Raba, a Levite a month old who released an Israelite firstborn a month old in the wilderness should therefore release himself from the necessity of redemption, while a Levite firstborn less than a month old who did not release a firstborn Israelite of* the same age should not release himself. Also a Levite's daughter who gave birth to a firstborn should not be exempt from the law. [Miller & Simon: Abbayye and Raba concur that we argue a fortiori that the firstborn of a Levite is exempt from the requirement of redemption. As to the Levite a month old, if the holiness of a Levite a month old who was not a firstborn released from holiness an Israelite firstborn a month old, as only the firstborn of a month old were counted, how much more so should the Levite firstborn a month old release himself from the requirement of being redeemed. But why does Scripture not say that the firstborn Levites in the wilderness who were at the time of counting less than a month old were to be redeemed? As to the Levite's daughter, married to an Israelite, why should she not be exempt from the rule, since females were not included in the count in the wilderness?] *But why, in light of all this, did R. Ada bar Ahbah say, 'A Levite woman who gave birth – her son is exempt from the requirement to present five selas to a priest [to redeem the son]'?"*

H   That is no problem, for it is in accord with that which Mar b. R. Joseph in the name of Raba said, "'the opening of the womb' (Num. 18:15) is what Scripture has said, meaning that the All-Merciful has made the obligation to redeem the firstborn depend upon the opening of the womb. [Miller & Simon: We go by the status of the mother, and since she comes of a tribe that is exempt from the requirement of redeeming the firstborn, we link the son with the mother and not the father, that is provided the exemption in the wilderness extended to all Levites, even those who were not a month old at the time]."

I   *And what of Aaron, who was not counted in that census of the Levites, the firstborn of his asses should not be released from the law of redeeming the firstborn. For it has been taught on Tannaite authority:* Why in the Hebrew Scriptures are dots placed over the name of Aaron in the book of Numbers [at Num. 3:39]? It indicates that he was not counted in that census.

J.   Scripture has said, "The Levites...," drawing a comparison among all Levites. [Miller & Simon: All Levites without regard to age, including anybody performing sacred functions, such as the priests, were exempt from the requirement to redeem the firstborn of an ass; this answers all the questions raised above.]

K.   *How do we know the rule for the priests?*

L.   It is in accord with that which R. Joshua b. Levi said, for said R. Joshua b. Levi, "In twenty-four passages priests are called Levites, and this is one of them: 'But the priests the Levites sons of Zadok'" (Ezek. 44:15). [So priests are called Levites, and when the word "Levites" occurs, it covers priests as well.]

I.2   A.   [4B] *How do we know that the exemptions of priests and Levites from the requirement to redeem firstborn applies for generations to come?*

B.   Scripture states, "and the Levites shall be mine" (Num. 3:45) – "and they shall be" means that the Levites will retain their status for all time.

C.   *And how do we know that the Levites exempted the Israelite's asses' firstborn in the wilderness with a sheep?* [Miller &Simon: Perhaps the verse, "and the cattle of the Levites instead of all the firstlings among the cattle of the children of Israel" (Num. 3:41) means that the firstborn of the Levite's ass exempted the Israelite's ass's firstborn, but not the sheep?]

D.   Said R. Hisda, "We find reference to 'money' (Num. 18:16) with reference to redemption of the firstborn throughout all generations, and we find 'a sheep' written in connection with the redemption of the firstborn of an ass for all time. Just as with 'money' prescribed for all time they redeemed the firstborn at all times and also at that particular time, in the wilderness, so with sheep prescribed for all time the Levites redeemed firstlings at all times and also redeemed them at that particular time in the wilderness."

E.   But the distinctive trait of "money" is that it was with money that they redeem Holy Things and Second Tithe [Miller & Simon: whereas we do not as a rule redeem Holy Things with a sheep].

F.   Rather, Scripture has said, "Nevertheless the firstborn of a man you shall surely redeem and the firstling of unclean beasts you shall redeem" (Num. 18:15) – just as, in the case of redeeming the firstborn of man, you have made no distinction between doing so for all generations to come and doing so at that particular moment in the wilderness, in both instances it is being done with money, so in respect to unclean beasts, you should make no distinction between doing so for generations to come and doing so at that particular time, its being done with a sheep.

I.3 A.   Said R. Hanina, "A single sheep of a Levite exempted any number of firstborn of asses for Israelites."

B.   Said Abbayye, "You may know that that is so, for lo, Scripture has counted the surplus of men [firstborn Israelites who had to be redeemed with money] [over the Levites, but it does not count the surplus of Israelite animals over Levite animals]. [Since Scripture does not mention the surplus of Israelite animals over Levite animals, we can infer that one Levite sheep exempted many Israelite animals.]"

C.   *But what sort of proof is derived from that fact? Perhaps the Israelites in the wilderness did not own all that many asses that required redemption [Miller & Simon: and this being the case, one Levite sheep did not have to redeem many firstborn of asses].*

D.   *Perish the thought! For it is written,* "Now the children of Reuben and the children of Gad had a very great multitude of cattle" (Num. 32:1).

E.   *But even so, the ordinary [animals, not firstborn] of the Israelites may still have corresponded to the number of the firstborn of the Israelites [so there still was no surplus, and so there is no evidence that the Israelites' firstlings outnumbered the animals of Levites who were not firstborn].*

F.   Scripture has said, "And the cattle of the Levites instead of their cattle" (Num. 3:45) – one beast in place of a great many beasts.

G.   *And might I say the word* "cattle" *means* "a great many beasts"?

H.   *If so, Scripture should have written,* "cattle instead of cattle" *or* "their cattle instead of their cattle." *Why say,* "cattle of...instead of their cattle"? *It is to make the point that a single sheep of a Levite exempted any number of firstborn of asses for Israelites.*

I.   Said Raba, "We also have learned the same ruling: 'and **he may redeem with a sheep many times the firstborn of asses.'**"

J.   *And R. Hanina ['s explanation for the fact that the Mishnah states explicitly what he wishes to prove from Scripture]?*

K.   *He is setting out the scriptural basis for the position of the Mishnah, and this is the sense of his statement: what is the reason that* **he may redeem with a sheep many times the firstborn of asses?** *It is because [in Scripture], a single sheep of a Levite exempted many asses' firstborn that belonging to Israelites."*

I.4   A.   It has been stated:

B.   R. Yohanan said, "The firstborn [of men and beasts] in the wilderness were sanctified."

C.   R. Simeon b. Laqish said, "The firstborn [of men and beasts] in the wilderness were not sanctified."

D.   R. Yohanan said, "The firstborn [of men and beasts] in the wilderness were sanctified: *for the All-Merciful has said that they are to be sanctified:* 'Sanctify to me all the firstborn'" (Ex. 13:2).

E.   R. Simeon b. Laqish said, "The firstborn [of men and beasts] in the wilderness were not sanctified: for it is written, 'And it shall be when the Lord shall bring you into the land of the Canaanites...you shall set apart to the Lord all that opens the womb' (Ex. 13:11, 12). From that formulation you may draw the conclusion that prior to their entering the land, the firstborn was not sanctified [and the reference 'sanctify to me all the firstborn' refers to those born in Egypt (Miller & Simon)]."

F.   R. Yohanan objected to R. Simeon b. Laqish, "**Before the tabernacle was set up, the high places were permitted, and the sacrificial service was carried out by the firstborn (Num. 3:12-13, 8:16-18) [M. Zeb. 14:4A].** [This indicates that the firstborn had been sanctified.]"

G.   He said to him, "It was done by those who had gone forth from Egypt. *That conclusion stands to reason, for if you do not say this, is a one-year-old suitable for carrying out the sacrificial service?*"

H.   *So if the other raised such an argument, on what basis could he have done so?*

I.   *This is the question that he raised: "Now if you take the view that the sanctification of the firstborn did not cease in the wilderness, there are no problems, because then those firstborn were originally born in Egypt and did not have their sanctification nullified. But if you hold that their sanctification did cease, that is to say, those firstborn produced in the wilderness were not sanctified, then the sanctification of the firstborn who were produced in Egypt should also have been nullified!"*

J.   *And the other?*

K.   *The ones who were originally sanctified [having been born in Egypt] remained sanctified, and those who were not sanctified were never sanctified.*

L.   [Yohanan] raised the following objection: "On that day on which the tabernacle was raised, in Israel were sacrificed offerings brought by reason of vows, thanksgiving-offerings, sin-offerings, guilt-offerings, firstlings, and animals designated as tithe of the flock or the herd" [and the tabernacle was raised in the wilderness, so firstborn were consecrated in the wilderness].

M   "Here, too, reference is made to those who had gone forth from Egypt, *and from the statement itself you may draw that same conclusion:* 'On that day on which the tabernacle was raised, in Israel were sacrificed' – *meaning, from that day firstlings were sacrificed, but from that time onward in the wilderness there was no sacrifice of firstlings.*"

N   *There are those who say that R. Simeon b. Laqish objected to R. Yohanan,* "On that day on which the tabernacle was raised, in Israel were sacrificed offerings brought by reason of vows, thanksgiving-offerings, sin-offerings, guilt-offerings, firstlings, and animals designated as tithe of the flock or the herd – *meaning, from that day firstlings indeed were sacrificed, but from that time onward in the wilderness there was no sacrifice of firstlings.*"

O   *Might I say,* "From that day and onward"? *And what does the framer of the passage propose to tell us? From that day onward, such sacrifices were made, but prior to that time they had not been made. Therefore obligatory sacrifices were not offered on a high place [encompassing sin-offerings, firstlings, and the like].*

P.   *Come and take note:* You turn out to say, in three places firstlings were sanctified in Israel: in Egypt, in the wilderness, and when the Israelites entered the Land.   In Egypt: "Sanctify to me all the firstlings" (Ex. 13:2); in the wilderness: "For the firstborn of the children of Israel are mine" (Num. 8:17); when they entered the Land of Israel: "And it shall be when the Lord shall bring you into the land of the Canaanites...that you shall set apart..." (Ex. 13:11, 12). [Miller & Simon: We see therefore that, contrary to the view of Simeon b. Laqish, the firstlings were sanctified in the wilderness.]

Q   Said R. Nahman bar Isaac, "The sense is, 'in three places the Israelites were admonished concerning firstlings, that they should be sanctified, though they were not at that moment sanctified.'"

R.   *But were the firstborn in Egypt not sanctified? Have we not said that they were holy?*

S   *This is the sense of the passage:* "In some of the three places the firstborn were sanctified, and in some they were not sanctified [in the wilderness in particular]."

T.   *R. Pappa objected,* "And in the wilderness were the firstborn not sacrificed?   And has it not been written, 'Number all the firstborn males of the children of Israel' (Num. 3:40)?"

U.   *Rather, if such a statement of matters ever was made, this is how it was made:*

V.   R. Yohanan said, "The firstborn [of men and beasts] in the wilderness were sanctified and did not cease to be sanctified."

W.   R. Simeon b. Laqish said, "The firstborn [of men and beasts] in the wilderness were sanctified [5A] but they ceased to be sanctified."

X.   *Now the position of R. Simeon b. Laqish poses no problems, for he has given scriptural support for his position (Ex. 13:11, 12). But what scriptural support exists for the position of R. Yohanan?*

Y.   *Said R. Eleazar,* "*R. Yohanan appeared in a dream to me, saying, 'I said an excellent thing, for Scripture has said,* "Mine shall they be" (Num. 3:13) [Miller & Simon: indicating that there was no break in their holiness, even in the wilderness]. *They shall remain as is.*'"

Z.   *And how does R. Yohanan interpret the verse, "*And it shall be when the Lord shall bring you into the land of the Canaanites...that you shall set apart..." (Ex. 13:11, 12)?

AA.   *He requires that verse in connection with that which has been set forth by the Tannaite authority of the household of R. Ishmael:* "Carry out this religious duty, for on its account you will enter the land."

BB.   Said R. Mordecai to R. Ashi, "You have repeated the matter to us in that way, but for our part, we repeat it contrariwise:

CC.   "R. Yohanan said, 'The firstborn were not sanctified in the wilderness.'

DD.   "And R. Simeon b. Laqish said, 'The firstborn were sanctified in the wilderness.'"

EE.   *He said to him, "And do you plan also to reverse the name of the source of the refutation [Yohanan refuted Simeon b. Laqish] in regard to the statement of R. Eleazar?"*

FF.   He said to him, "'They were not sanctified' [in my version of Yohanan's statement] means, *it was not necessary for the firstborn to be sanctified in the wilderness [since they were sanctified at birth, as Yohanan said above, so no firstborn was sanctified in the wilderness]."*

GG.   *He said to him, "If so, then that is the same version as ours!"*

HH.   Thus we learn that a person is obligated to state a teaching in the exact language of his master.

I.5   A.   General Quntroqos asked Rabban Yohanan b. Zakkai, "When the Levites were counted out, you find the total to be 22,300, but in the sum total you find only 22,000. What happened to the other three hundred?"

B.   He said to him, "Those three hundred were firstborn, and a firstborn cannot cancel the holiness of a firstborn."

C.   *How come?*

D.   Said Abbayye, "It suffices for a firstborn to cancel out the sanctification that pertains to him himself."

E.   And further he asked him, "With reference to the collection of money [when every Israelite gave half a sheqel] you count out two hundred and one kikkars [talents of silver. Each *kikkar* contains sixty *manehs*, each *maneh*, twenty-five *selas* or holy sheqels; so we have 1500 in a *kikkar*. 603,550 half sheqels were collected from the people, to make 301,775 sheqels. Divide 1500 into this and we have two hundred and one kikkars, with the remainder of 275 sheqels, eleven *maneh* (Miller & Simon)]. For it is written, 'A beka for every man, that is, half a sheqel after the sheqel of the sanctuary' (Ex. 38:26). But when the money was handed over and accounted for, you find only one hundred kikkars: 'And the hundred talents of silver were for casting' (Ex. 38:27). Your lord, Moses, was a thief or he was a swindler or he was bad at numbers. He gave half, took half, and did not even hand over a complete half [Miller & Simon: for a complete half would have been one hundred and a half kikkars and five and a half *manehs*, and he only returned one hundred *kikkars*]."

F.   He said to him, "Our lord, Moses, was a faithful trustee and expert at numbers, but the *maneh* of the sanctuary was double the ordinary one [and therefore 120 *maneh* made up a *kikkar*; the hundred *kikkar* were really two hundred, and the remaining *kikkar* and eleven *maneh* were 1,775 sheqels mentioned, from which hooks were made (Miller & Simon)]."

G. *R. Ahai considered the matter: "Now what was the general's problem?* 'And the hundred talents that were for casting' – *these were used for casting* [and would be separate from the 201 *kikkars* that are mentioned]. *And the other [201 kikkars] were for the treasury."*

H. *Scripture presented yet another verse:* "And the silver of those who were numbered of the congregation was a hundred talents" (Ex. 38:25) [Miller & Simon: and here no mention is made of being used for casting purposes].

I. *And as to his reply,* "but the *maneh* of the sanctuary was double the ordinary one," *how did he know that fact? If you say [that it derives from the verse at hand],* for here we have seventy-one *manehs*, since Scripture has said, "And of the thousand seven hundred seventy-five sheqels he made hooks for the pillars" and he counted them only in units of sheqels, if the value of the *maneh* is not higher, Scripture should have written, "One hundred and one kikkars and eleven manehs" [Miller & Simon: if all *manehs* consisted of sixty sheqels, then seventy-one *manehs* is one *kikkar* more, plus eleven *manehs*]. But since Scripture records them only in units of sheqels, you may deduce from here that the sacred *maneh* was double the ordinary one [Miller & Simon: and therefore the seventy-one *manehs*, the one thousand seven hundred seventy-five sheqels, could not be counted in terms of *kikkars*, as there would then be one hundred and twenty manehs in a *kikkar*].

J. *But perhaps it is the intention of Scripture to count only the sum total of a hundred kikkars, but the change of a kikkar or so is not counted?*

K. *Then prove the same point from the following [which will also show that the sacred maneh was twice the ordinary one]:* "And the brass of the offering was seventy talents and two thousand and four hundred sheqels" (Ex. 38:29) – for here are ninety-six manehs, and Scripture records them only in units of sheqels. Derive from here the fact, therefore, that the sacred maneh was double the ordinary one [Miller & Simon: one hundred twenty *manehs* in a *kikkar*, and therefore Scripture could not count this in terms of *kikkars*].

L. *Bur perhaps while Scripture will record a large odd number of kikkars* [Miller & Simon: like seventy *kikkars*, although they cannot be counted in terms of one hundred *kikkars*], *a small odd number it will not record?*

M. *Rather, said R. Hisda, "Proof derives from here:* 'And the sheqel shall be twenty gerahs, twenty sheqels, five and twenty sheqels, fifteen sheqels shall be your maneh' (Ezek. 45:12). [Miller & Simon: We therefore see that there were sixty sheqels in a maneh.]"

N. [5B] *And lo, would this maneh not be two hundred and forty denars* [Miller & Simon: and a *maneh* has only one hundred *denars* or *zuz*, for there are twenty-five sheqels to a *maneh*, and four *denars* to a sheqel]? Therefore draw the conclusion that the sacred maneh was double the ordinary one [fifty sheqels would add up to a maneh; this is two hundred *denars*, and the remaining forty were added later on] (Miller & Simon)].

O. *And this further yields the proposition that* measures may be augmented, but not by more than a sixth.

P. *And this further yields the proposition that* the added sixth is a sixth of the total [over and above the principal, that is, to five portions one is added, that is, 20 percent; here, too, the addition to the two hundred denars which add up to the maneh used by the sanctuary was 20 percent, that is, forty].

I.6 A. Said R. Hanina, "I asked R. Eliezer *in the great session:* 'what differentiates firstborn of asses from firstborn of horses and camels?'

B. "He said to me, 'It is merely a scriptural decree.

C. "'Moreover, asses helped the Israelites when they left Egypt, for not a single Israelite failed to possess ninety Libyan asses loaded with the silver and gold of Egypt.'

D. "And I further asked him, 'What is the meaning of the word "Rephidim"'?

E. "He said to me, 'It is a place name.'"

F. *A Tannaite dispute concerns the same matter:*

G. R. Eliezer says, "Rephidim is a place name."

H. R. Joshua says, "They relaxed [a word that uses the same letters as the word] their hold on the teachings of the Torah, and so Scripture says, 'The fathers shall not look back to the children on account of feebleness of hand' (Jer. 47:3)."

I. "I further asked him, "What is the meaning of the word, 'Shittim'?"

J. "He said to me, 'It is a place name.'"

K. *A Tannaite dispute concerns the same matter:*

L. R. Eliezer says, "Shittim is a place name."

M. R. Joshua says, "It means that they gave themselves up to stupidity [a word that uses the same consonants as Shittim]: 'And they called to the people to the sacrifices of their gods' (Num. 25:2)."

N. R. Eliezer says, "That verse means that the Israelites came into contact with naked bodies [since 'they called them' uses the same letters that stand for 'meet']."

O. R. Joshua says, "All of them were affected with seminal emissions."

I.1 amplifies the Mishnah's allusion to an argument a fortiori. No. 2 carries forward the inquiry of No. 1. No. 3 continues the interest of Nos. 1, 2, and No. 4 addresses the same subject. The issue of importance to the Bavli is the contrast between the laws that prevailed in the wilderness and those that prevailed once the Israelites had entered the land and for all time thereafter. To that interest, which is paramount, the Tosefta contributes nothing; and what interests the Talmud's framers, as to substance and scale alike, simply bears no relationship with the program of Tosefta's authorship, which is brief and episodic. No. 4 gives us three versions of the same matter. I see no compelling reason for the inclusion of No. 5; it intersects with the basic composition only in the rather generalized theme of the census of the wilderness. No. 5 carries No. 6 in its wake.

1:2A-H

A.   A cow which bore [an offspring] like an ass, or an as which bore [an offspring] like a horse –

B.   it [the offspring] is exempt from the law of the firstling,

C.   since it is said, *The firstling of an ass* (Ex. 13:13), *The firstling of an ass* (Ex. 34:20) –

D.   two times, [meaning that the rule applies] only when that which gives birth is an ass and that which is born is an ass.

E.   What is their rule as to eating [the offspring of such a union]?

F.   A clean beast which bore [an offspring] like an unclean beast – it [the offspring] is permitted as to eating.

G.   And an unclean beast which bore [an offspring] like a clean beast – it [the offspring] is prohibited as to eating.

H   For that which comes forth from the unclean is unclean, and that which comes forth from the clean is clean.

This pericope is as pellucid in contest as in form. Despite the blatant character of E as joining language, the whole is a conceptual unity, since the principle of the appended rule, E-H, given below as Bavli separates the passage from the foregoing, is identical to that of the principal part, A-D, and the appendix to E-H, I-K, is essential in the proper interpretation of E-H, and indeed conforms to the formulary pattern of E-H. The point of A-D is made clear by D. But that is only one side to the picture, for H clarifies A-B as much as its own unit. So reason, not exegesis, substantiates A-B. I-K further clarify F-H. The apocopation of F, G, is carried forward at I, J. The clean fish found in the belly of the unclean one is permitted to be eaten, by contrast to F, and for obvious reasons (K).

A.   R. Yosé the Galilean says, "Behold, Scripture says, *But the firstborn of an ox or the firstborn of a sheep or the firstborn of a goat you shall not redeem. They are holy* (Num. 18:17).

B.   *"The firstborn of an ox* [means that the rule applies] only when that which gives birth and that which is born are an ox.

C.   *"The firstborn of a sheep* [means that the rule applies] only when that which gives birth and that which is born are a sheep.

D.   *"The firstborn of a goat* [means that the rule applies] only when that which gives birth and that which is born are goats" [M. 1:2A-D].

E.   And if it [the offspring] exhibits some of the traits of the dam, it is liable to the law of the firstborn.

T. 1:5 Z p. 534, lines 24-27

A.   *A clean beast which bore an offspring like an unclean beast – it [the offspring] is permitted for eating* [M. Bekh. 1:2F].

B.   And if it exhibits some of the traits [of the dam], it is liable to the law of the firstborn.

C.   *And an unclean [beast] which bore an offspring like a clean beast – it is prohibited for eating* [M. Bekh. 1:2G].

D.   *For that which comes forth from the unclean is unclean, and that which comes forth from the clean is clean* [M. Bekh. 1:2H].

T. 1:6 Z p. 534, lines 27-29

A.   On what account [then] did they rule that the honey of bees is permitted?

B.   For they do not bring it forth [from their own bodies] but store it up.

C.   The honey of gazin bees is prohibited, for it is only saliva.

T. 1:8 Z p. 534, lines 30-32

A.   R. Simeon says, "Why does Scripture say, *Camel, Camel* (Lev. 11:4, Deut. 19:7) – two times?

B.   "To encompass the camel which is born of a cow as equivalent to one born of a camel.

C.   "And if its head and the greater part of its body are similar to those of its dam, it is permitted for eating."

D.   And sages say, *"That which goes forth from the unclean is unclean, and that which goes forth from the clean is clean* [M. Bekh. 1:2H].

E.   "For an unclean beast does not produce offspring form [mating with] a clean one, nor does a clean one produce offspring form [mating with] an unclean one, nor does a large one produce offspring from [mating with] a small one, nor does a small one produce offspring from [mating with] a large one, nor does a human being produce offspring from [mating with] any of them, nor does any of them produce offspring from [mating with] a human being."

T. 1:9 Z p. 534, lines 32-36

Tosefta's complement to M. 1:2 begins with Yosé the Galilean's exegetical proof of the proposition of M. 1:2A-D, an alternative to M.'s. But M. will hardly concede the qualification of T. 1:5E, which T. 1:6 wishes to read into M. The Bavli for the foregoing Mishnah passage now follows.

I.1   A.   *We have learned in the Mishnah there:* **A sheep which gave birth [to an offspring] something like a goat, or a goat which gave birth [to an offspring] something like a sheep – it [the offspring] is exempt from the law of the firstling. But if it bears some of the traits [of the mother], it is liable [M. Bekh. 2:5A-D].**

B.   *What is the source of this rule?*

C.   Said R. Judah, "Scripture has said, 'But the firstling of an ox' (Num. 18:17) – both it and the firstling must be an ox; 'firstling of a sheep' – both it and its firstling must be a sheep; 'firstling of a goat' – both it and its firstling must be a goat.

D.   "Might one suppose that even if the offspring possesses only some of the traits similar to the mother [the rule of the firstling applies]? Scripture states, 'but...,' so imposing a distinction [between total physical difference between the offspring and the mother and partial resemblance]."

E. *And lo, the Tannaite tradition contains a different proof, namely, the proof
    from the exemption of a cow that gave birth to a species of an ass* [since it
    is said, *"The firstling of an ass"* (Ex. 13:13), *"The firstling of an ass"*
    (Ex. 34:20) – two times, [meaning that the rule applies] only when
    that which gives birth is an as and that which is born is an ass] [so
    why does Judah present a different proof?]

F. *He states matters in accord with the view of R. Yosé the Galilean, for it has
    been taught on Tannaite authority:*

G. R. Yosé the Galilean says, "Scripture has said, 'But the firstling of an
    ox' (Num. 18:17) – both it and the firstling must be an ox; 'firstling
    of a sheep' – both it and its firstling must be a sheep; 'firstling of a
    goat' – both it and its firstling must be a goat.

H. "Might one suppose that even if the offspring possesses only some
    of the traits similar to the mother [the rule of the firstling applies]?
    Scripture states, 'but...,' so imposing a distinction [between total
    physical difference between the offspring and the mother and
    partial resemblance]."

I. *What is at issue between these two ways of proving the same proposition?*

J. *The Tannaite framer of our Mishnah takes the view that the All-Merciful
    reveals to us the rule that applies in the case of that which is consecrated
    for its value that if there is a change in the offspring from the appearance of
    the mother, the offspring is exempt from the law of the firstling, and the
    same is so of that which itself was consecrated* [Miller & Simon: the case
    of a cow or any clean animal where it is holy as such and is
    irredeemable; in such an instance, the law of the firstling should
    certainly apply only where the offspring resembles its mother, since
    it is irredeemable, the offspring should be required all the more to
    resemble its mother]. *R. Yosé the Galilean maintains the view that
    Scripture has revealed the rule governing a beast that is sanctified as to its
    body, and the same rule pertains to the consecration of the value of the
    beast, and he derives the law governing the consecration of the value of the
    beast from the rule governing the consecration of the body of the beast.*

K. *And our Mishnah's Tannaite framer – how does he deal with the
    duplicated reference to "firstling" [the threefold repetition of firstling at
    Num. 18:17]?*

L. He requires it with reference to that which R. Yosé b. R. Hanina
    stated, for said R. Yosé b. R. Hanina, "Why does Scripture speak of
    the portion of the animal that is sacrificed on the altar ['You shall
    dash their blood against the altar and shall make their fat smoke for
    an offering by fire,' a verse that refers to all three cases of firstlings
    mentioned in the text; a single allusion would have sufficed for all
    three] in referring to the firstling of an ox, the firstling of a sheep,
    and the firstling of a goat? *All three references are absolutely necessary.
    For if Scripture had referred only to the firstling of an ox, which is
    accompanied by a great volume of libations, [I might have supposed that
    that is the reason that the sacrificial parts have to be sacrificed on the altar,
    but the same rule would not apply to the firstlings of sheep or goat, which
    are not accompanied by substantial libations]. And as to the sheep, the
    special reason might have been that the fat tail is also offered up [which
    would not pertain in the other cases]. And if Scripture had spoken only of
    the goat, the special reason is that a great many goats are offered up in*

connection with unwitting acts of idolatry by an individual. Accordingly, one could not have derived one case from any other case.

M "Then could one have derived the rule governing one from that governing the two others? If I should propose that route, which two should I take? Let Scripture not speak of the rule governing the firstling of the ox, and derive it from the other two [sheep, goat]? But the exceptional characteristic of these other two species of firstling, accounting for the fact that their sacrificial parts have to be burned up on the altar, is that they may serve as Passover-offerings [but an ox may not]. If Scripture should omit reference to the sheep, so that we may derive the rule governing the firstling of the sheep from these others, one may respond that the exceptional trait of the others is that they serve as suitable offerings for the sin of idolatry when it is committed by the community [a bull for a burnt-offering, a goat for a sin-offering]. And if Scripture should omit reference to the goat, the rule governing the disposition of the firstling of which would then derive from the other two, it might be countered that the exceptional trait of the other two, accounting for the fact that they are offered on the altar, is that in common these others have the quality that they involve substantially greater offerings on the altar [the ox has the larger volume of libations, the sheep contributes in addition its fat tail]. Therefore all three cases have to be explicitly set forth."

N And R. Yosé the Galilean [how does he explain the multiple references to the sacrifice of the offerings on the altar that derive from all three species of firstlings]?

O If that were the operative consideration, Scripture could just as well have written, "But the firstling of an ox, sheep, and goat." Why bother to write, "But the firstling of an ox, the firstling of a sheep, and the firstling of a goat"? Is it not to bear the inference: 'But the firstling of an ox' (Num. 18:17) – both it and the firstling must be an ox; 'firstling of a sheep' – both it and its firstling must be a sheep; 'firstling of a goat' – both it and its firstling must be a goat."

P. And how does R. Yosé the Galilean interpret the references to [A cow which bore [an offspring] like an ass, or an ass which bore [an offspring] like a horse – it [the offspring] is exempt from the law of the firstling, since it is said,] "The firstling of an ass" (Ex. 13:13), "The firstling of an ass" (Ex. 34:20) – [two times, meaning that the rule applies only when that which gives birth is an ass and that which is born is an ass]?

Q He requires it in line with that which has been taught on Tannaite authority:

R. R. Yosé the Galilean says, "Since it is said, 'But the firstborn of man you shall surely redeem, and the firstling of unclean beasts you shall redeem' (Num. 18:15), might I infer that even the firstborn of horses and camels [are subject to the rule of the firstborn]? Scripture states, 'the firstborn of the ass.' 'It is in particular of the firstling of an ass that I have spoken when I required an act of redemption, but not the firstling of horses and camels.' And still might I say, 'the firstborn of an ass is to be redeemed with a sheep, but the firstborn of horses and camels may be redeemed with anything at all'? [6A] Scripture states, 'The firstling of an ass' (Ex. 13:13), 'The firstling of an ass' (Ex. 34:20) – two times, meaning, 'I have spoken to you concerning the firstlings of asses, and not concerning the firstlings of horses or camels."'

S.   *R. Ahai raised a problem with that proof, "[The repetition of 'firstling of an ass' had to be set forth,] for if the All-Merciful had made reference to that matter only one time, I might have thought that* the law governing the firstling of an ass's requiring redemption is a matter that had been covered in an encompassing rule and then was made subject to an explicit statement, so that the explicit statement is not limited to its own class alone but pertains to the entire class of unclean animals, with the result that in all cases of unclean animals, redemption is to be carried out with a sheep. *Scripture elsewhere therefore made reference to 'the firstling of an ass,' to make the point that only firstlings of asses are to be redeemed with sheep, but not the firstlings of horses and camels."*

T.   *But might I say that the purpose of the limitation with respect to horses and camels was only to indicate that redemption is not to be done with a sheep, but they may be redeemed with any object?*

U.   *If so, Scripture should have written, "The firstling of an ass you shall redeem with a sheep," and "an ass you shall redeem with a sheep." Why did Scripture repeat the matter: "The firstling of an ass you shall redeem with a sheep"* (Ex. 13:13), "the firstling of an ass you shall redeem with a sheep" (Ex. 34:20)? It was to indicate, it is the firstlings of asses of which I have spoken to you, and it is not the firstlings of horses or camels.

V.   *And as to the Tannaite authority of our Mishnah [who uses the repetition for his own purposes, as we have seen], how does he prove the proposition that horses and camels are not subject to the same law?*

W.   Said R. Pappa, "'And of all the cattle you shall sanctify the males' (Ex. 34:19) forms a general proposition; 'the firstling of an ox and sheep...and the firstling of an ass you shall redeem' is a particularization of the foregoing. When you have a generalization followed by a particularization, the generalization encompasses only what is covered by the particularization. That then indicates that the ox, sheep, *and ass are subject to the law of the firstling, but no other animal."*

X.   And R. Yosé the Galilean [who derives the ruling that the horse and camel are not subject to the law of the firstling in the way that the ass is, why does he not derive that proposition from the verse quoted by Pappa]?

Y.   "The word 'firstborn' interrupts the subject." [Miller & Simon: We do not interpret the verse as a general proposition complemented by a particularization, as the word firstborn indicates a break in the subject.]

Z.   And rabbis?

AA.   The "and" that occurs joins it again to the prior verse.

BB.   And R. Yosé the Galilean?

CC.   *Then let Scripture not write either the "and" or the "firstborn."*

DD.   And rabbis?

EE.   *Since the general proposition ["All that opens the womb" is mine, including the ass, which is not holy as such and must be redeemed with a sheep] deals with objects that are holy in respect to their value [but not offered up on the altar], and the other part deals with objects that are holy in themselves [not only as to their value], Scripture at first interrupts the subject and then reconnects it with the prior verse.*

I.2   A.   *The question was raised:* "If a cow gave birth to a species of an ass, which had some of the traits of the mother, what is the law? If a goat gave birth to a species of a ewe, and a ewe gave birth to a species of a goat, the rule is that, when the offspring has some of the traits of the mother, it is subject to the law of the firstling, *since the mother is clean and the offspring is clean, the mother is consecrated as to its body, and the offspring is consecrated as to the body. But here, where the offspring is unclean while the mother is clean, the mother can be consecrated as to her body, but the offspring can be consecrated only as to its value, so the ruling should not be the same. Or perhaps, since in both cases, the offspring belong to a category of animals that are subject to the sanctity of the firstborn, may we say that it is sanctified?*

B.   *"And if you should conclude that, since both of them belong to a category of animals that are subject to the sanctity of the firstborn, it is sanctified, then, if an ass gave birth to a species of a horse, what is the law? In this case, most certainly, the offspring does not belong to the class of animals that are sanctified as firstlings. Or perhaps we say that since the horse belongs to the same class, namely, that of unclean animals, it is sanctified?*

C.   *"And if you should conclude that since the horse belongs to the same class, namely, that of unclean animals, it is sanctified, then if a cow gave birth to a species of a horse, what is the law? Here the cow certainly belongs to the class of a clean animal, while the offspring is an unclean animal, the cow belongs to the class of animals that are subject to the sanctification of the firstling, and the horse does not belong to the category of animals that are subject to the sanctification of the firstling. Or perhaps we invoke the criterion of the distinguishing traits of the mother?"*

D.   *Come and take note:* **A clean beast that gave birth to a species of an unclean beast – the latter is exempt from the law of the firstling. If it possesses some of the traits of the mother, it is liable to the law of the firstling [cf. T. Bekh. 1:6B].** *Does this not mean,* even in the case of a cow that gave birth to a species of a horse?

E.   No, it refers to the case of a cow that gave birth to a species of an ass.

F.   *Come and take note:* **A cow which bore [an offspring] like an ass, or an ass which bore [an offspring] like a horse – it [the offspring] is exempt from the law of the firstling. [M. above]. If it exhibits some of the traits of the dam, it is liable to the law of the firstborn [T. 1:6B].** *Does this not refer to both cases [where a cow gave birth to a species of an ass or an ass gave birth to a species of a horse, if the offspring resembled the mother, it is liable to the law of the firstling]?*

G.   No, this refers only to a cow that gave birth to a species of an ass.

H.   Then an ass that gave birth to a species of a horse – *for what purpose is that case introduced anyhow? If it is to declare it exempt from the laws of the firstling, that is self-evident. If a cow which produced a species of an ass, both of which are subject to sanctification as firstlings, is adjudicated so that if it possesses the traits of the mother, it is subject to the law of the firstling, and if not, it is not subject to the law of a firstling, then an ass that gave birth to a species of a horse should surely not be a question at all!*

I.   *It was indeed necessary to raise that question, for otherwise I might have thought that in the case of the cow that gave birth to the species of an ass, the operative consideration is that the cow has horns but the ass has no horns, the cow has cloven hoofs but the ass's hooves are closed. But here, in regard to the ass that gave birth to a species of a horse, in both instances the beasts have no horns and the hooves of both are closed, I might have said that the offspring, a species of horse, was merely a red ass* [not a horse at all, since it is assumed that a horse is red and an ass is black, so the horse has some features of the parents and we ought to regard it as a kind of red ass, making it liable to the law of the firstling (Miller & Simon)]. *So we are informed that that is not the case.*

II.1 A.   **What is the rule as to eating them? A clean beast which bore [an offspring] like an unclean beast – it [the offspring] is permitted as to eating. And an unclean beast which bore [an offspring] like a clean beast – it [the offspring] is prohibited as to eating. [For that which comes forth from the unclean is unclean, and that which comes forth from the clean is clean]:**

      B.   *What need was there to specify,* **For that which comes forth from the unclean is unclean, and that which comes forth from the clean is clean?**

      C.   *It serves as a mnemonic, so that you should not revise the Mishnah's version and so that you should not say, "follow the status of the offspring, and this is a perfectly clean animal and that is a perfectly unclean animal"* [Miller & Simon: therefore where a clean animal is born from an unclean animal, it should be available for eating]. *Rather, follow the status of the mother.*

II.2 A.   *And what is the scriptural source for this rule?*

      B.   *It accords with that which our rabbis have taught:*

      C.   "Nevertheless, these you shall not eat of them that chew the cud or of them that divide the hoof" (Lev. 11:4) – there are beasts that chew the cud and divide the hoof that you are not to eat. And what is it? It is a clean beast that is born of an unclean beast.

      D.   But perhaps it is only an unclean beast that is born of a clean beast?

      E.   And how might one interpret the verse, "Nevertheless, these you shall not eat of them that chew the cud or of them that divide the hoof" (Lev. 11:4)?

      F.   [6B] This is the sense of the verse: That which is born of those that chew the cud and divide the hoof you shall not eat.

      G.   But the text goes on to say, "The camel...he is unclean" (Lev. 11:4), bearing the implication, he is unclean, but an unclean animal born from a clean animal is not unclean but clean.

II.3 A.   R. Simeon says, "The word camel occurs twice [at Lev. 11:4 and at Deut. 14:7], once referring to a camel born from a camel, which is forbidden, the other, to a camel born of a cow."

      B.   *And as to rabbis who disagree with R. Simeon, how do they interpret the repetition of the word camel?*

      C.   One serves to prohibit utilization of the camel itself, the other to prohibit its milk.

      D.   *And as to R. Simeon, how does he know on the basis of Scripture that there is a prohibition against the use of the camel's milk?*

E.   *He derives it from the use of the accusative particle, "et," [deemed an augmentative] with the word "camel."*

F.   *And rabbis?*

G.   *They derive no lessons from the use of the accusative particle. That is in accord with what has been taught on Tannaite authority:*

H.   Simeon the Imsonite would derive a lesson from the use of every accusative particle that is in the Torah. When he reached the verse that places the accusative particle before the word "Lord," namely, "the Lord your God you shall fear" (Deut. 10:20), he refrained from doing so [since he did not wish to suggest there was more than one God]. He disciples said to him, "My lord, what then will be the fate of all the other accusative particles from which you have drawn lessons [if you pick and choose among them]?"

I.   He said to them, "Just as I have received a reward for the lessons that I have derived, so I shall receive a reward for refraining from deriving a lesson."

J.   [And that was the situation that prevailed] until R. Aqiba came along and taught concerning the verse that places the accusative particle before the word "Lord," namely, "the Lord your God you shall fear" (Deut. 10:20), "The accusative particle serves to encompass within the commandment the disciples of sages themselves."

K.   [Reverting to the discussion broken off at G,] *Said R. Aha b. Raba to R. Ashi, "Then if the operative consideration of rabbis derives from the duplication of the word "camel," and that of R. Simeon derives from the use of the accusative particle prior to the word camel, then, were it not for these modes of demonstration of the particular rule, should I have derived the conclusion that the milk of an unclean domesticated beast is permitted for Israelites? Then how is the camel's milk differentiated from the classification of milk dealt with in that which has been taught on Tannaite authority?"*

L.   "These are unclean" (Lev. 11:31) – that statement serves to prohibit [not only the unclean beasts themselves but also] brine, soup, and jelly [made from their parts].

M.   *It was necessary [to prove the prohibition of milk in its own terms nonetheless,] for otherwise I might have reached the conclusion that since the fact that it is permitted to use the milk even of clean domesticated beasts is itself an [Miller & Simon:] anomaly, for* a master has said, "[The reason there is no menstruation during nursing is that] blood during the nursing period decomposes and turns into milk" [so milk derives from what is classified as otherwise prohibited!], *and, since permitting milk is itself anomalous, the milk of an unclean beast likewise ought to be permitted. So we are informed that that is not the case.*

N.   *That argument is fine for him who maintains,* "Blood during the nursing period decomposes and turns into milk," *but in accord with the view of him who says* [that the reason there is no menstruation during nursing is that] the mother's limbs become disjointed and she does not return to normality for twenty-four months [so the milk does not derive from blood, and the use of milk is not an anomaly at all (Miller & Simon)], *what is to be said?*

O.   *It was necessary nonetheless to provide such a proof [as rabbis and Simeon have formulated concerning camel's milk, for] otherwise what might I have supposed? Since there is nothing that derives from a living being that the All-Merciful has permitted, and yet milk is comparable to a part of a living beast and is permitted, so along these lines, even milk from an unclean animal likewise is to be permitted. So we are informed that that is not the case.*

P.   *And how on the basis of Scripture do we know that milk that derives from a clean animal is permitted?*

Q.   *Might I say that, since the All-Merciful has forbidden eating meat together with milk, lo, milk by itself is permitted? But I might take the position that milk by itself would be forbidden for eating, but permitted only for sale to third parties, while meat together with milk would be forbidden for all purposes. And even in line with the position of R. Simeon, who maintains that meat together with milk is permitted for sale to third parties, the prohibition itself can be interpreted as required so as to indicate the sanction of lashes that are inflicted on account of the act of cooking meat in milk in any event!*

R.   Rather, since the All-Merciful revealed in the context of Holy Things that have become unfit, "Nonetheless, you may kill" (Deut. 12:15) – but not shear; "meat" but not milk, *this bears the implication that milk from an unconsecrated beast for its part is permitted.*

S.   *But [as before] might I say that that which derives from unconsecrated beasts is forbidden as to consumption but permitted only as to sale to third parties, while that which derives from Holy Things is forbidden also as to sale to third parties?*

T.   *But rather, since it is written,* "And you shall have goats' milk enough for your food, for the food of your household and for the maintenance of your maidens" (Prov. 27:27) [we learn that the milk of clean animals is permitted for consumption].

U.   *But perhaps this means, only in connection with commerce [in milk, not in connection with use]?*

V.   *But rather, since it is written,* "And carry these ten cheeses to the captain of their thousand" (1 Sam. 17:18) [Miller & Simon: and Jesse instructs David to bring them to the captain of their thousand in the war, which shows that it is permitted to eat milk].

W.   *But perhaps this means, only in connection with commerce [in milk, not in connection with use]?*

X.   Is it commonplace in war time to sell [food to the other side]?

Y.   *And if you prefer, proof derives from the following:* "A land flowing with milk and honey" (Ex. 3:8) – *if milk were not permitted, would Scripture commend to us a country rich in something not suitable for eating?*

Z.   *And if you prefer, proof derives from the following:* "Come and buy and eat, yes, come buy wine and milk without money and without price" (Isa. 55:1).

AA.   [Now if, according to rabbis and Simeon, who derive lessons from the fact that Scripture speaks twice of the camel,] *how about the equivalent repetition* [in Leviticus and in Deuteronomy] of "rockbadger," two times, "hare," two times, "pig," two times – *is there some purpose in these repetitions as well?*

BB.   *Rather, it is in accord with that which has been taught on Tannaite authority:*

CC.   Why does Scripture repeat the lists of clean and unclean animals in Leviticus and in Deuteronomy? It is on account of the shesuah-beast [which has two backs and two spinal columns, not mentioned in Leviticus as forbidden]. Why with reference to birds? On account of the raah [an unclean bird not in Leviticus].

DD.   *Then perhaps camel is repeated for the same purpose [that is, only to accommodate the inclusion of one new animal and bird not mentioned in Leviticus]?*

EE.   *Wherever we can derive a lesson from a verse of Scripture we do derive that lesson.*

II.4   A.   *Our rabbis have taught:*

B.   **A sheep which gave birth [to an offspring] something like a goat, or a goat which gave birth [to an offspring] something like a sheep – it [the offspring] is exempt from the law of the firstling. But if it bears some of the traits [of the mother], it is liable [M. Bekh. 2:5A-D].**

C.   R. Simeon says, "That is the case only if its head and the greater part of its body bear the traits of the mother."

D.   *The question was raised: To settle the question of whether or not the animal may be eaten, does R. Simeon require that the head and the greater part of the body bear the traits of the mother? As to the law of the firstling, Scripture says,* "But the firstling of an ox" (Num. 18:17), *meaning, that the law of the firstling applies only if the mother is an ox and the firstling is an ox, too [in that the head and the greater part of the body must be like those of the mother]. But when it comes to whether or not a beast is permitted for eating, Scripture has said that it is the camel that is forbidden.* [7A] *The meaning then is that, if it was changed from that form and does not look like a camel, there is no problem. Or perhaps, there is no difference at all [even for permission to eat the beast, and here too, we require that the head and greater part of the body resemble the mother's].*

E.   *Come and take note:* A clean beast that gave birth to a species of an unclean beast – the latter is forbidden as to eating. But if the head and greater part of the body resemble that of the mother, it is liable to the law of the firstling. *That yields the inference, then, that as to whether or not it can be eaten, the same criteria are required by R. Simeon.*

F.   *Not at all, it is in particular with reference to the status of the beast as to a firstling that these criteria pertain. That conclusion may be derived from a close reading of the text, which has omitted reference to eating altogether and addressed itself only to the matter of the firstling. That proves that it is specifically with reference to the status as to the firstling that R. Simeon requires that the head and greater part of the body resemble those of the mother, but as to eating, he does not invoke that criterion at all.*

G.   *Not at all, quite to the contrary, I shall tell you that also as to whether or not the beast may be eaten, he requires the same traits to be in evidence. But it was necessary to make reference in particular to the matter of the firstling. For otherwise I might have thought that, since it is written,* "But the firstling of an ox" (Num. 18:17), *the rule is that only if it is an ox and its offspring is an ox does the rule apply, so it does not suffice that only the head and greater part of the body resemble those of the mother, but the whole of the beast must resemble the mother. So we are informed to the contrary.*

H   *Come and take note:* "'Nevertheless these you shall not eat of them that chew the cud or of them that divide the hoof' (Lev. 11:4) – This you must not eat [for instance, a camel born of a cow], but you may eat an animal which bears one of the two validating traits that its mother has. And what is a beast that has one of the two validating traits? It is an unclean animal that was born of a clean animal that had been impregnated by a clean animal.

I   "Might one suppose that the same rule would apply even if the mother had been impregnated by an unclean animal?

J.   "Scripture says, 'A sheep born from a pair of lambs, a goat born from a pair of goats' (Deut. 14:4) – the father must be a sheep and the mother a sheep," the words of R. Joshua.

K.   R. Eliezer says, "This verse of Scripture does not come in order to permit what is already permitted, but to add to the list of what is already permitted. And what might that be? It is an unclean beast born of a clean beast that had been impregnated by an unclean beast.

L.   "But might the passage refer only to one that had been impregnated by a clean beast? Scripture states, 'a sheep of lambs,' a sheep of goats, in any circumstance [Miller & Simon: from the repetition of the word for sheep, it is inferred that even if the unclean animal has only a mother that is a clean animal, the father being an unclean animal, it is still permitted]."

M   *So he refers to the beast as unclean, just as does R. Simeon* [Miller & Simon: the language used, "an unclean animal," but not "that which issues from a clean animal," is in accordance with the view of Simeon, who forbids the offspring as definitely unclean if it has not got marks resembling the mother; and it says here that if it has one mark similar to its mother, it is permitted; hence we see that we do not require the head and so on to resemble the mother, so far as Simeon is concerned], and he goes on to say, "But you may eat an animal that possesses one validating trait like that of its mother."

N   *The Tannaite version at hand accords with R. Simeon in one aspect but differs from him in another.*

O.   *There are those who present this question and work it out in a different way, as follows:*

P.   *Is it possible for impregnation to take place by an unclean animal?* For has not R. Joshua b. Levi said, "Impregnation does not take place of an unclean mother by a clean father, or of a clean mother by an unclean father, or of a fat beast by a thin one, or of a thin beast by a fat one, or of a domesticated beast by a wild beast, or of a wild beast by a domesticated beast, except for the case under discussion by R. Eliezer and those who differ from him, for they would say, "A wild beast may be impregnated by a domesticated beast." And in this connection, said R. Jeremiah, "It refers to a case in which the mother became pregnant by an animal with closed and uncloven hoofs, born of a cow," *and that view is in accord with the position of R. Simeon [who holds that an unclean animal born of a clean animal is unclean].*

And the passage further states, "But you may eat an animal that possesses one validating trait like that of its mother."

Q. *The Tannaite version at hand accords with R. Simeon in one aspect but differs from him in another.*

R. *Does this formulation then bear the implication that R. Eliezer takes the view that the product of two heterogeneous factors is permitted* [the offspring is the result of the impregnation from an unclean animal, because since it is a produce of combined causes, and one of these, the mother, is clean, the animal is permitted (Miller & Simon)], *while R. Joshua maintains the view that the product of two heterogeneous factors is forbidden? Now lo, we have a tradition from them that reverses these positions:*

S. **The offspring of a terefah animal – R. Eliezer says, "It is not to be offered on the altar." And sages [Bavli: R. Joshua] say, "It is to be offered" [M. Tem. 6:5B-D].**

T. *In general, R. Eliezer takes the view that the product of two heterogeneous factors is permitted, but he treats the present case as exceptional, for if the rule applied here, Scripture should write,* "the sheep of lambs and goats." Why say, "the sheep" two times? That yields the conclusion – sheep, under all circumstances.

U. And R. Joshua?

V. *He will say to you, "In general, the product of two heterogeneous factors is permitted, but the present case is exceptional, for if it were the case, Scripture should have written, 'Ox, sheep of a lamb, sheep of a goat.' Why write, 'lambs, goats'? That yields the deduction that* the father must be a sheep and the mother likewise must be a sheep."

W. *Come and take note:* R. Simeon says, "Scripture states, 'camel' two times, one to refer to a camel that is born of a camel, the other to refer to a camel that is born of a cow. But if the head and the greater part of the body resemble those of the mother, then it is permitted to eat such a beast."

X. *That statement yields the conclusion, does it not, that whether or not one may eat the beast, R. Simeon requires that the head and the greater part of the body resemble those of the mother?*

Y. *That indeed settles the question.*

III.1 A. **For that which comes forth from the unclean is unclean, and that which comes forth from the clean is clean:**

B. *The question was raised before R. Sheshet, "As to the urine of an ass, what is the law?"*

C. *Why not ask about the urine of horses or camels?*

D. *The urine of horses and camels is not a question, for it is not turbid and so is not like milk. It is water coming in, water going out. But the question does pertain to the urine of an ass, which is turbid and like milk.*

E. *What is the rule? Since it is drained from the body of the ass itself, is it forbidden? Or perhaps it is water coming in and water going out, and the thickness is because of the body's exhalation?*

F. *Said to them R. Sheshet, "You have yourselves learned the rule of the Mishnah:* that which comes forth from the unclean is unclean, and that which comes forth from the clean is clean. *What the Mishnah states is not,* 'from what is unclean' *but rather,* [7B] from the unclean. This, too, is from that which is unclean."

G.   *There are those who say:*

H.   *The urine of horses and camels is not a question, for it is not something that people drink, but that from asses is a question, because that is something that people drink and that is good for jaundice. So what is the law?*

I.   *Said to them R. Sheshet, "You have yourselves learned the rule of the Mishnah:* that which comes forth from the unclean is unclean, and that which comes forth from the clean is clean. *This, too, is from that which is unclean."*

J.   *The following objection was raised:* On what account [then] did they rule that the honey of bees is permitted? For they do not bring it forth [from their own bodies] but store it up. [The honey of gazin bees is prohibited, for it is only saliva] [T. Bekh. 1:8]. [If the substance that proceeds from an unclean creature is thick, although it does not drain from the body, it is prohibited; but here in the case of honey the reason that it is allowed is that it does not drain from the body; honey comes from an unclean creature and so should be forbidden].

K.   *This accords with R. Jacob, who said, "It is the All-Merciful that, in Scripture, permitted honey,"* [so divine law explicitly permits honey, although it may come from the body of the beast, and no reason is given at all], *for it has been taught on Tannaite authority:*

L.   R. Jacob says, "'Yet these you may eat among all the winged swarming things' (Lev. 11:21) – this you may eat, but you may not eat an unclean winged swarming thing.

M.   *"Now does not Scripture explicitly mention as forbidden an unclean winged swarming thing? Rather, this is the sense of the passage:* An unclean fowl that swarms you must not eat, but you may eat an unclean fowl that casts forth something from its body, and what might that be? It is bees' honey.

N.   "Might one think that one is permitted also to eat gazin honey or hornets' honey? Hardly. Then why include bees' honey but exclude gazins' honey and hornets' honey? I include bees' honey, which has no special name, but I exclude gazins' honey and hornets' honey, since they have a special name."

O.   *According to whom is the following statement:* The honey of gazin bees is prohibited, for it is only saliva?

P.   It is not R. Jacob.

III.2 A. [The honey of gazin bees is prohibited, for it is only saliva] – It is clean, *and therefore it requires intention that it be used as a food [since it is not ordinarily regarded as food].*

B.   *So, too, it has been taught on Tannaite authority:*

C.   Honey that is in its honeycomb imparts uncleanness as food, without an intervening stage of intentionality.

III.3 A. *As regards* [Miller & Simon:] *the gall-like concretions in a fallow deer, rabbis considered stating that they are classified as eggs and therefore are forbidden* [like a limb from a living animal, having been communicated from the male organ to the womb (Miller & Simon)].

B.   *Said R. Safra, "It is the seed of a deer that went after a hind, but since the hind's womb is narrow, the deer is unable to copulate and so couples with a fallow deer, releasing the semen into the latter's womb* [Miller & Simon:

owing to the delay in copulation, the semen has hardened, and although it enters the womb, it has no effect and issues later in the animal's excrements, in the form of ball concretions]."

III.4 A. Said R. Huna, "The skin that covers the face of an ass at birth may be eaten."

B. *How come?*

C. *It is [Miller & Simon] a mere secretion.*

D. *Said to him R. Hisda, "There is a Tannaite version that supports your position:* Skin that covers the face of man, whether alive or dead, is clean [not a source of uncleanness]. *Does this not mean,* whether the offspring and the mother are alive, or the offspring and the mother are dead [Miller & Simon: and even if both are dead, the skin is clean; so it is a false membrane and not considered an afterbirth of either the mother or the offspring]?"

E. No, what it means, is whether it is alive and the mother is dead, or it is dead and the mother is alive.

F. *But is it not taught on Tannaite authority:* "Whether the offspring and the mother are alive, or the offspring and the mother are dead"?

G. *If that has been taught on Tannaite authority, so it has been taught.*

I.1 immediately directs our attention to the pertinent passage of the Mishnah that intersects with the one under consideration. We begin by finding the scriptural source for the rule of that passage. No. 2 proceeds to ask a question on a particular case, amplifying the general principle of the Mishnah. **II.1** again clarifies the language of the Mishnah, and No. 2 proceeds to identify the source for the ruling at hand. No. 3 complements No. 2. It is really a protracted appendix, parachuted here because it can serve to fill out an otherwise fairly thin discussion. No. 4 reverts to the problem of **I.1**. **II.1** provides a concrete problem in response to the abstraction of the Mishnah's statement. No. 2 serves as a minor footnote to **I.1.O**. No. 3 pursues the basic problem of the clause of our Mishnah that is under discussion here. No. 4 follows suit.

1:2I-K

I. An unclean fish which swallowed a clean fish – it [the clean fish] is permitted as to eating.

J. A clean fish which swallowed an unclean fish – it [the unclean fish] is prohibited as to eating,

K. for it is not its product [Danby: "Since it was not bred from the other"].

A. *An unclean fish which swallowed a clean fish – it [the clean fish] is permitted as to eating.*

B. And a clean fish which swallowed an unclean fish – it [the unclean fish] is prohibited as to eating, for it is not its product [M. Bekh. 1:2I-K].

T. 1:7 Z p. 534, lines 29-30

A. [Delete: *Even though they have said]* A small clean beast gives birth at five months. A large clean beast gives birth at nine months. A large unclean beast gives birth at twelve months, the dog at fifty days; the cat at fifty-two; the pig at sixty days; the fox and all creeping things at six months; the wolf, the lion, the bear, the panther, the leopard, the elephant, the baboon, and the ape at three years; and the snake at seven years.

T. 1:10 Z p. 534, lines 36-39, p. 535, line 1

A.   Dolphins give birth and raise [their young] as does man.
B.   An unclean fish casts forth young.
C.   A clean fish lays eggs.

T. 1:11 Z p. 535, lines 1-2

A.   The innards of fish and the foetus [thereof] are eaten only on the advice of an expert.
B.   Fowl are eaten in accord with tradition [as to which are clean],
C.   A hunter is believed to state, "This fowl is clean."

T. 1:12 Z p. 535, lines 2-3

T.'s first complement to the concluding lines of the Mishnah paragraph is at T. 1:8, since T. 1:7 simply cites and lightly glosses the Mishnah's language. T. 1:9 goes over the ground of M. 1:2 E-H. T. 1:10-12 then supplement the foregoing with marginally relevant information. T. 1:10 differentiates the various beasts; it has no bearing on the Mishnah and leads nowhere. T. 1:11 continues the foregoing. T. 1:12 seems to me a miscellany. T. 1:8 appears casually in the Bavli's treatment of our Mishnah, but T. 1:9 finds a large and important counterpart in what follows.

I.1   A.   *The operative consideration [that allows eating the clean fish] is that we have seen that the unclean fish swallowed it. But if we had not seen it, we might say that the clean fish had been bred by an unclean fish. How do we know that fact? It is in line with that which is taught on Tannaite authority:*

       B.   **An unclean fish casts forth young. A clean fish lays eggs [T. Bekh. 1:11].**

       C.   *If that is the case, then even if we see that the unclean fish had actually swallowed the clean one, we still should say that the clean fish has been absorbed, and the fish found inside had been bred by the unclean fish [which should be ruled unclean as the offspring of an unclean beast].*

       D.   Said R. Sheshet, "For instance, if one found it in the bowels [not in the womb]."

       E.   [Miller & Simon omit:] R. Pappa said, "For example if one found it in the esophagus."

       F.   R. Nahman said, "For example, if one found it whole."

I.2   A.   R. Ashi said, "Most fish breed their own species, so [if we discover a different kind of fish inside] *it is as though* the unclean fish had swallowed the clean one in our very presence."

I.3   A.   *Our rabbis have taught on Tannaite authority:*

B.   **An unclean fish casts forth young. A clean fish lays eggs [T. Bekh. 1:11].**

C.   Any creature that gives birth also gives suck.

D.   Whatever lays eggs supports the brood by picking up food for it, except for the bat, for, while it lays eggs, it gives suck to the brood.

E.   **[8A] Dolphins give birth and raise [their young] as does man [T. Bekh. 1:11A].**

F.   *What are dolphins?*

G.   Said R. Judah, "They are human beings in the sea [half fish, half human]."

H   Any creature that has its testicles outside gives birth, and any creature that has its testicles inside casts forth eggs.

I.   *Is this so? But has not Samuel said, "The domestic goose and the wild goose are classified as hybrids if they are paired." And we gave thought to the matter: what is the operative consideration here?*

J.   *Said Abbayye, "This one has its testicles on the outside, and that one has its testicles on the inside, but both of them lay eggs."*

K.   Rather, [the statement of H should be as follows:] Any species the male of which has its penis on the outside gives birth, and any that has its penis on the inside lays eggs.

L.   Any species that has sexual relations by day gives birth by day, and any that does so by night gives birth by night, and any that does so by day and by night gives birth whether by day or by night.

M   Any species that has sexual relations by day gives birth by day: the cock.

N.   And any that does so by night gives birth by night: the bat.

O.   And any that does so by day and by night gives birth whether by day or by night: man *and all species that are like man.*

P.   *What are the practical consequences of these facts?*

Q.   *The answer accords with what R. Mari b. R. Kahana said for* said R. Mari b. R. Kahana, "If one inspected the chicken coop on the eve of the festival day and found no egg therein, and the next day he got up early and found an egg therein, it is permitted to eat the egg on the festival." [Miller & Simon: Since the hen does not lay eggs at night, the egg must have been laid on the previous day. A newly laid egg on a festival cannot be eaten on that day.]

R.   But did the man not search?

S.   I might say that he did not search carefully.

T.   But lo, he searched carefully?

U.   I might say that the greater part had come forth and then retreated.

V.   *And that accords with what R. Yohanan said, for* said R. Yohanan, "An egg the greater part of which emerged on the eve of the festival and then retreated may be eaten on the festival."

W.   All animals that copulate and are pregnant in accord with a common rule [e.g., dogpatch style, pregnancy for five months, such as sheep and goats] give birth from one another and can nurse one another's offspring.

X.   All animals have intercourse dogpatch style, except three, which do it face to face: fish, man, and serpent.

Y.   *Why are these three exceptional?*

Z.   When R. Dimi came, [he said,] "In the West, they say, 'Since with them the Presence of God engaged in speech.'"

AA.   *A Tannaite authority states:*

BB.   The camel does it back to back.

I.4   A.   *Our rabbis have taught on Tannaite authority:*

B.   A chicken lays eggs after twenty-one days, and corresponding to the hen is the almond tree among trees [from the time it blossoms to when the fruits ripen, twenty-one days pass].

C.   A dog takes fifty days, and its counterpart among trees is the fig tree.

D.   A cat takes fifty-two days, and its counterpart among trees is the mulberry.

E.   A pig takes sixty days, and corresponding among trees is the apple tree.

F.   A fox and all kinds of snakes take six months, and corresponding among trees is wheat.

G.   Small clean animals take five months, and corresponding among trees is the vine.

H.   Large unclean cattle take twelve months, and corresponding among trees is the palm.

I.   Clean large cattle take nine months, and corresponding among trees is the olive.

J.   The wolf, lion, bear, leopard, hyena, elephant, monkey, and long-tailed ape take three years, and corresponding among trees is the white fig.

K.   A viper takes seventy years, and corresponding among trees is the carob.

L.   From the time of planting the carob to its ripening takes seventy years, and its pregnancy [from the blossoming to the ripening of the fruit] takes three years.

M.   A serpent is pregnant for seven years, and for that wicked animal there is no counterpart among trees.

N.   Some say that there is a corresponding tree, the white fig.

O.   *How do we know it?*

P.   Said R. Judah said Rab, *and some assign it to the name of R. Joshua b. Hanania,* "Because Scripture has said, 'You are more cursed than all other cattle and all the beasts of the field' (Gen. 3:14) – if it is more cursed than a cattle, then all the more so than a wild beast! But the purpose is to tell you, just as the animal is cursed to be pregnant longer than a wild beast in the proportion of one to seven – *and how so? An ass is pregnant longer than a cat* – so the serpent is cursed to be pregnant in a proportion of one in seven, *hence seven years.*"

Q.   *Then why not phrase matters in this way:* "Just as a wild beast is cursed with pregnancy more than a domesticated beast by a ratio of one to three – *and what is an example? a lion is pregnant more than an ass, three years to one* – so it is cursed more than a wild beast in the ratio of one to three, which is then nine years"?

R.   [8B] Does Scripture state, "More than all beasts and more than all cattle"? What it states is, "More than all cattle and more than all beasts," meaning, the serpent is cursed by pregnancy more than all animals that are cursed, [Miller & Simon: in that it takes longer to produce their young] than the beasts.

S. *Then why not phrase matters in this way: "Just as a domesticated beast has been cursed with pregnancy more than a wild beast in the ratio of one to three – and what is an example? a goat is pregnant longer than a cat, three years to one –* so the serpent has been cursed in the proportion of one to three, *thus fifteen months"?*

T. *If you wish, I shall reply: "Scripture states, 'More than all cattle'* [Miller & Simon: the animal most cursed, an unclean large animal, like an ass, pregnant longer than the beast, i.e., the cat, thus the ratio is one to seven as stated earlier]."

U. *If you wish, I shall reply: "It is a curse, and therefore we assign the curse so far as is possible to the snake."*

I.5 A. *Said Caesar to R. Joshua b. Hananiah, "How long is the pregnancy and parturition of a snake?"*

B. *He said to him, "It takes seven years."*

C. *"But did not the sages of the Athenian academy mate a male serpent with a female and the pregnancy and parturition took three years?"*

D. *"They had already been pregnant for four years."*

E. *"But did the sages not see that they had sexual relations?"*

F. *"They are like human beings."*

G. *"But are the Athenian sages not wise?"*

H. *"We are smarter than they are."*

I. *"If you are so smart, go and win an argument with them and bring them to me."*

J. *He said to him, "How many are there?"*

K. *"Sixty."*

L. *"Then make me a ship with sixty compartments, each compartment with sixty cushions."*

M. *He did it for him.*

N. *When R. Joshua got to Athens, he found a slaughter house and said to a certain man who was dressing an animal, "Is your head for sale?"*

O. *He said to him, "Yes."*

P. *He said to him, "How much?"*

Q. *He said to him, "Half a zuz."*

R. *He paid the money.*

S. *In time he said to him, "Give me your head."*

T. *[He gave him the animal's head.] R. Joshua said, "Did I say the head of an animal? I said, your head."*

U. *Joshua said to him, "If you want me to give up the case, walk in front of me and show me the door of the academy of the Athenian sages."*

V. *The man replied, "I am afraid to do so, for whoever points them out is put to death."*

W. *Joshua said to him, "Take a bundle of reeds and when you get there, throw it down as if to take a rest."*

X. *He went and found guards inside and guards outside the academy; for when the sages saw somebody come in, they would kill the guards outside, and when they saw someone leave, they killed the guards inside.*

Y. *He reversed the heel of his shoe and they killed the inside guards.*

Z. *He reversed the shoe to the normal position, and they killed all of them.*

AA.   *He went along and found the young men sitting high up and the elders below.*

BB.   *He said, "If I greet the ones below, the young men will kill me, saying, 'we are the more important, for we sit high up and they sit down below. And if I greet the young men, the elders will kill me, saying, 'we are older and they are younger.'"*

CC.   *He said, "Peace be unto you."*

DD.   *They said to him, "What are you doing here?"*

EE.   *He said to them, "I am the sage of the Jews, I want to learn wisdom from you."*

FF.   *"If so, we will ask you questions."*

GG.   *He said to them, "Well and good. If you defeat me then do to me anything you like, but if I defeat you, eat bread with me in a ship."*

HH.   *They said to him, "If a man went and asked a woman to marry him and did not get consent, can he seek someone of higher birth?"*

II.   *He took a peg and stuck it below on a stone wall, and it would not join, but he stuck it higher up and it went in.*

JJ.   *He said, "Here, too, it may be that the second woman is the one that is destined for him."*

KK.   *"If a man lends money and is forced to seize what is owing to him by force, will he be expected to lend again?"*

LL.   *"A man goes into a forest, cuts the first load of wood and cannot lift it; he continues cutting until someone comes along and helps him lift the bundle."*

MM.   *They said to him, "Tell us some jokes."*

NN.   *He said to them, "There was a mule that gave birth, and around its neck was a document in which was inscribed, 'there is a claim against my father's house of one hundred thousand zuz.'"*

OO.   *They asked him, "Can a mule give birth?"*

PP.   *He said to them, "It's just one of those jokes."*

QQ.   *"When salt loses its flavor, how do you salt the salt?"*

RR.   *He said to them, "With the afterbirth of a mule."*

SS.   *"And does a mule have an afterbirth?"*

TT.   *He said to them, "And does salt lose its flavor?"*

UU.   *"Build a house in the sky."*

VV.   *He pronounced the Divine Name and suspended himself between heaven and earth. He said to them, "Bring me bricks and clay from down there."*

WW.   *"And is it possible to do that?"*

XX.   *"And is it possible to build a house between heaven and earth?"*

YY.   *"Where is the center of the world?"*

ZZ.   *He raised his fingers and said to them, "Here."*

AAA.   *They said to him, "Prove it."*

BBB.   *He replied, "Bring ropes and a measure."*

CCC.   *They said, "We have a pit in the field. Bring it to town."*

DDD.   *He replied, "Knot ropes of bran flour for me and I will bring it."*

EEE.   *"We have a broken millstone. Fix it."*

FFF.   *[Miller & Simon: He took a detached portion from it and threw it before them,] saying, "Take out the threads for me like a weaver and I shall mend it."*

GGG.   *"A bed of knives – how can we cut it?"*

HHH.   *"With the horns of an ass."*

III.   *"But does an ass have horns?""*

JJJ.   *"And is there a bed of knives?"*

KKK.   *They brought him two eggs: "Which comes from the black clucking hen, which from the white?"*

LLL.   *He brought them two cheeses: "Which is from a black goat and which is from a white one?"*

MMM *"A chicken dead in its shell – where has the spirit gone?"*

NNN.   *"From whence it came, to there it went."*

OOO.   *"Show us something the value of which is not worth the loss that it causes."*

PPP.   *He brought a mat of reeds and spread it out. It could not get through the door.*

QQQ.   *He said, "Bring a rake and a pickaxe," and he demolished the door. "Here is an example of something the value of which is not worth the loss that it causes."*

RRR.   *He brought them to a meal on the ship, each one into his own chamber. When they saw the sixty cushions, each thought that everyone was coming to this room. He ordered the captain to set sail. As they were about to make the trip, he took some earth from their native soil. [9A] When they came to the straits, they filled a jug of water from the waters of the straits. When they arrived, they were presented to Caesar. He noticed that they were depressed. He said, "These are not the same people."*

SSS.   *He took some of the earth of their country and threw it at them. They acted in a haughty way towards Caesar. He said to R. Joshua, "Do whatever you want to them."*

TTT.   *He took water that the Athenians had taken from the straits and poured it into a ditch. He said to them, "Fill this and go your way."*

UUU.   *They tried to fill it by casting water in it, one after another, but it was absorbed. So they went on filling it until the joints of their shoulders became dislocated and they perished.*

I.1 clarifies the law of the Mishnah by appeal to information in the Tosefta. No. 2 takes its own tack on the interpretation of the Mishnah and need not be read as a continuation of the foregoing. No. 3 reverts to the analysis of the Tosefta's complement, and then moves on to a list of further observations along the same lines. No. 4 continues with further collections of well-organized facts on the same general theme. No. 5 is a free-standing entry, tacked on for obvious reasons. The framers of the Bavli cannot lay claim to have formed an intellectually very engaging composition in response to our Mishnah paragraph, but they did have a plan, which was to cite and gloss the Tosefta's materials in small part, to cite and re-present a rather substantial corpus of equivalent materials in larger part, but in largest measure, simply to record here, rather than somewhere else, an entirely free-standing composition. The theory of the Bavli's framers encompasses the principle that, where we have access to a large and well-crafted composition, which intersects in some way with an otherwise unrelated discussion, we will insert that composition whole and complete. The Tosefta's framers rarely do the same. So like those responsible for the Tosefta as we know the document, the Bavli's authorship has a plan of its own, one that, as we see, it follows.

1:3-4

I.	A.	An ass which had not given birth and which bore two males [and it is not known which of them came forth first] –
	B.	one gives a single lamb to the priest.
	C.	[If it bore] male and female [and it is not known which of them came forth first] –
	D.	one separates a single lamb for himself.
II.	E.	Two asses which had not given birth and which bore two males –
	F.	one gives two lambs to the priest.
	G.	[If they bore] (1) a male and a female or (2) two males and a female,
	H.	one gives a single lamb to the priest.
	I.	[If they bore] (1) two females and one male, (2) or two males and two females,
	J.	there is nothing whatsoever here for the priest.
III.	A.	[Two asses], one [of which] had given birth and one which had not given birth, and which bore two males –
	B.	one gives a single lamb to the priest.
	C.	[If they produced] a male and a female, one separates a single lamb for himself.
	D.	For it is said, "*And every firstling of an ass you shall redeem with a lamb*" (Ex. 34:20) –
	E.	(1) [a lamb deriving] from sheep or from goats,
	F.	(2) male or female,
	G.	(3) large or small,
	H.	(4) blemished or unblemished.
	I.	(1) And one redeems with it many times [Danby: "With it he may redeem more firstlings"].
	J.	(2) And it enters the fold to be tithed.
	K.	(3) And if it dies, they derive benefit from it.

M. 1:3-4C present three situations, the first of each of which begins with mild apocopation, and each of which then continues with implied-*if* clauses. All three are fully articulated, covering all possibilities. Formal considerations require the interpolations at M. 1:4A; *Two asses* of course is implied from M. 1:3E, and draws in its wake the S before BKRH, in the model of M. 1:3A, E. M. 1:4D-K bear no necessary relationship to the foregoing, and the joining particle, S, is hardly a propos.

The problem of the first unit, M. 1:3-4C, is a situation of doubt as to which offspring is the firstborn. The first case is the simplest. We have a single ass which has not yet given birth. If it produces two males, then, whichever of them has come forth first, one of them certainly is a firstborn male and belongs to the priest. If it produces a male and a female, one does not know whether or not he has to give a lamb in place of the firstborn ass. He therefore sets aside a lamb, with which he redeems the ass. But the lamb remains with the owner, because the burden of proof that the lamb belongs to priests is borne by the priest. The second case is more complicated, since we have two asses which produce firstborn. Obviously, if they bear two males, both are firstborn and belong to the priest (M. 1:3E-F). If one produces a male, and the other, a female, when the two are confused, then the male certainly is the firstborn of one of the ases and must be redeemed with a lamb. If they bore two females and one male, I, then we invoke the principle of C-D. It is entirely possible that the two males came forth first, and the priest must prove otherwise (J). G's secondary case (G2) has the two asses produce two males and a female. One is certainly a firstborn. But the other may have followed the birth of the first male or of the female. So the other male is subject to doubt and is redeemed with the lamb covering the firstborn which is not subject to doubt. The third case repeats the first, but with two asses. One ass has given birth, the other has not. If there are two males, one of them assuredly is the firstborn of one of the two asses. The priest is given a lamb for its redemption. M. 1:4C is familiar from M. 1:3C-D. Now we do not know for sure that the male is a firstborn. Since it may be a firstborn, a lamb is set aside for its redemption; but since it may not be a firstborn, the priest has no claim on the lamb.

M. 1:4D-K then provide facts on the lamb used for redemption of the firstborn of an ass. D-K are not to be read solely as a continuation of the foregoing. The lamb's character is spelled out at E-H. I-K then add a triplet of rules. With a single lamb (Rashi: returned by a priest to an Israelite) one may redeem the firstborn of a number of asses, releasing them from their status of sanctity. If an Israelite has set aside a lamb for the redemption of the firstborn of an ass but kept it for himself, along the lines of the foregoing rules, when he gives a tithe of his flock and herd (M. 9:4), he includes the lamb therein. If the lamb used for redemption dies, one does not have to give the carcass to a priest. B. Bekh. 11B understands the subject of M. 1:4K to be priests: From the time it is set aside, it falls into the domain of the priest. But M. is clear as stated, for the supposition of K cannot conflict with that of J.

A.   *An ass which had not given birth and which gave birth to two males* [and it is not known which is the firstborn] –

B.   *one gives [for redemption] a single lamb to the priest.*

C.   *[If it gives birth to] a male and a female, one separates a lamb.* But it is *for himself* [M. Bekh. 1:3A-D].

D.   *Two asses which had [not] given birth and which gave birth to two males – one gives two lambs to the priest.*

E.   *[If they gave birth to] a male and a female or to two males and a female, one gives a single lamb to the priest.*

F.   [*If they gave birth to*] *two females and a male or to two males and two females*, and one does not know [which is which], *there is nothing whatsoever here for the priest* [M. Bekh. 1:3E-J].

G.   But one separates a single lamb and redeems with it each one by itself [M. Bekh. 1:4I].

T. 1:19 Z p. 535, lines 16-20

T. cites M. and glosses at G, on which see S. Lieberman, *Tosefet Rishonim* II, pp. 266-7, to lines 19/20.

A.   A cow which gave birth to a kind of lamb – they do not redeem therewith [the kind of lamb] the firstborn of an ass.

B.   For every place in which *lamb* is stated encompasses *sheep and goats, large and small, males and females, unblemished and blemished* [M. Bekh. 1:4E-H].

C.   One redeems [the firstborn of an ass] with it [a redemption lamb], does it a second and a third time [with the same lamb] [M. Bekh. 1:4I].

D.   And he brings it in fulfillment of a vow and as a thank-offering, for his sin-offering and for his guilt-offering.

E.   And it is liable to the law of the firstborn and to the priestly gifts [the two cheeks, shoulder, and maw].

T. 1:13 Z p. 535, lines 3-6 (continued)

T. augments M. 1:4D-K. The lamb is not sacred and may be used as the owner decides (D-E), but it then belongs to the owner, not the priest, and is liable to the priestly gifts (E). T. thus clearly understands M. 1:4D-K to refer to M. 1:4C. We may say that, in general, both the Tosefta's and the Bavli's authorships have in mind a commentary to the Mishnah. But while the plan of the Tosefta for its Mishnah commentary involves clarification of words and phrases, that of the Bavli's authorship directs attention to quite other matters altogether. The one group is mainly philological, in a broad sense to be sure, the other, principally intellectual and philosophical. And the distinctive characteristics of the program of the one call attention to the different, but equally well-formed and crafted, characteristics of the program of the other.

A.   What is the least one gives?

B.   R. Yosé bar Judah says, "One should give no [redemption lamb] of less than the value of a sheqel."

C.   What is [the sort of lamb used for] the redemption of the firstborn of an ass which *enters the fold for tithing* [M. Bekh. 1:4J]?

D.   (1) An Israelite who had [firstborn asses] the status of which was in doubt and who redeemed them [M. Bekh. 1:4C];

E.   (2) and so, too, a priest who inherited [the redemption lamb of] his mother's father, an Israelite [so *TR*, II, p. 266, lines 10/11];

F.   (3) or if one gives him [a priest] the firstborn of an ass as a gift to redeem it [and the priest redeemed it] –

G.   this [lamb, used for redemption] is the redemption lamb of a firstborn of an ass which *enters the fold for tithing*.

H   Lo, [if] one has a firstling and does not have [a lamb] with which to redeem it,

T. 1:15 Z p. 535, lines 8-12

I.   [and] a priest said to him, "Give it to me, and I shall redeem it,"

J.   lo, this one should give it to him only if he knows that he will [most certainly] redeem it.

T. 1:16 Z p. 535, lines 12-14

T. 1:15C-H augment M. 1:4J. The sort of redemption lamb which is subject to tithing is one which is deemed in the domain of the Israelite owner, not of the priest (D), or which, while in doubt, had its status resolved (E), or one which belongs to a priest (F). H-J go on to clarify F. This concludes the Tosefta's response to the cited paragraph. The Talmud's is vast but equally distinctive in its approach to the same task.

I.1   A.   *Who is the Tannaite authority behind this formulation of the rule* [an ass which had not given birth and which bore two males and it is not known which of them came forth first – the farmer gives a single lamb to the priest]?

      B.   *Said R. Jeremiah, "It does not accord with the principle of* R. Yosé the Galilean, who has said, "It is possible to determine exactly [what both heads came forth simultaneously, in which case, both would be deemed firstborn]."

      C.   Said Abbayye, 'You may even claim that it accords with the principle of R. Yosé the Galilean. The case here is exceptional when it deals with the firstborn of a clean animal, for Scripture is explicit in referring to the plural, 'The males shall be the Lord's' (Ex. 13:12) [even two males, but in the case of firstborn of asses, the singular is used throughout, so even if it were possible to make sure both heads came forth simultaneously, they are not sanctified (Miller & Simon)]."

      D.   *But why not derive the case of the firstborn of an unclean animal from the firstborn of a clean animal?*

      E.   *Lo, Scripture itself has excluded that possibility when it refers with the definite article to* "the males."

      F.   *Some state matters in this way:*

      G.   *May one say that this does not accord with the principle of R. Yosé the Galilean, for if it accorded with the principle of R. Yosé the Galilean, lo,* he has said, "It is possible to determine exactly [what both heads came forth simultaneously, in which case, both would be deemed firstborn]."

      H.   Said Abbayye, 'You may even claim that it accords with the principle of R. Yosé the Galilean. The case here is exceptional when it deals with the firstborn of a clean animal, for Scripture is explicit in referring to the plural, 'The males shall be the Lord's' (Ex. 13:12)."

      I.   *Now there is no problem for R. Jeremiah, who does not propose to maintain that the passage accords with R. Yosé the Galilean, since that explains why the Mishnah does not make explicit,* "And both their heads came forth simultaneously." *But from the viewpoint of Abbayye, should not the passage state, "And both their heads came forth simultaneously"?*

J.   *And furthermore, has it not been taught on Tannaite authority:*

K.   In the case of one's ass, which had not given birth before, which gave birth to two males, and the two of their heads came forth simultaneously –

L.   R. Yosé the Galilean says, "Both of them are given to the priest, as it is said, 'The males shall be the Lord's' (Ex. 13:12)."

M   *But does not the verse of Scripture refer to the consecration of the body of the animal itself [and that can only be a clean animal, so how can this prove anything about the ass, which is an unclean animal]?*

N   Rather, because it is written, "The males are the Lord's" [Miller & Simon: the inference from the verse is indirect. Since Scripture has indicated in this verse that it is possible to ascertain that both heads came forth simultaneously in connection with a clean animal, we apply the same to the firstborn of an ass; it is clear then that Yosé's ruling refers even to the firstborn of an ass.]

O.   *Does that not represent a refutation of Abbayye's view?*

P.   *It indeed represents a refutation of Abbayye's view.*

Q   [9B] *And as to rabbis [represented by the rule,* **An ass which had not given birth and which bore two males [and it is not known which of them came forth first] – the farmer gives a single lamb to the priest],** *may one say that rabbis take the view that even if a portion of the womb has touched the firstling, it consecrates the beast? For if it consecrates only when the whole womb has touched the firstling, while it is impossible to ascertain that both heads came forth at once, still, there is an interposition* [Miller & Simon: for before one male wholly emerges, the other is on its way out; therefore although one came forth prior to the other and was sacred, it did not have the whole womb to consecrate it, owing to the other male, which was coming out at the same time; there was, consequently, an interposition between the first male and the womb].

R.   Said R. Ashi, "Where it is a pair of the same species, we do not deem one to form an interposition to the other."

II.1 A   **[If it bore] male and female [and it is not known which of them came forth first] – one separates a single lamb [but keeps it] for himself.**

B.   *Since he keeps the lamb for himself, why does he have to bother to designate it in any event?*

C.   *It is so as to remove from the beast the prohibitions that attach to the firstborn of an ass [not to work with it, not to shear it].*

D.   *It follows that, until it is released from those prohibition, it is subject to the prohibitions against beneficial use. Then who is the authority behind our Mishnah's rule? It is R. Judah, for it has been taught on Tannaite authority:*

E   "It is forbidden to derive benefit from the firstborn of an ass," the words of R. Judah.

F.   R. Simeon declares it permitted.

G.   *What is the operative consideration behind the position of R. Judah?*

H Said Ulla, "Do you have something that has to be redeemed and nonetheless is permitted for benefit even before it has been redeemed?"

I And is there no such thing? And lo, there is the firstborn of man, who has to be redeemed, and yet who is permitted prior to redemption [in that, even if unredeemed, one may derive benefit from him].

J Rather, "Do you have something concerning which the Torah has explicitly specified that the redemption must be with a sheep, and yet which can be used prior to redemption?"

K And has the Torah been so meticulous as to the character of that which must be used for redemption? *And did not R. Nehemiah b. R. Joseph redeem an ass through an exchange of boiled herbs of equivalent value?*

L *[Redeeming the firstling of an ass is not subject to restrictions of a more severe order than redeeming other consecrated objects, and, therefore] at issue here is not redeeming it with an object of equivalent value. What is at stake here is redeeming the object not with its equivalent value, and the point of Ulla is as follows:* "Is there anything concerning which the Torah has shown special concern *in such a way as to release the prohibitions affecting it only with a sheep — even though not its equivalent in value — and yet which one may use for one's own benefit?*"

M Lo, there is the redemption of produce that has been designated as second tithe, concerning which the Torah has shown special interest in specifying that it is to be redeemed with coined money, and yet we have learned on Tannaite authority: R. Judah says, "If one has deliberated betrothed a woman with produce in the status of second tithed, she has been validly betrothed." [Miller & Simon: Therefore we see that it is permitted to benefit from an object even before its appropriate redemption; we conclude that, according to R. Judah, it is permitted to use it.]

N *Also with a firstborn of an ass a woman can be betrothed, in line with the view of R. Eleazar, for R. Eleazar said,* "A woman knows that produce that has been designated second tithe through being exchanged with her as a token of betrothal has not been rendered secular in such an exchange, so she for her part will take the produce with her up to Jerusalem and eat it there." *Here too, a woman knows that the firstborn of an ass is subject to prohibitions, so she redeems it with a lamb, and she is betrothed with the difference in the value between an ass and a sheep* [Miller & Simon: therefore no objection can be cited to Ulla's reading of Judah's views from the case of second tithe].

O *And as to R. Simeon, what is the operative consideration behind his position?*

P Said Ulla, "Is there something the redemption exchange for which is permitted for use while the object itself remains forbidden?" [Miller & Simon: Here the lamb with which the ass is redeemed is permitted for secular purposes.]

Q And is there no such thing? And lo, there is the matter of produce of the Seventh Year, for that which is given to redeem it may be used, but the produce itself remains forbidden. [Miller & Simon: If one sold fruit of the Sabbatical Year, the object purchased may be used, but the produce itself is forbidden and must be removed from the house when the beasts in the field have consumed the produce in the field.]

R.   That which is given in redeeming produce of the Seventh Year in point of fact also is forbidden, for a Master has said, "The prohibition attaching to produce of the Sabbatical Year affects the very last thing bought." [Miller & Simon: If one purchased meat in exchange for fruit of the Sabbatical Year, both are liable to the law of removal pertaining to the Sabbatical Year; if he then bought wine in exchange for the meat, the meat may be used but not the wine; if he exchanged oil for the wine, the oil is forbidden, as well as the produce of the Sabbatical Year itself.]"

S.   *And if you prefer, I shall say, "R. Judah and R. Simeon differ as to the interpretation of verses of Scripture. For it has been taught along those lines on Tannaite authority":*

T.   "'You shall not do work with the firstling of your ox' (Deut. 15:19) – but you may do work with an ox that belongs to you and to a gentile.

U.   "'You shall not shear the firstling of your flock,' (Deut. 15:19), but you may shear what belongs to you and to a gentile," the words of R. Judah. [Miller & Simon: Since the verse does not exclude the firstborn of an ass, we do not permit its use prior to its redemption and it is on a par with a firstling of a clean animal.]

V.   R. Simeon says, "'You shall not do work with the firstling of your ox' (Deut. 15:19) – but you may do work with the firstling of man.

W.   "'You shall not shear the firstling of your flock,' (Deut. 15:19), but you may shear the firstling of an ass."

X.   *Now there is no problem, from R. Simeon's perspective, in the fact that Scripture has set forth two verses. But from the perspective of R. Judah, why did Scripture have to employ two verses so as to exclude a firstling belonging to both you and to a gentile, and, moreover, from R. Judah's perspective, in the case of the firstborn of man, also, we should say that it is forbidden to work with that class of persons before redemption? Rather, all parties must concur that the reference to "your ox" suffices to exclude the firstborn of man [which one may use for work, even though he has not been redeemed]. Where there is a dispute, it concerns the reference to "your flock." The opinion of R. Judah is consistent with views expressed elsewhere, for he has said, "A beast held in partnership with a gentile is liable to the law of a firstborn," on account of which a verse of Scripture is required to indicate that it is permitted to shear and work a firstling subject to such a partnership. R. Simeon takes the position, "A beast held in partnership with a gentile is exempt from the law of a firstborn," on account of which a verse is hardly required to exempt the matter of sheering and working the beast. Where a verse is needed, it has to do with the firstborn of an ass.*

Y.   *That poses no problem from the perspective of R. Judah, for that explains why Scripture had to specify, "your sheep," and "your ass" is added because of the reference to "your ass." But in the perspective of R. Simeon, why make reference to "your ox and your sheep"? [Miller & Simon: If Scripture had merely written, "the firstling of an ox and* the firstling of a sheep, Simeon could still have expounded the verse in the manner that he does.]

Z. *That is a real question.*

II.2 A. Said Rabbah, "R. Simeon concedes that after the breaking of the neck [of an ass that is a firstborn which has not been redeemed with a lamb], it is forbidden to derive benefit from it. *What is the scriptural basis for his opinion? He derives that lesson from the analogy to be drawn with 'the breaking of the neck' stated also with reference to the heifer the neck of which is to be broken in the case of a neglected corpse."* [One cannot make use of the carcass of that heifer, so also not of this one.]

B. *Said Rabbah, "On what basis do I make that claim? It is on the basis of that which has been taught on Tannaite authority:*

C. "The fruit of fruit trees in the first three years after planting, mixed seeds in a vineyard, an ox that is to be put to death by stoning, a heifer that has had its neck broken, the birds of the leper's offering, the firstborn of an ass, and a mixture in which meat and milk have been boiled together – all of them are in the class of food so far as the rules of uncleanness are concerned [even though they may not be used for any sort of benefit, they still contract and convey uncleanness as food].

D. "R. Simeon says, 'None of them receives uncleanness as food. [What cannot be eaten also is not deemed food so far as cultic uncleanness is concerned.' [Thus in any event after the breaking of the neck [of an ass that is a firstborn which has not been redeemed with a lamb], it is forbidden to derive benefit from it.]

E. "But R. Simeon concedes in respect to the mixture of meat and milk that it does receive uncleanness as soon, since at one point it was suitable to be subject to such uncleanness [before the cooking took place]." And R. Assi said R. Yohanan said, "What is the operative consideration of R. Simeon? It is written, 'All food therein which may be eaten' (Lev. 11:34) – food you can give to gentiles to eat is classified as food, but food you cannot give to gentiles to eat is not classified as food."

F. *[10A] If so, then in respect to the mixture of meat and milk, why invoke the consideration that at one point it was valid? Derive the rule from the fact that it is food that you can feed to gentiles! For it has been taught on Tannaite authority:*

G. R. Simeon b. Judah says in the name of R. Simeon, "Meat cooked in milk may not be eaten, but one may derive benefit from it [e.g., by selling it to gentiles to eat], as it is said, 'For you are a holy people to the Lord your God' (Deut. 14:21), [which is followed by the prohibition of cooking a kid in its mother's milk, bearing the sense that you may not eat it but you may give it to others to eat]. And further, 'And you shall be holy to me' (Ex. 22:30) [in regard to terefah meat]." Just as in that latter case, the food may not be eaten but one may derive benefit from it, so here too, the food may not be eaten but one may derive benefit from it."

H. [In reply to the question of F:] the sense of the matter is, "This and yet another proof...": first of all comes the reason, "food you can give to gentiles to eat is classified as food, but food you cannot give to gentiles to eat is not classified as food," and, furthermore, comes the reason, for the Israelite himself, too, there was a time before boiling when this food was susceptible to uncleanness as food [Miller & Simon: unlike the case of the ox and heifer mentioned above, since they have forbidden status when alive].

I.   *Now if it is the fact that R. Simeon declares the beast permitted [for benefit] after the breaking of the neck, then the passage cited should state,* "And R. Simeon concurs in the case of the firstborn of an ass as well as in the case of meat in milk that they are subject to the uncleanness of food."

J.   *If one had determined to use the ass as food, it would be as you say* [Miller & Simon: that the ass with a broken neck would have received the uncleanness relating to food]. *But here with what sort of a case do we deal? It is one in which he had formed no such intention* [Miller & Simon: and that is the reason that the passage does not include the case of an ass in the statement of Simeon on receiving uncleanness as food, for ordinarily, without expressing the intention of regarding it as food, it is not considered food].

K.   *And for what reason do rabbis [contrary to Simeon] declare it unclean?*

L.   *Rabbis stated before R. Sheshet,* "The fact that Scripture declares it prohibited makes it sufficiently important to be classified as food."

M.   *But from the viewpoint of rabbis, do we really invoke the conception,* "The fact that Scripture declares it prohibited makes it sufficiently important to be classified as food"? *And have we not learned in the Mishnah:* Thirteen matters regarding the carrion of the clean bird: (1) It requires intention and does not require preparation. And (2) it renders unclean with food uncleanness when it is the size of an egg, and (3) [it conveys food uncleanness] when it is the size of an olive in the [eater's] gullet. And (4) he who eats it requires waiting until sunset. And (5) they are liable on its account for entering the sanctuary. And (6) they have heave-offering on its account. And (7) he who eats a limb from the living [bird] from it is smitten with forty stripes. "Slaughtering it and wringing its neck render it no longer unclean even if it is terefah, " the words of R. Meir. R. Judah says, "They do not render it clean." R. Yosé says, "Slaughtering it renders clean but not wringing its neck" [M. Toh. 1:1]. And this is then one of them: It requires intention and does not require preparation. Now if it were the case that the fact that Scripture declares it prohibited makes it sufficiently important to be classified as food, why in the world would I require intentionality here?

N.   *Lo, who is the authority of the passage? It is none other than R. Simeon himself.*

O.   *Come and take note of the following:* The carrion of an unclean beast located anywhere, and the carrion of clean fowl in the villages require intention but do not require preparation [M. Uqs. 3:3]. Now if it were the case that Scripture declares it prohibited makes it sufficiently important to be classified as food, why in the world would I require intentionality here?

P.   *Lo, who is the authority of the passage? It is none other than R. Simeon himself.*

Q   *Come and take note of the following:* **The carrion of a clean beast located anywhere, and the carrion of clean fowl, and fat in the markets do not require intention or preparation [M. Uqs. 3:3].** *Lo, that which is unclean does require intention, and should you claim once more, lo, who is the authority of the passage? It is none other than R. Simeon himself, since R. Simeon makes his appearance at the conclusion of the same passage,* **R. Simeon says, "Also: the [carcass of] a camel, rabbit, cony, and pig do not require intention or preparation,"** *the opening lines of the passage cannot also represent him as well!* And R. Simeon further spelled matters out: "What is the operative consideration? Since these classes of animal exhibit the marks of a clean animal...." [Miller & Simon: The first passage with reference to the carcass of an unclean animal's requiring intention of being used as food must accord with the view of rabbis. Hence we infer that rabbis do not hold that its prohibition marks it out as fit to receive food uncleanness, and therefore the passage cited by Rabbah, where rabbis say that the firstborn of an ass receives uncleanness as food, must deal with a case in which a person has expressed the intention of using it as food. Simeon maintains that it does not receive uncleanness as food, because it is food that cannot be given to a gentile to eat and therefore cannot be used. Rabbah therefore is able to deduce from this that an ass that had its neck broken because it was not redeemed may not be used for any sort of benefit.]

R.   *Rather, said Rabbah, "All parties concur that we do* not *invoke the principle,* 'The fact that Scripture declares it prohibited makes it sufficiently important to be classified as food.' *And as to rabbis' reason, if the ass's neck is broken, it would be the fact [Miller & Simon: that rabbis would concur that it does not receive uncleanness as food, since it was not intended for use as food].* **[10B]** *But here with what sort of a case do we deal?* A case in which the animal was slaughtered for the purpose of learning how to carry on the act of slaughter [but not for the purpose of eating the meat at all]. *And at issue is the dispute between Onymus and R. Eleazar. For it has been taught on Tannaite authority:*

S.   "Said R. Yosé, 'Onymus, brother of R. Joshua the grits dealer, said to me, **"He who slaughters a raven in order to practice slaughtering on it – its blood imparts susceptibility to uncleanness."** And R. Eleazar says, **"All blood deriving from slaughter invariably imparts susceptibility to uncleanness"'**[T. Makh. 3:13E, 3:14A-C]. *Now R. Eleazar's view is the same as that of the opening authority [Onymus]! So is it not the case that at issue between the two of them is whether or not we invoke the principle,* 'The fact that Scripture declares it prohibited makes it sufficiently important to be classified as food.' *The first Tannaite authority before us takes the position,* its blood imparts susceptibility to uncleanness to other food, *but, as to the raven itself, there must be intention to use the raven as food. Now R. Eleazar comes along to say,* **'All blood deriving from slaughter invariably imparts susceptibility to uncleanness,'** *and even as to the body of the raven itself, there is no requirement of intentionality to render the beast susceptible to uncleanness as food."*

T. *But what makes you so sure? Perhaps the operative consideration of R. Eleazar in the dispute with Onymus concerns the case of the raven in particular, since that is exceptional in that it bears marks of cleanness* [having a crop, a mark of a clean bird]. [Miller & Simon: Hence it is considered food as regards levitical uncleanness; but in the case of a firstborn of an ass, which has none of the marks of cleanness, unless the man intended to use it as food, rabbis would not hold that it receives uncleanness pertaining to food, and Simeon would maintain that even if he had thought of it as food, it is not subject to uncleanness as food, since it may not be used after the neck is broken.]

U. *The reason I am so sure is that it says in connection with the passage cited above [Q],* R. Simeon further spelled matters out: "What is the operative consideration? Since these classes of animal exhibit the marks of a clean animal...." *And should you object that, if the reason were only because of marks of cleanness, then why should the passage say, he killed the raven in order to practice slaughtering, since, even if he had slaughtered it unintentionally, the case would be the same, the answer is this: indeed so, but it is on account of the position of Onymus that he does not make that statement.*

V. *An objection was raised:*

W. "If one did not want to redeem the ass, one breaks its neck with a hatchet from the back, and one buries it, and it is not permitted for any sort of advantage," the words of R. Judah. But R. Simeon permits it to be used [and this yields the opposite of Rabbah's thesis on Simeon's position concerning the disposition of the ass that had its neck broken. For said Rabbah, "R. Simeon concedes that after the breaking of the neck [of an ass that is a firstborn which has not been redeemed with a lamb], it is forbidden to derive benefit from it"].

X. *State matters in this way:* "When it is alive, it is forbidden to be used, and R. Simeon permits doing so."

Y. *But since the second part of the cited passage speaks of the beast when it is alive, the first part should refer to the beast when it is not alive. For the second part states:* "He should not kill it with a cane, sickle, spade, or saw; nor may he let it go into an enclosure to be locked in and left to die; and one may not shear it or work with it," the words of R. Judah. And R. Simeon permits.

Z. *Both the opening clause and the concluding clause refer to the ass when it is alive; the first permit refers to deriving benefit from the value of the beast [renting out the beast or selling it to others], the second part, to benefit deriving from the body of the beast [shearing it and working with it]. And it is necessary to make both points, for if the Tannaite version made reference only to deriving benefit from the value of the beast, I should have thought that it is in particular in that case that R. Simeon permits doing so, but as to deriving benefit from the body of the beast itself, I might have supposed that he concurs with R. Judah. And if the Tannaite authority had referred only to deriving benefit from the body of the beast, I might have thought that it is in particular in that matter that R. Judah prohibits deriving benefit, but as to deriving benefit from the value of the beast, I might have supposed that he concurs with R. Simeon.*

AA. And so said R. Nahman said Rabbah bar Abbuha, "R. Simeon concurs that, after the breaking of the ass's neck, it is forbidden."

BB. *And said R. Nahman, "On what basis do I make that statement? For it has been taught on Tannaite authority:*

CC. *""Then you shall break its neck"* (Ex. 13:13) – We find a reference to breaking of the neck here, and elsewhere in connection with the heifer the neck of which is broken in the case of the discovery of a neglected corpse] we find reference to breaking the neck as well. Just as in that case the beast may not be used for any beneficial purpose, so here the beast may not be used for any beneficial purpose.' *Now whose position does that formulation represent? Shall I say that it represents the view of R. Judah? But since he forbids utilization of the beast even when it is alive, [why would he have to say that it is forbidden when it is dead, which is an obvious point from his perspective]? Rather, you must say, it stands for the position of R. Simeon."*

DD. *Said to him R. Sheshet, "Our colleague Safra sets matters out in this way: In point of fact, the formulation may be that of R. Judah, but it is necessary to make that point nonetheless. For I might have thought that since the breaking of the neck stands instead of redemption, just as redeeming the beast renders it available for beneficial use, so breaking the neck renders it permissible for beneficial use. So he tells us that it is not the case."*

EE. *Said R. Nahman, "On what basis then do I maintain that Simeon agrees that it is forbidden to use the beast after the neck is broken? It derives from what R. Levi taught on Tannaite authority: 'He has caused a loss of money to the priest, therefore let him lose some money too.' Now who stands behind this statement? Shall I say it is R. Judah? Lo, so far as he is concerned, the loss is well established [even when the ass is alive, it is forbidden for beneficial use anyhow]. Rather, is it not R. Simeon?"*

FF. *If you wish, I shall say it represents the view of R. Judah, and if you wish I shall say it represents the position of R. Simeon.*

GG. *If you wish, I shall say it represents the view of R. Judah: He makes reference to the loss [Miller & Simon:] entailed in the difference [between the value of the beast when alive and when dead; for while when alive, although it could not be used, it could be redeemed, but now he loses everything].*

HH. *And if you wish I shall say it represents the position of R. Simeon: He speaks of the loss incurred by its death [for it can be fed to the dogs alone and there has been a considerable loss (Miller & Simon)].*

II. And so did R. Simeon b. Laqish state, "R. Simeon agrees that it is forbidden to use the beast after the neck is broken."

JJ. And R. Yohanan and some say, R. Eleazar, said, "The disagreement remains in force."

KK. *There are those who report R. Nahman's ruling in the context of the following:*

LL. He who betroths a woman in exchange for the firstborn of an ass – the woman is not deemed betrothed.

MM. *May I say that that formulation of the Tannaite rule is not in accord with R. Simeon?*

NN. Said R. Nahman said Rabbah bar Abbuha, "This passage refers to the disposition of the animal the neck of which had been broken, and all parties concur."

OO. *There are those who say, "Now who is the authority behind this ruling? It is not R. Judah nor is it R. Simeon.*

PP. *"It is not R. Simeon, for in his view, let her become betrothed with the entire value of the ass [all of which may be utilized for gain], nor is it the position of R. Judah, for in his view, let her be betrothed with the difference in value [between the ass of the value of a sheqel and a sheep of the value of a sixth of a denar]."*

QQ. Said Rabbah bar Abbuha said Rab, "It indeed does represent the position of R. Judah, and it deals with a case in which the beast is worth no more than a sheqel." *And he concurs with that which R. Yosé b. R. Judah has said, as has been taught on Tannaite authority:* "You shall redeem...you shall redeem" (Ex. 13:13) – "you shall redeem" the beast immediately; "you shall redeem the beast" at any unspecified value [there being no fixed sum; and redemption may be done with even less than a sheqel].

RR. "R. Yosé b. R. Judah says, 'Redemption cannot take place with something worth less than a sheqel.'"

II.3 A. A master has said, "'You shall redeem...you shall redeem' (Ex. 13:13) – 'you shall redeem' the beast immediately; 'you shall redeem' the beast at any unspecified value [there being no fixed sum; and redemption may be done with even less than a sheqel]."

B. *Is this not self-evident?*

C. *It was necessary and had to be spelled out. For otherwise I might have thought that since an unclean animal is treated as comparable to the firstborn of man, it would follow that, just as the firstborn of man is to be redeemed after the passage of thirty days and for the sum of five selas, so the redemption here of the ass should take place after thirty days and with the sum of five selas. So Scripture states,* "You shall redeem...you shall redeem" (Ex. 13:13) – "you shall redeem" the beast immediately; "you shall redeem" the beast at any unspecified value [there being no fixed sum; and redemption may be done with even less than a sheqel].

II.4 A. R. Yosé b. R. Judah says, "Redemption cannot take place with something worth less than a sheqel."

B. *Which way do you want it? If the matter is treated as comparable to the firstborn of man, then he should require the sum of five sheqels. And if the matter is not treated as comparable, then how does he know that a sheqel is involved at all?*

C. In point of fact, he draws no such comparison.

D. Said Raba, "Scripture has said, 'And all your valuations shall be according to the sheqel of the sanctuary' (Lev. 27:25) – all valuations that you make shall be worth at least a sheqel." [That proves Yosé b. R. Judah's proposition.]

E. *And rabbis?*

F. *That verse* **[11A]** *is written with reference to assessing the amount of one's means* [and if one vows his own value, his valuation is accepted only if his means are worth more than a sheqel. But in respect to the redemption of the firstling of an ass, it may be with anything of any value whatsoever (Miller & Simon)].

II.5 A. Said R. Nahman, "The decided law is in accord with the opinion of sages."

B.   And how much [must be the worth of the lamb exchanged for the ass's firstborn]?

C.   *Said R. Joseph, "Even [Miller & Simon:] a puny lamb, worth no more than a danqa."*

D.   *Said Raba, "We, too, have learned [the same rule on Tannaite authority:]* **[a lamb deriving] from sheep or from goats, male or female, large or small, [blemished or unblemished]."**

E.   *That [statement, that it can be a puny lamb, worth no more than a danqa] is perfectly obvious!*

F.   *What might you otherwise have supposed? That if it were of such slight value it would not be adequate, or that a puny lamb would not be acceptable at all? So we are told that that is perfectly acceptable for the purpose.*

II.6   A.   *R. Judah Nesiah had the firstborn of an ass. He sent it to R. Tarfon and said to him, "How much do I have to give to a priest?"*

B.   He said to him, "Lo, sages have said: a liberal person gives a sela; a stingy person, a sheqel; an average person, a rigia."

C.   Said Raba, "The decided law is that it must be with a rigia."

D.   *And how much is that? It is three zuz, one zuz less than a sela, one zuz more than a sheqel.*

E.   *Is there not a conflict between one statement of the decided law and another [that it may be something worth as little as a danqa]?*

F.   *There is no contradiction, the one rule refers to how one advises someone who comes and consults about the matter, the other speaks of someone who acts on his own initiative.*

II.7   A.   Said R. Simeon b. Laqish, "One who has the firstling of an ass and has no sheep with which to redeem it may redeem it with something of equivalent value."

B.   *According to whom does he make this ruling? Shall I say it is R. Judah [who says a lamb must be used]? Lo, he has said, "The Torah was meticulous in the matter in insisting that a lamb must be used."* Then it must be in accord with R. Simeon.

C.   *This is how R. Aha repeated the matter. But Rabina raised this difficulty:* "When there is a dispute between R. Judah and R. Simeon, the decided law is in accord with R. Judah. And the Tannaite version in hand gives the anonymous version of the law [which is the authoritative version] in accord with R. Judah. And yet you maintain that the decided law accords with R. Simeon? Rather, you may even maintain that it is the view of R. Judah. For the rules governing the redemption of the firstborn of an ass should not be more strict than those governing other Holy Things [which may be redeemed by what is equivalent to their value, not necessarily something of their own species or some other specified species]. And the reason that the Torah has spoken of a lamb is not to impose a strict ruling on the farmer but to impose a lenient ruling on him."

D.   *R. Nehemiah b. R. Joseph redeemed the firstborn of an ass with boiled herbs equivalent in value to it.*

II.8   A.   Said R. Shizbi said R. Huna, "He who redeems the firstling of an ass belonging to another party – his act of redemption is valid."

B.   *The question was raised: Is it the rule that his act of redemption is valid for the one who carries out the act of redemption [who then* owns the ass], or perhaps his act of redemption is valid for the owner of the firstling itself [who then retains ownership of the firstling, so the one who has redeemed it may not dispose of it]? *The question is not raised with respect to the position of R. Simeon, for he has said, "The ass is permitted for benefit," it is classified as the property of the owner. Where we do have to raise the question, it is vis à vis R. Judah, who has said, "It is forbidden to be used for one's own benefit." Does he compare it with Holy Things, concerning which the All-Merciful has said,* "And he shall give money and it shall be assured to him" (Lev. 27:19), *or perhaps, since the owner retains the possession of the difference between the value of the ass and that of a sheep, it is not comparable to Holy Things at all?*

C.   *Said R. Nahman, "Come and take note:* He who steals the firstborn of an ass belonging to another party has to pay the double payment to the owner, for even though he had not got the right of ownership in the beast now, he will have it in time to come [after it is redeemed]. *Now who stands behind this rule? If we should suppose it is R. Simeon, why has he not got rights of ownership even now? But it is obvious that in hand is the opinion of R. Judah. And if you then say that we compare the matter to the case of Holy Things, then what Scripture has said is,* 'if it be stolen out of a man's house' (Ex. 22:6) – not out of the sanctuary [which is not compensated with double payment]. [So we do not compare the case to the redemption of a Holy Things,] and there is nothing else on the subject."

III.1 A. **Two asses, one [of which] had given birth and one which had not given birth, and which bore two males – one gives a single lamb to the priest. [If they produced] a male and a female, the farmer separates a single lamb for himself. For it is said, "And every firstling of an ass you shall redeem with a lamb"** (Ex. 34:20) – **(1) [a lamb deriving] from sheep or from goats, (2) male or female, (3) large or small, (4) blemished or unblemished. (1) And one redeems with [a single lamb] many firstlings. (2) And it enters the fold to be tithed:**

B.   *Our rabbis have taught on Tannaite authority:*

C.   Under what circumstances is it the case that **it enters the fold to be tithed?** You cannot maintain that the firstling has come into the possession of a priest [and then went back to an Israelite, e.g., as a gift], for lo, we have learned in the Mishnah: **a beast that is purchased or given to him as a gift is exempt from the law of tithing animals** [M. Bekh. 9:3A]. Rather, we speak of an Israelite who possessed in his household ten firstlings of asses that were subject to doubt, in which case he sets aside as their counterparts ten lambs, tithes them, but then keeps them.

D.   This supports the view of R. Nahman, for R. Nahman said Rabbah bar Abbuha said, "An Israelite who possessed in his household ten firstlings of asses that were subject to doubt sets aside as their counterparts ten lambs, tithes them, but then keeps them."

III.2 A. And said R. Nahman said Rabbah bar Abbuha, "An Israelite who possessed in his household ten firstlings of asses that were in no way subject to doubt, which he received as an inheritance from his maternal grandfather, who was a priest, who himself had received the animals from his maternal grandfather who was an Israelite [and therefore was required to redeem the animals, which were born in the domain of an Israelite] sets aside as their counterparts ten lambs, tithes them, but then keeps them."

B. And said R. Nahman said Rabbah bar Abbuha, "An Israelite who possessed in his household produce from which the priestly and levitical dues had not yet been set aside, which had been piled up and smoothed [and so is liable for tithing], received as an inheritance from his maternal grandfather, a priest, who had received it from his maternal grandfather, an Israelite, tithes it and retains possession of the tithes."

C. *And it was necessary to specify the rule for these several cases, for had we had only the initial ruling, I might have supposed that the operative consideration was that the lambs and asses had already been designated* [Miller & Simon: therefore it is as if the asses and the lambs had come to him by inheritance from his maternal grandfather, a priest, already separated]. *But in the second case, we deal with gifts for the priests that had not yet been taken by the priest, and they are not treated as thought they have been given, so I might have assumed that the same rule does not pertain* [Miller & Simeon: and the tithes have to be given to the priest; so we are told that the tithes belong to the man, and he does not have to give them to another priest]. *And had we been given only the second case, I might have supposed that the reason that the man keeps the tithes of the produce is that he can tithe the untithed but liable produce as is, for it lies there in hand, but in the other case, since the lamb derives from some other source, we do not maintain that it is as though it were already set aside* [Miller & Simon: for special action is needed to procure the lamb in order to redeem the firstlings of the asses with it, while in the case of the untithed produce, no such effort is necessary]. *So it was important to give the rule in both cases.*

III.3 A. Said R. Samuel bar Nathan said R. Hanina, "He who purchases from a gentile produce from which the priestly and levitical dues had not yet been set aside, [11B] which had been piled up and smoothed [and so is liable for tithing], tithes the produce but keeps ownership of the part of the crop designated for the required tithes. [Miller & Simon: The priest's share of the crop he sells to a priest.]"

B. *Now who was it who had piled up the produce [and so rendered it liable for the separation of tithes]? If we say that a gentile had done so,* Scripture states, "your grain" (Deut. 14:23), meaning, not the grain of a gentile! *So, rather, it is a case in which Israelites had smoothed out the pile in the domain of the gentile [the Israelite being a sharecropper; he had stored up the grain, and the Israelite had acquired the grain in exchange for his labor].*

C. "He tithes it," on the principle that a gentile has no valid right of possession of any land in the Land of Israel in such wise as to release from produce the obligation of tithing.

D. "...But keeps ownership of the part of the crop designated for the required tithes," *for he says to the priest, "I have gained my rights to this crop from someone against whom you cannot establish a claim in law."*

E. *There in the Mishnah we have learned:* [He who brings his tithed wheat to a Samaritan miller or to an am haares miller – the wheat remains in its presumed status with regard to tithes and with regard to Seventh-Year produce; to a gentile miller – the wheat is deemed to be demai.] He who leaves his tithed produce in the keeping of a Samaritan or an am haares – the produce remains in its presumed status with regard to tithes and with regard to Seventh-Year produce; [if it is left] in the keeping of a gentile – the produce is deemed to be like his [viz., the gentile's] produce. R. Simeon says, "It is deemed to be demai [doubtfully tithed produce]" [M. Dem. 3:4A-I].

F.   *Said R. Eleazar, "All parties concur that the priest's share has to be set aside from the produce. They differ on whether or not it has to be handed over to the priest [in line with the principle of D, above]. The initial Tannaite authority takes the view that since he has certainly exchanged the produce for his own, the farmer has to handed over the priest's share to the priest, and R. Simeon takes the view that it is deemed to be subject to doubt and hence doubtfully tithed produce."*

G.   *R. Dimi was in session and stating this tradition. Said Abbayye to him, "The operative consideration then is that we are in doubt as to whether or not he has exchanged the produced. But if he had certainly exchanged the produce, all parties would concur that he has to give the priest's share to the priest? And yet did not R. Samuel say R. Hanina said, 'He who purchases from a gentile produce from which the priestly and levitical dues had not yet been set aside, which had been piled up and smoothed [and so is liable for tithing], tithes the produce but keeps ownership of the part of the crop designated for the required tithes'?"*

H   *"Perhaps the one rule [Dimi's] refers to the principal heave-offering, and R. Samuel's speaks of the heave-offering of tithe [owed to the priest]?"*

I.   *"That matter reminds me of something that R. Joshua b. Levi said, namely, 'How do we know that one who bought untithed grain, properly piled up, from a gentile, is exempt from having to designate the heave-offering of tithe? Because Scripture has said, "Moreover, you shall speak to the Levites and say to them, when you take of the children of Israel" (Num. 18:26) – from untithed grain that you purchase from the children of Israel to you separate the heave-offering of the tithe and hand over to the priest; but from untithed grain that you purchase from a gentile, you do not have to separate heave-offering of the tithe and hand it over to the priest.'"*

IV.1 A. **And if it dies, they derive benefit from it:**

B.   *How shall we say that it died? If we say that it died when in the domain of a priest, and he is permitted to derive benefit from the beast, that is self-evident, since the beast belongs to him anyhow! Rather, that it died in the domain of the owner and the priest derives benefit from it? This, too, is obvious!*

C.   *You might have thought that so long as the beast has not reached the possession of the priest, the priest does not really possess it. So we are informed that, from the moment that the Israelite has designated the beast for that purpose, the beast is held to be within the domain of the priest.*

I.1 begins with a question on the Tannaite authority behind the rule, which helps us to identify the principle embedded within the rule. II.1

goes through exactly the same process, with the same result. No. 2 complements the foregoing, though it sets off in its own direction. The composition is entirely independent of the program of II.1, and it has its own focus and direction. Nos. 3, 4, 5 form footnotes to No. 2. No. 6 then brings the matter to a close with a case, followed by some secondary rules dealing with special cases or problems, Nos. 7, 8. III.1 clarifies one of the Mishnah's clauses by appeal to an appropriate amplification of the matter. No. 2 is of course integral to 1.C, but I treat it as separate from the foregoing for an obvious reason: the exposition of 2.A, B, ignores 1.C entirely. No. 3 is tacked on to No. 2. IV.1 asks an obvious question about the clarification of the Mishnah's statement. That the Bavli's program is quite coherent hardly requires much comment at this point, with a rather vast, sometimes tedious composition giving much evidence of careful planning, point by point.

1:5

A. They do not redeem [a firstling of an ass] with (1) a calf, or (2) with a wild beast, or (3) with an animal which has been properly slaughtered, or (4) with an animal which is terefah, or (5) with a hybrid [of a he-goat and a ewe], or (6) with a koy [the offspring of a he-goat and a hind].

B. R. Eleazar permits in the case of a hybrid, because it is deemed a lamb, and prohibits in the case of the koy, because it is a matter of doubt [whether it is deemed a lamb].

C. [If] one gave it [the offspring of an ass] to the priest, the priest is not permitted to keep it unless he will separate [set aside and designate] a lamb in its place.

Continuing M. 1:4D-K, A presents three pairs, 1-2, 3-4, and 5-6. The dispute concerns only the last one. We require a lamb of sheep or goats; the lamb must not be slaughtered, nor may it be one which, even alive, is deemed terefah; not the hybrid of a goat and a sheep. Eleazar will have had a list of five items, for the reasons given at B.

C is a separate rule entirely. If one gave the offspring of an ass to the priest, the priest can keep it only if he separates a lamb for its redemption.

F. R. Eleazar says, "The hybrid of a ewe and a goat – they redeem therewith [the firstborn of an ass].

G. "That of a koy – they do not redeem therewith [the firstborn of an ass]" [M. Bekh. 1:5B].

T. 1:13 Z p. 535, lines 6-7

A. Just as they do not redeem [the firstborn of an ass] with a slain [lamb], so they do not redeem the firstborn of an as which died [M. Bekh. 1:5A/3].

T. 1:14 Z p. 535, lines 7-8

T. restates M. 1:5B and 1:5A3 and adds, at T. 1:14, sages' view, M. 1:6F, H. The clear plan is once more to gloss the Mishnah in some minor ways. The Talmud's ambitions are considerably greater, but an equally clear plan governs.

I.1 A.   *Who is the authority behind the anonymous rule of the Mishnah? It is Ben Bag Bag, for it has been taught on Tannaite authority:*

      B.   Ben Bag Bag says, "Here we find a reference to 'lamb' [Ex. 13:13, with reference to the redemption of the firstborn of an ass], and elsewhere, with reference to the Passover-offering, we find reference to the word 'lamb' (Ex. 12:5). Just as in that context excluded are all those who have been named in the Mishnah, none of which may be used for the Passover-offering, so lamb here is meant to exclude all those classes of beasts listed in the Mishnah, which may not serve in redemption of the firstling of an ass.

      C.   "Might one say, just as the Passover-offering must be a male, unblemished, a year old, so here too, the beast used for the redemption of the firstborn of an ass must be a male, unblemished, a year old?

      D.   "Scripture states, 'you shall redeem...you shall redeem,' in that way encompassing a beast that is not male, blemished, and not a year old."

      E.   If then the language, "you shall redeem...you shall redeem," serves to encompass, *then why not include all of these classes of beasts as well?*

      F.   *If so, why refer to the analogous meaning of the references to "lamb" in both contexts? [That analogy excludes the proposition just now proposed.]*

I.2 A.   *The question was raised: How about redeem the firstborn of an ass with an animal that has been taken live from the slaughtered mother's womb? That question cannot be raised within the premises of R. Meir, for, since R.* Meir has said, "An animal taken live from a slaughter mother's womb has itself to be slaughtered," *here we have a perfectly valid sheep. The question arises only within the premises of rabbis, who have said,* "The act of slaughter of the mother renders the beast valid, as though it were flesh in the cooking pot" *[and since this beast is then deemed properly slaughtered, we cannot use it to redeem the firstborn of an ass]. Or perhaps, since at this moment, the beast is there running and walking about, it may be classified as a lamb?*

      B.   Mar Zutra said, "It may not be used for redeeming the firstling of an ass."

      C.   And R. Ashi said, "It may be used for redeeming the firstling of an ass."

      D.   *Said R. Ashi, "What's in your mind? Do you infer this from the case of the Passover-offering [which cannot be made from an animal taken live from its slaughtered mother's womb]? Then why not go further:* just as the Passover-offering must be a male, unblemished, a year old, so here too, the beast used for the redemption of the firstborn of an ass must be a male, unblemished, a year old? Scripture states, 'you shall redeem...you shall redeem,' in that way encompassing a beast that is not male, blemished, and not a year old – and if that is the case, then even a beast removed live from its slaughtered mother's womb should be acceptable!"

E. "If that were the case, then why derive the analogy from the repeated reference to 'lamb'?" [Miller & Simon: And since that is the case, we include the beast taken live from the slaughtered mother's womb as unsuitable, for this falls into the category of a properly slaughtered beast.]

I.3 A. *The question was raised:* What is the law as to redeeming the firstling of an ass with an animal that appears to be a hybrid [the father a ram, the mother a ewe, and the offspring looks like some other species]? *The question cannot be raised within the premises of R. Eliezer, for if he actually permits redemption with a hybrid beast, will the beast that merely appears to be a hybrid cause him any problems? The question may be raised only within the premises of rabbis. We may say that it is in particular with hybrids that we may not redeem the firstling of an ass, but with a beast that merely looks like a hybrid, we do so. Or perhaps there is no difference anyhow?*

B. Come and take note: A cow that gave birth to a species of a goat — they do not redeem the firstling of an ass with it. *Then it follows that if a ewe gave birth to a species of a kid, we do redeem the firstling of an ass with it. Whose opinion is before us? If we say that it is R. Eliezer, so far as he is concerned, we also redeem the firstling of an ass with a hybrid. So is it not the view of rabbis [and that answers our question]?*

C. *No, in point of fact it is the view of R. Eliezer, and this is the very point that he wishes to teach us [without any further deduction as to redeeming with an offspring that looked like a kid produced by a ewe], that* if a cow gave birth to a species of a goat, one may not redeem with it, *and you are not to say, 'make the decision by appeal to the criterion of the traits of the offspring itself, and this is a genuine kid,' but rather say, 'make the decision by appeal to the criterion of the traits of the mother, and this is a calf.'"*

D. *Come and take note: for Rabbah bar Samuel taught as a Tannaite version:* "What is the definition of a hybrid? A ewe that gave birth to a species of a kid, though the father was a sheep."

E. But if the father was a sheep is this a hybrid? Is it not merely a beast that appears to be a hybrid? Rather: "What is the definition of that which is so similar to a hybrid that rabbis have treated it as equivalent to a hybrid? A ewe that gave birth to a species of a kid, though the father was a sheep." *Now for what purpose have rabbis treated it as equivalent to a hybrid? Should I say that it is in respect to sanctifying it for the purpose of an offering [indicating that a beast that looks like a hybrid may not be offered as a sacrifice]? The very passage that excludes the use of hybrids from the altar also yields the exclusion of the beast that appears to be a hybrid as well. For it has been taught on Tannaite authority:*

F. "When a bullock of a sheep" (Lev. 22:27) – excluding a hybrid; "or a goat" (Lev. 22:27) – excluding a beast that looks like a hybrid.

G. And if it is for the purpose of excluding a beast that appears to be a hybrid from the rule of the firstling, Scripture has said, "But the firstling of an ox" (Num. 18:17) – the All-Merciful has said that the beast must be an ox, and its firstborn must also be an ox.

H   And if it is for the purpose of excluding a beast that appears to be a hybrid from the rule of tithing the herds, Scripture has expressly excluded both the hybrid and the beast that appears to be a hybrid from that classification because the word "under" appears in both contexts.

I   So it must be that the purpose of that statement can only have been to refer to the firstborn of an ass [and to indicate that one may not use a beast that appears to be a hybrid for that purpose].

J   *No, in point of fact at issue is the matter of tithing of the herd, and we deal with a case in which the beast that appears to be a hybrid still has some of the characteristics of the mother. You might have said that, because the word "under" appears in both contexts, [it is liable to tithing], but so we are informed that that is not the case, for we draw an analogy between the use of the word "under" here and that same usage in connection with Holy Things [so we exclude the animal that appears to be a hybrid from the tithe of the herd, comparing it with a hybrid].*

I.4 A   *The question was raised:* What is the law as to redeeming the firstling of an ass with beasts that are invalid for serving as Holy Things [and that have been redeemed]? *Within the premises of R. Simeon it is not a question, for, since he has said,* "Such beasts are available for one's own benefit," *he deems them to be unconsecrated. The question arises solely from the position of R. Judah, who has said,* "Such beasts are not available for one's own benefit [but have to be redeemed]." What is the rule? Do we maintain that since the beast is forbidden for use for one's own benefit, we invoke the principle that one prohibition does not take effect where another prohibition is already in place [Miller & Simon: the prohibition attaching to the firstborn of an ass cannot be transferred to a consecrated animal that is unfit for the altar which is liable to the prohibitions regarding shearing or working]? *Or perhaps, since the redemption serves only for releasing the ass from being subject to a prohibition [and to allow people to use the firstling of the ass, but the sanctity of the ass does not then affect the object with which the ass has been redeemed], [and so it would be permitted to use the invalid Holy Things for that purpose]?*

B   *Said R. Mari b. R. Kahana, "And do we treat as inconsequential what is written in regard to beasts that were consecrated but became unfit for use on the altar: 'As the gazelle and the hart'* (Deut. 12:22)? Just as we do not redeem the firstling of an ass with a gazelle or a hart [but only with a sheep], so we do not redeem the firstling of an ass with animals that were sanctified but then became unfit for the altar."

C   *Now that you have come so far,* **[12B]** *then even according to the view of R. Simeon, it should be forbidden to redeem the firstling of an ass with animals that were sanctified but then became unfit for the altar* [Miller & Simon: for although it is permitted according to him to benefit from the firstborn of an ass, we are still not allowed to redeem it with an animal of that classification], since, after all, Scripture states, "As the gazelle and the hart" (Deut. 12:22). [Just as we do not redeem the firstling of an ass with a gazelle or a hart but only with a sheep, so we do not redeem the firstling of an ass with animals that were sanctified but then became unfit for the altar.]

I.5   A.   *The question was raised:* what is the law as to redeeming the firstling of an ass with an animal purchased with produce of the Seventh Year? *With respect to an ass that is beyond doubt a firstborn, there is no basis for raising the question, since the All-Merciful has specified that the produce of the Seventh Year is to be used* "for food" (Lev. 25:6), meaning, for food but not for commerce. *The question arises with regard to a firstborn of an ass that is subject to doubt as to its status.*

  B.   *And in regard to the position of R. Simeon, there is no basis for raising the question, for he maintains that a firstborn of an ass that is subject to doubt is not subject to redemption.*

  C.   *Where there is a basis for raising the question, it is within the premise of R. Judah. Now what is the ruling? Since one sets aside a lamb and it remains for the farmer's own use, we may say that it meets the criterion of being used for food. Or perhaps, since so long as the prohibition affecting the ass has not been nullified the ass is not permitted, the act is tantamount to commercial trading with produce of the Seventh Year?*

  D.   *Come and take note, for* said R. Hisda, "With a beast that has been purchased with produce of the Seventh Year, one may not redeem the firstling of an ass that is not subject to doubt, but one may redeem with such produce the firstling of the seventh year that is subject to doubt."

  E.   And said R. Hisda, "The beast purchased with produce of the seventh year is exempt from the law of the firstborn and it is liable for the designation of the gifts that are owing to the priesthood.

  F.   "It is exempt from the law of the firstborn, for the All-Merciful has said, 'for food,' but not for burning [and certain portions of the firstling are burned on the altar].

  G.   "It is liable for the designation of the gifts that are owing to the priesthood for in that case, we can meet the requirement that the beast be used only for food [the priest will eat the meat]."

  H.   *An objection was raised:* He who eats from dough made from produce of the Seventh Year prior to the dough-offering's having been designated and removed is liable to the death penalty. *But why should that be the rule? The rule is that if the dough became unclean, it would have to be burned, but the All-Merciful has said, 'for food,' but* not for burning, [so there should be no liability to dough-offering at all]!

  I.   *That case is exceptional, for* Scripture says, "Throughout your generations" (Num. 15:21) [Miller & Simon: implying that even in the Seventh Year, dough-offering must be given].

  J.   *So, too, it has been taught on Tannaite authority:*

  K.   How on the basis of Scripture do we know that he who eats from dough made from produce of the Seventh Year prior to the dough-offering's having been designated and removed is liable to the death penalty? It is because it is said, "Throughout your generations" (Num. 15:21).

  L.   *Then why not derive the rule that the firstling bought with the produce of the Seventh Year is liable to the law of the firstling from the case of dough-offering itself?*

M   *The difference is that, in the case of dough-offering, one designates dough
     as dough-offering principally so the priests can eat it, but in the case of the
     firstling, the principal purpose of the firstling is to yield the part that is
     burned on the altar.*

II.1 A   **If] one gave it [the offspring of an ass directly] to the priest, the
           priest is not permitted to keep it unless he sets aside and
           designates a lamb in its place [which he also, of course, keeps]:**

      B.   *We have learned here as a Tannaite version that which our rabbis have
           taught:*

      C.   An Israelite who had in his household a firstling of an ass, and a
           priest said to him, "Give it to me and I shall redeem it" – lo, he
           should not hand it over to him unless the priest redeems the animal
           in his presence.

      D.   Said R. Nahman said Rabbah b. Abbuha, "That is to say that priests
           are suspect concerning the redemption of firstlings of asses."

      E.   *Obviously!*

      F.   *No, you might otherwise have thought that that is so only where the priest
           is known to be under suspicion, but, in general, we do not suspect priests.
           So we are told that the priest will commonly decide that it is entirely
           legitimate [not to set aside a lamb for the redemption of the firstling of an
           ass, since the lamb remains his property].*

I.1 goes through the familiar process of clarifying the authorship of
the passage, and in that way, identifying the operative principle or
consideration. No. 2 presses a secondary problem suggested by the
classes of beasts listed in the Mishnah, and Nos. 3, 4, 5 do the same. A
single pattern governs throughout. II.1 raises a minor point of extension
of the rule. What is important for our purpose is the uniform character
of much of this – again, protracted – discussion. Any notion that our
document's framers simply collect and arrange whatever they have
received and do not find guidance in a well-crafted program of their own
is belied by the clearly coherent character of these long and well-
developed discussions.

1:6

      A.   He who separates a redemption lamb for a firstborn of an ass and
           who died –

      B.   R. Eliezer says, "(1) They [the heirs] are responsible for it [to give
           the redemption lamb to the priest], (2) as [the heirs are liable for]
           the five selas [paid in the redemption of the firstborn] son."

      C.   And sages say, "(1) They are not liable for it [to give the
           redemption lamb to the priest], (2) as [the are not liable in the case
           of] the redemption of second tithe."

      D.   Testified R. Joshua and R. Sadoq concerning the redemption
           lamb which was set aside for the firstling of an ass [and] which
           had died,

      E.   that there is nothing whatsoever for the priest here [= C].

      F.   [If] the firstling [of an ass] died,

G.   R. Eliezer says, "It is to be buried. And [the owner] is permitted to derive benefit from the lamb [which had been set aside to redeem it]."

H.   And sages say, "It need not be buried. And the lamb belongs to the priest."

The pericope is in three parts, A-C, D-E, and F-H. A-C, F-H follow a single, highly disciplined form. The man who has separated a redemption lamb for the firstborn of an ass has died. Does the lamb then belong to a priest? Eliezer maintains that it does, along the lines of the analogy specified at B2 [= M. 8:8]. Sages say that the lamb is not given over to the priest. Their analogy is somewhat askew. They refer to food set aside as second tithe, which is either to be eaten in Jerusalem or redeemed for coins to be spent on food there. If the produce is lost, the owner is not liable for it; he has nothing to bring up to Jerusalem. Accordingly, Eliezer's conception is that the liability inheres not in the owner but in the animal, which still is in hand and not redeemed. D-E raise the question, What if the lamb set aside for the redemption of the firstborn of an ass itself dies? The priest has no claim to it (exactly as has been stated by M. 1:4K). D-E concur with sages, C. Once the lamb is set aside, the firstling is redeemed.

The dispute of A-C then is joined by a parallel one, F-H. If the firstling dies, how do we dispose of the lamb which has been set aside for its redemption? Eliezer has the firstling buried, as if it has not been redeemed. Why? Because the owner is liable for the redemption lamb, B; it is deemed in his possession; the firstling therefore is not redeemed. The lamb does not have to be given to the priest. Sages say that the firstling need not be buried; it is as if it were redeemed (C, D-E). But then the redemption lamb, once set aside, is deemed to belong to the priest (C), for the firstling of the ass is redeemed thereby. So A-C are continued at F-H, in which case the intrusion of D-E is for thematic reasons only: (1) the owner dies; (2) the redemption lamb dies; (3) the firstling itself dies. The Tosefta contains nothing to complement or supplement this passage. But the Bavli's framers have their usual inquiry, into the scriptural basis for the rule at hand; that inquiry then bears its own secondary expansion.

B.   The firstborn of an ass – its religious requirement is that one keep it for thirty days.

C.   Thereafter one must either redeem it or break its neck.

T. 1:14 Z p. 535, lines 7-8

T. complements M. 1:7A-B. This same item figures in the following Talmud.

I.1 A. Said R. Joseph, "What is the scriptural basis for the position of R. Eliezer? It is written, 'Nevertheless the firstborn of man you shall surely redeem and the firstling of unclean beasts you shall redeem' (Num. 18:15) – just as in the case of the firstborn of man, one is responsible to make up the redemption money that has been set aside, should it get lost, so in the case of the firstborn of an unclean animal, he is responsible to make up the lamb set aside for redemption if it dies."

B. Said to him Abbayye, "Might one then say, 'just as in the case of the firstborn of man, one is permitted to derive benefit from the person before he is redeemed, so in the case of the firstborn of an unclean animal, it should be permitted likewise to derive benefit from it'? *And if you should say, that is indeed so, have we not learned,* **[If] the firstling [of an ass] died, R. Eliezer says, 'It is to be buried'?** *What is the meaning of,* **It is to be buried?** *Is it not, it is forbidden to derive benefit from it?"*

C. "No, simply, **It is to be buried** as the firstling of man is to be buried."

D. *"And is it only the firstborn of man that is to be buried but an ordinary one does not have to be buried? And has it not been taught on Tannaite authority,* R. Eliezer concedes that one who has in his household a firstling of an ass that is subject to doubt, one designates a lamb on its account, but the lamb remains his? [Miller & Simon: And while with reference to an ass that is a firstborn beyond doubt, he maintains that so long as the lamb is not in the possession of the priest, the firstborn is not redeemed, he agrees with regard to a firstborn subject to doubt that he need not give its redemption to the priest but sets aside a lamb, thus implying that the firstborn of an ass otherwise cannot be used; and since we do not compare an unclean animal with the firstborn of a man in this respect, the same should apply in respect to his responsibility to make it up if it should be lost. So what is the reason behind Eliezer's position?]

E. Rather, said Raba, "Scripture says, 'Nevertheless the firstborn of man you shall surely redeem and the firstling of unclean beasts you shall redeem' (Num. 18:15) – it is in particular in connection with the responsibility for redemption that I have drawn a comparison between an unclean animal and the firstborn of man, but not with respect to any other matter."

I.2 A. *It has been taught on Tannaite authority in another regard:*

B. Valuations are assessed in accord with the situation prevailing when he made the pledge of valuation [even though the pledge is paid later on]; the redemption of a firstborn son is to take place after thirty days have passed; the redemption of the firstborn of an ass takes place immediately.

C. Is it the fact that the redemption of the firstborn of an ass takes place immediately? *But a contradiction to that position may be cited in the following:* at least thirty days must be assigned to the period of valuation, redemption of the firstborn, spell of Naziriteship, and redemption of the firstborn of an ass, and one may add to the time in which action is taken in each of these matters indefinitely [so, valuation accords with the increase in one's age, a Nazirite can vow for years, the firstborn of an ass may be redeemed even after years; the contradiction is that the redemption of the firstborn of an ass takes place only thirty days after birth, not immediately].

D.   Said R. Nahman, "The statement, 'the redemption of the firstborn of an ass takes place immediately,' indicates that if one has actually redeemed it forthwith, the act of redemption is valid."

E.   Does this then imply that in the case of his son, if he redeemed him immediately [and not after thirty days], the act of redemption is invalid? *And has it not been stated:* He who redeems his son within the first thirty days – Rab said, "His son is validly redeemed."

F.   *But has it not been stated in that same connection, said Raba, "All parties concur [that if he said that the firstborn will be redeemed] from now [before thirty days have passed], his son is not validly redeemed."*

G.   [13A] R. Sheshet said, "The passage indicates that if one has done so, he does not violate the law."

H.   Rami bar Hama objected, "'**The religious duty pertains for the first thirty days. After that time has passed, the farmer must either redeem the firstling or break its neck' [T. 1:14B-C].** *Is the meaning not,* The religious duty is to retain the animal for the entire period of thirty days?"

I.   No. It is, the religious duty is to redeem it during the thirty days.

J.   If so, then the passage should read, "from that point on, the farmer must either redeem the firstling or break its neck."

K.   *Rather, said Raba, "There is no contradiction. The one statement [redemption is done after thirty days] is the opinion of R. Eliezer, who treats the unclean animal's firstborn as equivalent to that of man, and the other statement [that redemption takes place immediately] represents the opinion of rabbis, who draw no such analogy."*

I.1 commences with the usual inquiry into the scriptural basis for an aspect of the Mishnah's rule. No. 2 proceeds to clarify the span of time in which the firstborn of an ass may, or must, be redeemed, a detail that does not intersect with any salient point of our Mishnah paragraph. The reason for the inclusion is shown at the end, the dispute on the pertinent analogy.

1:7

A.   [If] one did not want to redeem it [the firstling of an ass], he breaks its neck from behind with a hatchet, and buries it.

I.   B.   The requirement of redemption takes precedence over the requirement of breaking the neck,

C.   since it is said, *And if you will not redeem it, then you will break its neck* (Ex. 34:20).

II. D.   The requirement of espousing [a Hebrew bondwoman] takes precedence over the requirement of redemption,

E.   since it is said, *So that he has not espoused her, then he shall let her be redeemed* (Ex. 21:8).

III. F.   The requirement of Levirate marriage takes precedence over the
                ceremony of *halisah* –
      G   at first, when they would consummate the Levirate marriage for
                the sake of fulfilling a commandment.
      H   But now, that they do not consummate the Levirate marriage for
                the sake of fulfilling a commandment, they have ruled:
      I.   The requirement of *halisah* takes precedence over the
                requirement of Levirate marriage.
      J.   The requirement of redeeming [an unclean beast dedicated to the
                Temple] is incumbent upon the master.
      K.   He takes precedence over every other person [M. Ar. 8:2],
      L   since it is said, [*Then he shall ransom it...*] *or if it is not redeemed,
                then it shall be sold according to thy estimation* (Lev. 27:27).

A is a simple declarative sentence, giving a rule which restates that
of Scripture, C. It then is joined with its sizable appendix, B-I, which
itself is given a supplement, J-L. The formal requirements of B-F are not
met at F-I, but are readily reconstructed. For in the model of B-C, D-E, F
should be followed by: Since it is said, *And if the man does not wish to take
his brother's wife, then his brother's wife shall go up to the gate...*(Deut. 25:7).
That is, here, too, Scripture explicitly specifies that the Levirate marriage
takes precedence over the rite of *halisah*. G-H are a complete saying unto
themselves, and H then links them to I. J-L ignore the form of the
foregoing, and the issue is quite distinct, as well.

      A   *One breaks its neck from behind with a hatchet and buries it* [M. Bekh.
                1:7A].
      B.   And it is prohibited for benefit.
      C   One should not kill it with a staff or a red, or lock the door in its
                face so that it will die.
      D.   And if one has done so, lo, he has not [*TR* II, p. 266] carried out his
                obligation.

                            T. 1:17 Z p. 535, lines 14-15

      A   While it is alive [and unredeemed], it is prohibited for shearing or
                for any sort of labor.
      B.   And R. Simeon declares permitted.
      C.   And the firstling of man is permitted in all instances.

                            T. 1:18 Z p. 535, lines 15-16

T. augments M. as indicated. The Bavli goes over these materials in
its own context, but offers nothing in the amplification of this Mishnah
paragraph in particular.

Now that we have compared the Bavli's and the Tosefta's treatment
of the same chapter of the Mishnah, we of course note various obvious
differences. But what is important is not only difference, but a pattern of
difference: the Bavli's framers differ in their theory of Mishnah
commentary from the Tosefta's framers, and the differences are
consistent throughout. In the contrast between the Tosefta and the

Talmud of Babylonia, we have seen over and over again, the Talmud of Babylonia emerges as a well-crafted and highly purposive document, and certainly not a mere compilation of this-and-that, the result of centuries of the accumulation, in a haphazard way, of the detritus of various schools or opinions. Any sample of the Talmud that we take presents itself as exceedingly carefully and well crafted, a sustained and cogent inquiry. Scarcely a single line is out of place; not a sentence in the entire passage sustains the view of a document that is an agglutinative compilation. Ordinarily, for example, at any given passage of the Bavli, we begin with the clarification of the Mishnah paragraph, turn then to the examination of the principles of law implicit in the Mishnah paragraph, and then broaden the discussion to introduce what I called analogies from case to law and law to case. These are the three stages of our discussion. It would be very easy to outline a given Talmudic discussion, beginning to end, and to produce a reasoned account of the position and order of every completed composition and the ordering of the several compositions into a composite. That result strongly points away from the picture of the Talmud as essentially agglutinative.

The facts do not indicate a haphazard, episodic, sedimentary process of agglutination and conglomeration. They point, quite to the contrary, to a well-considered and orderly composition, planned from beginning to end and following an outline that is definitive throughout. That outline has told the framers of the passage what comes first – the simplest matters of language, then the more complex matters of analysis of content, then secondary development of analogous principles and cases. We move from simple criticism of language to weighty analysis of parallels. True, we invoke facts treated elsewhere; but reference is always verbatim, so, with a modicum of information, we can follow the discussion. True, the Talmud is not an elementary primer of the law, but it does not pretend to be. It claims to discuss the Mishnah paragraph that it cites, and it discusses that Mishnah paragraph.

We may therefore speak of the Bavli as a composition, not merely a compilation, because of two facts. First, the Talmud's authors or authorship follow a few rules, which we can easily discern, in order to say everything they wish. So the document is uniform and rhetorically cogent. The highly orderly and systematic character of the Talmud emerges, first of all, in the regularities of language. The Talmud utilizes two languages, and a glance at the translation in Hebrew and Aramaic, as I have shown the difference, tells us the rules governing the resort to each. The Talmud speaks in Aramaic, represented, in the translation, in italics. Hebrew is used when the Talmud cites a received document in that language, particularly the Mishnah (and the Tosefta); and, second, when a rule of law is to be formulated in some sort of official and final form. So there is nothing at all haphazard about the bilingualism of the document, and that is a sign that the document's framers have made choices, effected throughout.

Second, the Talmud speaks through one voice, that voice of logic that with vast assurance reaches into our own minds and by asking the logical and urgent next question tells us what we should be thinking. So the Talmud's rhetoric seduces us into joining its analytical inquiry, always raising precisely the question that should trouble us (and that would trouble us if we knew all of the pertinent details as well as the Talmud does). The Talmud speaks about the Mishnah in essentially a single voice, about fundamentally few things. Its mode of speech as much as of thought is uniform throughout. Diverse topics produce slight differentiation in modes of analysis. The same sorts of questions phrased in the same rhetoric – a moving, or dialectical, argument, composed of questions and answers – turn out to pertain equally well to every subject and problem. The Talmud's discourse forms a closed system, in which people say the same thing about everything. The fact that the Talmud speaks in a single voice supplies striking evidence (1) that the Talmud does speak in particular for the age in which its units of discourse took shape, and (2) that that work was done toward the end of that long period of Mishnah reception that began at the end of the second century and came to an end at the conclusion of the sixth century.

Let us first turn to the Talmud's ubiquitous, monotonous, and, alas, I must admit, sometimes tedious "narrator": who is telling me these things? Whence the conceptual and rhetorical uniformities? When the Talmud speaks about a passage of the Mishnah, it generally takes up a single, not very complex or diverse, program of inquiry. The Talmud also utilizes a single, rather limited repertoire of exegetical initiatives and rhetorical choices for whatever discourse about the Mishnah the framers of the Talmud propose to undertake. Accordingly, as is clear, the Talmud presents us with both a uniformity of discourse and a monotony of tone. The Talmud speaks in a single voice. That voice by definition is collective, not greatly differentiated by traits of individuals.

When I say that the Talmud speaks in a single voice, I mean to say it everywhere speaks uniformly, consistently, and predictably. The voice is the voice of a book. The message is one deriving from a community, the collectivity of sages for whom and to whom the book speaks. The document seems, in the main, to intend to provide notes, an abbreviated script which anyone may use to reconstruct and reenact formal discussions of problems: about this, one says that. Curt and often arcane, these notes can be translated only with immense bodies of inserted explanation. All of this script of information is public and undifferentiated, not individual and idiosyncratic. We must assume people took for granted that, out of the signs of speech, it would be possible for anyone to reconstruct speech, doing so in accurate and fully conventional ways. So the literary traits of the document presuppose a uniform code of communication: a single voice. Our comparison of the Bavli's and the Tosefta's authorships response to the Mishnah underlines that choices have been made, decisions reached, so that a single intentionality governs, in both the one document and the other.

The ubiquitous character of this single and continuous voice of the Talmud argues for one of two points of origin. First, powerful and prevailing conventions may have been formed in the earliest stages of the reception and study of the Mishnah, then carried on thereafter without variation or revision. Or, second, I hold, the framing of sayings into uniform constructions of discourse may have been accomplished only toward the end of the period marked by the formation of the Talmud's units of discourse and their conglomeration into the Talmud of the Land of Israel as we know it. In the former case, we posit that the mode of reasoned analysis of the Mishnah and the repertoire of issues to be addressed to any passage of the Mishnah were defined early on, then persisted for four hundred years. The consequent, conventional mode of speech yielded that nearly total uniformity of discourse characteristic of numerous units of discourse of the Talmud at which the interpretation of a law of the Mishnah is subject to discussion. In the latter case we surmise that a vast corpus of sayings, some by themselves, some parts of larger conglomerates, was inherited at some point toward the end of the two hundred years under discussion. This corpus of miscellanies was then subjected to intense consideration as a whole, shaped and reworded into the single, cogent and rhetorically consistent Talmudic discourse.

As between these two possibilities, the character of the sustained and relentless inquiry we followed makes the latter by far the more likely. The reason is simple. I cannot find among the units of discourse in the Talmud evidence of differentiation among the generations of names or schools. There is no interest, for instance, in the chronological sequence in which sayings took shape and in which discussions may be supposed to have been carried on. That is to say, the Talmudic unit of discourse approaches the explanation of a passage of the Mishnah without systematic attention to the layers in which ideas were set forth, the schools among which discussion must have been divided, the sequence in which statements about a Mishnah law were made. That fact points to formation at the end, not agglutination in successive layers of intellectual sediment. In a given unit of discourse, the focus, the organizing principle, the generative interest – these are defined solely by the issue at hand. The argument moves from point to point, directed by the inner logic of argument itself. A single plane of discourse is established. All things are leveled out, so that the line of logic runs straight and true. Accordingly, a single conception of the framing and formation of the unit of discourse stands prior to the spelling out of issues. More fundamental still, what people in general wanted was not to create topical anthologies – to put together instances of what this one said about that issue – but to exhibit the logic of that issue, viewed under the aspect of eternity. Under sustained inquiry we always find a theoretical issue, freed of all temporal considerations and the contingencies of politics and circumstance.

Once these elemental literary facts make their full impression, everything else falls into place as well. Arguments such as the one we followed just now did not unfold over a long period of time, as one generation made its points, to be followed by the additions and revisions of another generation, in a process of gradual increment and agglutination running on for two hundred years. That theory of the formation of literature cannot account for the unity, stunning force and dynamism, of the Talmud's dialectical arguments. To the contrary, someone (or small group) at the end determined to reconstruct, so as to expose, the naked logic of a problem. For this purpose, oftentimes, it was found useful to cite sayings or positions in hand from earlier times. But these inherited materials underwent a process of reshaping, and, more aptly, refocusing. Whatever the original words – and we need not doubt that at times we have them – the point of everything in hand was defined and determined by the people who made it all up at the end. The whole shows a plan and program. Theirs are the minds behind the whole. In the nature of things, they did their work at the end, not at the outset. There are two possibilities. The first is that our document emerges out of a gradual increment of a sedimentary process. Or it emerges as the creation of single-minded geniuses of applied logic and sustained analytical inquiry. But there is no intermediate possibility.

One qualification is required. I do not mean to say that the principles of chronology were wholly ignored. Rather, they simply were not determinative of the structure of argument. So I do not suggest that the framers of the Talmud would likely have an early authority argue with a later one about what is assigned only to the later one. That I cannot and do not expect to instantiate. I do not think we shall find such slovenly work in the Talmud. These sages were painstaking and sensible. But no attention ever is devoted in particular to the temporal sequence in which various things are said. Everything is worked together into a single, temporally seamless discourse. Discussion will always focus upon the logical point at hand. The sequence of authorities in the pages we reviewed is not temporal but logical: which problem has to be addressed first, and which is logically next in sequence.

It follows that the whole is the work of the one who decided to make up the discussion on the atemporal logic of the point at issue. Otherwise the discussion would be not continuous but disjointed, full of seams and margins, marks of the existence of prior conglomerations of materials that have now been sewn together. What we have are not patchwork quilts, but woven fabric. Along these same lines, we may find discussions in which opinions of Palestinians, such as Yohanan and Simeon b. Laqish, will be joined together side by side with opinions of Babylonians, such as Rab and Samuel. The whole, once again, will unfold in a smooth way, so that the issues at hand define the sole focus of discourse. The logic of those issues will be fully exposed. Considerations of the origin of a saying in one country or the other will play no role whatsoever in the rhetoric or literary forms of argument. There will be no possibility of differentiation among opinions on the basis of where, when, by whom, or how they are formulated, only on the basis of what, in fact, is said.

Others take the view that sayings assigned to particular names circulated for a long time and only at the very end of a process of transmission were they given their place in a conglomerate or composite. This is a principal fact that leads them to see the document as a compilation and not a composition. While named authorities and sayings assigned to them do occur, the dialectic of argument is conducted outside the contributions of the specified sages. Sages' statements serve the purposes of the anonymous voice, rather than defining and governing the flow of argument. So the anonymous voice, "the Talmud," predominates even when individuals' sayings are utilized. Selecting and arranging whatever was in hand is the work of one hand, one voice. The materials are organized so as to facilitate explanations of the law's inner structure and potentiality, not to present a mere repertoire of ideas and opinions of interest for their own sake. The upshot is a sustained argument, not an anthology of relevant sayings. Such a cogent and ongoing argument is more likely the work of a single mind than of a committee, let alone of writers who lived over a period of ten or fifteen decades.

The role of individuals is unimportant. The paramount voice is that of "the Talmud." The rhetoric of the Talmud may be described very simply: a preference for questions and answers, a willingness then to test the answers and to expand through secondary and tertiary amplification, achieved through further questions and answers. The whole gives the appearance of the script for a conversation to be reconstructed, or an argument of logical possibilities to be reenacted, in one's own mind. In this setting we of course shall be struck by the uniformity of the rhetoric, even though we need not make much of the close patterning of language.

The voice of "the Talmud," moreover, authoritatively defines the mode of analysis. The inquiry is consistent and predictable; one argument differs from another not in supposition but only in detail. When individuals' positions occur, it is because what they have to say serves the purposes of "the Talmud" and its uniform inquiry. The inquiry is into the logic and the rational potentialities of a passage. To these dimensions of thought, the details of place, time, and even of an individual's philosophy, are secondary. All details are turned toward a common core of discourse. This, I maintain, is possible only because the document as whole takes shape in accord with an overriding program of inquiry and comes to expression in conformity with a single plan of rhetorical expression. To state the proposition simply: it did not just *grow*, but rather, someone *made* it up.

The Talmudic argument is not indifferent to the chronology of authorities. But the sequence in which things may be supposed to have been said – an early third century figure's saying before a later fourth century figure's saying – in no way explains the construction of protracted dialectical arguments. The argument as a whole, its direction and purpose, always govern the selection, formation, and ordering of the parts of the argument and their relationships to one another. The dialectic is determinative. Chronology, if never violated, is always subordinated. Once that fact is clear, it will become further apparent that "arguments" – analytical units of discourse – took shape at the end, with the whole in mind, as part of a plan and a program. That is to say, the components of the argument, even when associated with the names of specific authorities who lived at different times, were not added piece by piece, in order of historical appearance. They were put together whole and complete, all at one time, when the dialectical discourse was made up. By examining a few units of discourse, we shall clearly see the unimportance of the sequence in which people lived, hence of the order in which sayings (presumably) became available.

The upshot is that chronological sequence, while not likely to be ignored, never determines the layout of a unit of discourse. We can never definitively settle the issue of whether a unit of discourse came into being through a long process of accumulation and agglutination, or was shaped at one point – then, at the end of the time in which named authorities flourished – with everything in hand and a particular purpose in mind. But the more likely of the two possibilities is clearly the latter. It seems to me likely that the purposes of dialectical argument determined not only which available sayings were selected for inclusion, but also the order and purpose in accordance with which sayings were laid out. In my view it follows that the whole – the unit of discourse as we know it – was put together at the end. At that point everything was in hand, so available for arrangement in accordance with a principle other than chronology, and in a rhetoric common to all sayings. That other principle will then have determined the arrangement, drawing in its wake resort to a single monotonous voice: "the Talmud." The principle is logical exposition, that is to say, the analysis and dissection of a problem into its conceptual components. The dialectic of argument is framed not by considerations of the chronological sequence in which sayings were said but by attention to the requirements of reasonable exposition of the problem. That is what governs.

In this regard, then, the Talmud is like the Mishnah in its fundamental literary traits, therefore also in its history. The Mishnah was formulated in its rigid, patterned language and carefully organized and enumerated groups of formal substantive cognitive units, in the very processes in which it also was redacted. Otherwise the correspondences between redactional program and formal and patterned mode of articulation of ideas cannot be explained, short of invoking the notion of a literary miracle. The Talmud, too, underwent a process of redaction, in which fixed and final units of discourse were organized and put together. The probably antecedent work of framing and formulating these units of discourse appears to have gone on at a single period, among a relatively small number of sages working within a uniform set of literary conventions, at roughly the same time, and in approximately the same way. The end product, the Talmud, like the Mishnah, is uniform and stylistically coherent, generally consistent in modes of thought and speech, wherever we turn. That accounts for the single voice that leads us through the dialectical and argumentative analysis of the Talmud. That voice is ubiquitous and insistent.

By comparing the Tosefta's with the Bavli's treatment of the Mishnah, I have shown in these pages not only that the Bavli's approach to Mishnah commentary differs from the Tosefta's (which is hardly surprising), *but that the differences in the aggregate are uniform and predictable.* Comparison yields a fixed and coherent set of contrasts. The Bavli's authorship referred to a coherent and cogent program of exegetical principles when they turned to the Mishnah, which is shown by the fact that the differences between the two documents are fixed and predictable. Since the Bavli is commonly (mis)represented as a mere conglomeration of whatever people happen to have received – a sedimentary piece of writing, not a planned and considered one, the result of many centuries of accumulation, not the work of a generation or two of thoughtful writers – these results provide a detailed argument against one proposition and in favor of another. The upshot is that we may speak about "the Talmud," its voice, its purposes, its mode of constructing a view of the Israelite world. The reason is that, when we claim "the Talmud" speaks, we replicate both the main lines of chronology and the literary character of the document. These point toward the formation of the bulk of materials – its units of discourse – in a process lasting (to take a guess) about half a century, prior to the ultimate arrangement of these units of discourse around passages of the Mishnah and the closure and redaction of the whole into the document we now know and admire.

4

The Two Vocabularies of Symbolic Discourse in Judaism

In some of the canonical writings of the Judaism of the Dual Torah we find lists of different things joined with the words, "another matter." These different things cohere in two ways. First, all of them address the same verse of Scripture. Second, each of these other matters in its way proves to make the same statement as all the others. Appeal is made to what we shall see is a standard and fixed repertoire of things – events, named persons, objects or actions or attitudes. As these things combine and recombine, a thing appearing here next to one thing, there next to another, they appear to serve, as words serve, to make statements. Strung out in one selection of the larger vocabulary of symbols, they then say this, and in another set of choices made out of the same larger repertoire, they say that. How do people know which things to choose for which statement? Why combine this with that? These are the questions I bring to the examination of the numerous sets of "another matter" composites, scattered throughout the canonical literature. Along these same lines a restricted repertoire of persons, events, and objects is portrayed in synagogue art, mosaics, frescoes, carvings, and the like. Were we to compose a list of things that might have been chosen, it would prove many times longer than the list of things that in fact were selected and represented by the synagogue artists. Do these, too, make a statement, and if they do, how are we to discern what it is?

I. One Symbolic Language or Two?

In asking the literary and artistic evidence to tell us about shared convictions of a common Judaism attested for in late antiquity in both written and iconic representation, how are we to proceed? It is, first, by identifying the sort of evidence that serves. We limit our analysis to this public and official evidence: in literature, what anonymous, therefore genuine, authorities accepted as the implicit message of canonical and normative writings, on the one hand, in art, what synagogue communities accepted as the tacit message of the symbols in the presence of which they addressed God, on the other. Excluded then are expressions deriving from individuals, for example, letters or private writings, ossuaries and sarcophagi, which can have spoken for everyone, but assuredly spoke only for one person.

Second, within public evidence, what do we identify as potential evidence for a shared vocabulary, common to evidence in both media, written and iconic, and shared among all sponsors – artists and patrons, authors, authorships, and authorities of canonical collections alike? The answer must be, the evidence provided by symbolic discourse, which is the only kind of discourse that can be shared between iconic and literary expressions. By definition, iconic evidence does not utilize the verbal medium, and, it goes without saying, our documents are not illustrated and never were. But the two bodies of publicly accepted and therefore authoritative evidence on the symbolic structure of Judaism deliver their messages in the same way. So constant reference to a set of what we must classify as not facts but symbols will turn up evidence for a shared vocabulary.

We wish to bring the restricted iconic vocabulary of the synagogue into juxtaposition, for purposes of comparison and contrast, with that of the canonical books. What we want to know is first, whether the same symbols occur in both media of expression, literary and artistic. Second, we ask whether the same messages are set forth in the two media, or whether the one medium bears one message, the other a different message. If, as I claim, symbolic discourse in the fifth and sixth centuries took place in Judaic expression in both synagogues and among sages, the one in iconic, the other in written form, we naturally wonder whether the symbols were the same, and whether the discourse was uniform. To frame the question in simple terms: were the same people saying the same things in different media, verbal and iconic, or were different people saying different things in different media? At the present, elementary stage in our reading of the symbolic discourse, we cannot expect to reach a final answer to that question. But the outlines of an answer even now will emerge when we compare the symbolic language of synagogue iconography with the symbolic language framed in verbal terms in the rabbinic Midrash compilations.

Effecting that comparison, of course, requires us to frame in the same medium the two sets of symbols. But which medium – the visual (in our imagination at least) or the verbal? If it is to be the verbal, then we have to put into words the symbolic discourse portrayed for us on the walls and floors of synagogues. That is to say, we have to set forth in a manner parallel to symbolic discourse in words the symbols of the *etrog* and *lulab*, *shofar*, and *menorah*. And we have to do so in accord with the rhetoric forms that sustain symbolic discourse in verbal media. But by definition that cannot be done. First, symbolic discourse in verbal form requires us to identify and parse a verse of Scripture. But which verse for the items at hand? Second, we should require a clear notion of the meanings of the iconic symbols. But among the possible meanings, for example, for the *shofar* – the New Year and Day of Atonement, Abraham binding Isaac on the altar, the coming of the Messiah, Moriah and the Temple – which are we to choose? And, third, since the symbolic discourse in iconic form obviously joins the *etrog* and *lulab*, *shofar*, and *menorah*, translating the three (or four) into words demands a theory about what those symbols mean when they are joined in order, arrangement, and context. What do the symbols mean together that they do not mean when apart? The key is why certain combinations yield meaning, others, gibberish (Moses and Sennacherib on the same list, for example). Since we do not have that key for symbolic discourse in iconic form, we had best consider the alternative.

Since we cannot meet any one of those three conditions, we take the other road, which is open. That is, we must proceed to translate into visual images (in our imagination) the symbols in verbal form that we have. Here, by definition, we have access to the context defined by a parsed verse of Scripture. We have a fairly explicit statement of the meanings imputed to the symbols, that is, the use in communication that is made of them. And, finally, the combinations of symbols for symbolic discourse are defined for us by our documents – again by definition. So we can turn to written evidence and ask whether, in verbal form, symbolic discourse seems to converge with the counterpart discourse in the iconic medium.

II. Connections, Iconic and Verbal

To repeat: the key to a symbolic code must explain what connects with one thing but not with another, and how correct connections bear meaning, incorrect ones, gibberish. Now to carry forward that notion, we ask whether a single key will serve to decipher the code of symbolic discourse that governs symbols in both verbal and iconic form. The answer to that lies on the surface, in the connections that people made between and among symbols. If we find the same connections in both verbal and literary symbolic discourse, we may not know what message (if any) is supposed to be communicated, but we have solid grounds for thinking that a single code governs discourse in both media. On the other hand, if we find no combinations of the same symbols in both media of symbolic discourse, then we have no reason to suppose that a single key will explain what connects one thing with some other, or why one thing connects with this other, but not with that other. So the first test of whether or not we have a single discourse in two media or two distinct discourses, symbolic in both cases, but differentiated by media, is whether or not we find the same combination of symbols in both writing and iconography. We take as our test case symbols we now know are very commonly connected, the *etrog* and *lulab, shofar,* and *menorah.* Our question is simple: when in writing people refer to the *lulab* or to the *shofar,* do they forthwith think also of the *menorah* and *shofar,* along with the *lulab,* or the *lulab* and *menorah,* along with the *shofar*? Or do they think of other things – or of nothing? As a matter of fact, they think of other things, but not, in the case of the *lulab,* of the *menorah* and *shofar*; and not, in the case of the *shofar,* of the *lulab* and *menorah.* So the combinations that people make in writing are not of the same symbols as the combinations that people make iconically. In combination with these things that in iconic form clearly connect with one thing and not some other, they think of other things.[1]

To satisfy ourselves that the distinctive combination of symbols – the *etrog* and *lulab, shofar,* and *menorah* – does not occur in the literary form of discourse (whether symbolic or otherwise) I present a brief account of how the Midrash compilations treat two of the three items, the first and second. Here we shall see that the persistent manipulation of the three symbols as a group finds no counterpart in writing. The connections are different.

We begin with the *lulab* and ask whether representation of that symbol provokes discourse pertinent, also, to the symbols of the *shofar* and of the *menorah,* or even only of the *menorah.* The answer is negative. Other matters, but not those matters, are invoked. Leviticus Rabbah Parashah XXX treats the festival of Tabernacles (*Sukkot*), the sole point in the liturgical calendar at which the *etrog* and *lulab* pertain. The base verse that is treated is Lev. 23:39-40: "You shall take on the first day the fruit of goodly trees, branches of palm trees and boughs of leafy trees and willows of the brook," and that statement is taken to refer, specifically, to the *lulab.* When sages read that verse, they are provoked

---

[1] I state categorically that in no case of symbolic discourse in verbal form that I have examined do we find the combinations of the *etrog* and *lulab, shofar,* and *menorah.* I have taken the more difficult problem, therefore, of moving beyond the specific evidence of discourse of a symbolic character and treating propositional discourse as well.

to introduce the consideration of Torah study; the opening and closing units of the pertinent unit tell us what is important:

Leviticus Rabbah XXX

I.1   A   "[On the fifteenth day of the seventh month, when you have gathered in the produce of the land, you shall keep the feast of the Lord seven days....] And you shall take on the first day [the fruit of goodly trees, branches of palm trees and boughs of leafy trees and willows of the brook, and you shall rejoice before the Lord your God for seven days]" (Lev. 23:39-40).

      B   R. Abba bar Kahana commenced [discourse by citing the following verse]: "Take my instruction instead of silver, [and knowledge rather than choice gold]" (Prov. 8:10).

      C   Said R. Abba bar Kahana, "Take the instruction of the Torah instead of silver.

      D   "'Why do you weigh out money? Because there is no bread' (Isa. 55:2).

      E   "'Why do you weigh out money to the sons of Esau [Rome]? [It is because] "there is no bread," because you did not sate yourselves with the bread of the Torah.

      F.   "'And [why] do you labor? Because there is no satisfaction' (Isa. 55:2).

      G   "'Why do you labor while the nations of the world enjoy plenty? 'Because there is no satisfaction,' that is, because you have not sated yourselves with the wine of the Torah.

      H   "For it is written, 'Come, eat of my bread, and drink of the wine I have mixed'" (Prov. 9:5).

I.6   A   Said R. Abba bar Kahana, "On the basis of the reward paid for one act of 'taking,' you may assess the reward for [taking] the palm branch [on the festival of Tabernacles].

      B   "There was an act of taking in Egypt: 'You will take a bunch of hyssop' (Ex. 12:22).

      C.   "And how much was it worth? Four *manehs*.

      D   "Yet that act of taking is what made Israel inherit the spoil at the Sea, the spoil of Sihon and Og, and the spoil of the thirty-one kings.

      E   "Now the palm branch, which costs a person such a high price, and which involves so many religious duties – how much the more so [will a great reward be forthcoming on its account]!"

      F.   Therefore Moses admonished Israel, saying to them, "And you shall take on the first day..." (Lev. 23:40).

Whatever the sense of *lulab* to synagogue artists and their patrons, the combination with the *etrog, menorah,* and *shofar* was critical; nothing in these words invokes any of those other symbols. What would have led us to suppose some sort of interchange between iconic and verbal symbols? If we had an association, in iconic combinations, of the Torah shrine and the *etrog* and *lulab*, we might have grounds on which to frame the hypothesis that some sort of association – comparison, contrast for instance – between the symbols of the festival of Tabernacles and Torah study was contemplated. Here there is no basis for treating the iconic symbols as convergent with the manipulation of those same symbols in propositional discourse. It suffices to say that nowhere in Leviticus Rabbah Parashah XXX do we find reason to introduce the other iconic symbols.

What about the *shofar*? If we speak of that object, do we routinely introduce the *etrog, lulab, menorah*? The answer is negative. We introduce other things, but not those things. Pesiqta deRab Kahana *pisqa* XXIII addresses the New Year as described at Lev. 23:24: "In the seventh month on the first day of the month you shall observe a day of solemn rest, a memorial proclaimed with blast of trumpets." The combination of judgment and the end of days is evoked in the following. I give two distinct statements of the same point, to show that it is in context an important motif.

Pesiqta deRab Kahana XXIII

II.2 A *For I will make a full end of all the nations* (Jer. 30:11): As to the nations of the world, because they make a full end (when they harvest even the corner) of their field, concerning them Scripture states: *I will make a full end of all the nations among whom I scattered you.*

  B But as to Israel, because they do not make a full end (when they harvest, for they leave the corner) of their field, therefore: *But of you I will not make a full end* (Jer. 30:11).

  C *I will chasten you in just measure, and I will by no means leave you unpunished* (Jer. 30:11). I shall chasten you through suffering in this world, so as to leave you unpunished in the world to come.

  D. When?

  E. *In the seventh month, [on the first day of the month]* (Lev. 23:24).

Pesiqta deRab Kahana XXIII

V.1 A R. Jeremiah commenced [discourse by citing the following verse]: *"The wise man's path of life leads upward, that he may avoid Sheol beneath* (Prov. 15:24).

  B *"The path of life*: The path of life refers only to the words of the Torah, for it is written, as it is written, *It is a tree of life* (Prov. 3:18).

  C *"Another matter: The path of life*: The path of life refers only to suffering, as it is written, *The way of life is through rebuke and correction* (Prov. 6:23).

  D *"[The wise man's path]...leads upward* refers to one who looks deeply into the Torah's religious duties, [learning how to carry them out properly].

  E "What, then, is written just prior to this same matter (of the New Year)?

  F. *"When you harvest your crop of your land, you will not make a full end of the corner of your field* (Lev. 23:22).

  G "The nations of the world, because they make a full end when they harvest even the corner of their field, [and the rest of the matter is

> as is given above: *I will make a full end of all the nations among whom I have driven you* (Jer. 30:11). But Israel, because they do not make a full end when they harvest, for they leave the corner of their field, therefore, *But of you I will not make a full end* (Jer. 30:11). *I will chasten you in just measure, and I will by no means leave you unpunished* (Jer. 30:11)." When? *In the seventh month, on the first day of the month, [you shall observe a day of solemn rest, a memorial proclaimed with blast of trumpets]* (Lev. 23:24)].

What is now linked is Israel's leaving the corner of the field for the poor, Lev. 23:22, the connection between that verse and the base verse here is what is expounded. Then there is no evocation of the *menorah* or the *lulab* and *etrog* – to state the obvious. We can explain what is combined, and we also can see clearly that the combination is deliberate. That means what joined elsewhere but not here bears another message but not this one. An elaborate investigation of the role of *lulab* and *etrog*, *shofar* and *menorah* in the literary evidence of the Midrash compilations hardly is required to demonstrate what we now know: we find no evidence of interest in the combination of those items in literary evidence.

III. One Version of a Symbolic Structure of Judaism: Symbols in Verbal Form

Now that we have identified the iconic representations that form, if not a system, at least a structure – items that occur together in a given manner – let me set forth one example of what I conceive to be a fine statement of the symbolic structure of Judaism as symbols in verbal form set forth in such a structure. This will serve as an example of the kinds of symbols we find in general in symbolic discourse in verbal form.[2] Our further experiments will then draw on the symbolic repertoire that a single passage – counterpart to a single synagogue – has supplied. The character of the passage will explain why I have chosen it as representative:

Genesis Rabbah LXX

VIII.2 A. "As he looked, he saw a well in the field":

B. R. Hama bar Hanina interpreted the verse in six ways [that is, he divides the verse into six clauses and systematically reads each of the clauses in light of the others and in line with an overriding theme:

C. "'As he looked, he saw a well in the field': this refers to the well [of water in the wilderness, Num. 21:17].

---

[2]A reference to the materials gathered in *Symbol and Theology in Judaism*, Chapters Four through Seven will suffice to show that what follows is reasonably proposed as representative.

D. "'...and lo, three flocks of sheep lying beside it': specifically, Moses, Aaron, and Miriam.

E. "'...for out of that well the flocks were watered': for from there each one drew water for his standard, tribe, and family."

F. "And the stone upon the well's mouth was great":

G. Said R. Hanina, "It was only the size of a little sieve."

H [Reverting to Hama's statement:] "'...and put the stone back in its place upon the mouth of the well': for the coming journeys. [Thus the first interpretation applies the passage at hand to the life of Israel in the wilderness.]

VIII.3   A. "'As he looked, he saw a well in the field': refers to Zion.

B. "'...and lo, three flocks of sheep lying beside it': refers to the three festivals.

C. "'....for out of that well the flocks were watered': from there they drank of the Holy Spirit.

D. "'...The stone on the well's mouth was large': this refers to the rejoicing of the house of the water drawing."

E. Said R. Hoshaiah, "Why is it called 'the house of the water drawing'? Because from there they drink of the Holy Spirit."

F. [Resuming Hama b. Hanina's discourse:] "'...and when all the flocks were gathered there': coming from 'the entrance of Hamath to the brook of Egypt' (1 Kgs. 8:66).

G. "'...the shepherds would roll the stone from the mouth of the well and water the sheep': for from there they would drink of the Holy Spirit.

H "'...and put the stone back in its place upon the mouth of the well': leaving it in place until the coming festival. [Thus the second interpretation reads the verse in light of the Temple celebration of the festival of Tabernacles.]

VIII.4   A. "'...As he looked, he saw a well in the field': this refers to Zion.

B. "'...and lo, three flocks of sheep lying beside it': this refers to the three courts, concerning which we have learned in the Mishnah: **There were three courts there, one at the gateway of the Temple Mount, one at the gateway of the courtyard, and one in the chamber of the hewn stones [M. San. 11:2].**

C. "'...for out of that well the flocks were watered': for from there they would hear the ruling.

D. "The stone on the well's mouth was large': this refers to the high court that was in the chamber of the hewn stones.

E. "'...and when all the flocks were gathered there': this refers to the courts in session in the Land of Israel.

F. "'...the shepherds would roll the stone from the mouth of the well and water the sheep': for from there they would hear the ruling.

G. "'...and put the stone back in its place upon the mouth of the well': for they would give and take until they had produced the ruling in all the required clarity." [The third interpretation reads the verse in light of the Israelite institution of justice and administration.]

VIII.5   A. "'As he looked, he saw a well in the field': this refers to Zion.

B. "'...and lo, three flocks of sheep lying beside it': this refers to the first three kingdoms [Babylonia, Media, Greece].

C. "'...for out of that well the flocks were watered': for they enriched the treasures that were laid up in the chambers of the Temple.

D. "'...The stone on the well's mouth was large': this refers to the merit attained by the patriarchs.

E. "'...and when all the flocks were gathered there': this refers to the wicked kingdom, which collects troops through levies over all the nations of the world.

F. "'...the shepherds would roll the stone from the mouth of the well and water the sheep': for they enriched the treasures that were laid up in the chambers of the Temple.

G. "'...and put the stone back in its place upon the mouth of the well': in the age to come the merit attained by the patriarchs will stand [in defense of Israel].' [So the fourth interpretation interweaves the themes of the Temple cult and the domination of the four monarchies.]

VIII.6 A. "'As he looked, he saw a well in the field': this refers to the Sanhedrin.

B. "'...and lo, three flocks of sheep lying beside it': this alludes to the three rows of disciples of sages that would go into session in their presence.

C. "for out of that well the flocks were watered': for from there they would listen to the ruling of the law.

D. "'...The stone on the well's mouth was large': this refers to the most distinguished member of the court, who determines the law decision.

E. "'...and when all the flocks were gathered there': this refers to disciples of the sages in the Land of Israel.

F. "'...the shepherds would roll the stone from the mouth of the well and water the sheep': for from there they would listen to the ruling of the law.

G. "'...and put the stone back in its place upon the mouth of the well': for they would give and take until they had produced the ruling in all the required clarity." [The fifth interpretation again reads the verse in light of the Israelite institution of legal education and justice.]

VIII.7 A. "'As he looked, he saw a well in the field': this refers to the synagogue.

B. "'...and lo, three flocks of sheep lying beside it': this refers to the three who are called to the reading of the Torah on weekdays.

C. "'...for out of that well the flocks were watered': for from there they hear the reading of the Torah.

D. "'...The stone on the well's mouth was large': this refers to the impulse to do evil.

E. "'...and when all the flocks were gathered there': this refers to the congregation.

F. "'...the shepherds would roll the stone from the mouth of the well and water the sheep': for from there they hear the reading of the Torah.

G. "'...and put the stone back in its place upon the mouth of the well': for once they go forth [from the hearing of the reading of the Torah] the impulse to do evil reverts to its place." [The sixth and last

interpretation turns to the twin themes of the reading of the Torah
in the synagogue and the evil impulse, temporarily driven off
through the hearing of the Torah.]

Genesis Rabbah LXX

IX.1   A.   R. Yohanan interpreted the statement in terms of Sinai:

B.   "'As he looked, he saw a well in the field': this refers to Sinai.

C.   "'...and lo, three flocks of sheep lying beside it': these stand for the
priests, Levites, and Israelites.

D.   "'...for out of that well the flocks were watered': for from there they
heard the Ten Commandments.

E.   "'...The stone on the well's mouth was large': this refers to the
Presence of God."

F.   "...and when all the flocks were gathered there":

G.   R. Simeon b. Judah of Kefar Akum in the name of R. Simeon: "All of
the flocks of Israel had to be present, for if any one of them had
been lacking, they would not have been worthy of receiving the
Torah."

H   [Returning to Yohanan's exposition:] "'...the shepherds would roll
the stone from the mouth of the well and water the sheep': for from
there they heard the Ten Commandments.

I.   "'...and put the stone back in its place upon the mouth of the well':
'You yourselves have seen that I have talked with you from
Heaven' (Ex. 20:19)."

The six themes read in response to the verse cover (1) Israel in the
wilderness, (2) the Temple cult on festivals with special reference to
Tabernacles, (3) the judiciary and government, (4) the history of Israel
under the four kingdoms, (5) the life of sages, and (6) the ordinary folk
and the synagogue. The whole is an astonishing repertoire of
fundamental themes of the life of the nation, Israel: at its origins in the
wilderness, in its cult, in its institutions based on the cult, in the history
of the nations, and, finally, in the twin social estates of sages and
ordinary folk, matched by the institutions of the master disciple circle
and the synagogue. The vision of Jacob at the well thus encompassed the
whole of the social reality of Jacob's people, Israel. Yohanan's exposition
adds what was left out, namely, reference to the revelation of the Torah
at Sinai. The reason I have offered the present passage as a fine instance
of symbolic discourse is now clear. If we wished a catalogue of the kinds
of topics addressed in passages of symbolic, as distinct from
propositional, discourse, the present catalogue proves compendious and
complete. Our next experiment is now possible.

IV. Symbolic Discourse in Iconic and in Verbal Form: Convergence or Divergence?

A simple set of indicators will now permit us to compare the character of symbolic discourse in verbal form with that in iconic form. The question is now a simple one. Let us represent the Judaism – way of life, worldview, theory of who or what is "Israel"? – set forth by symbolic discourse in iconic form effected by the *lulab* and *etrog, shofar,* and *menorah*. Let us further represent the Judaism set forth by symbolic discourse in verbal form, treating as exemplary a discourse that will appeal to visual images appropriate to the themes of Israel in the wilderness, the Temple cult, the judiciary and government, Israel under the four kingdoms and at the end of time, the life of sages, ordinary folk and the synagogue. How do these statements relate?

The shared program will cover the standard topics that any symbolic structure of representing a religion should treat: holy day, holy space, holy word, holy man (or: person), and holy time or the division of time.

	ICONIC SYMBOLS	VERBAL SYMBOLS
Holy day	NewYear/Tabernacles/Hanukkah	
	Tabernacles/Pentecost/Passover	
Holy space	Temple	Temple/Zion
Holy man/person	No evidence	The sage and disciple
Holy time	Messiah (*shofar*)	Four kingdoms/Israel's rule
Holy event	Not clear	Exodus from Egypt

The important point of convergence is unmistakable: holy space for both symbolic structures is defined as the Temple and Mount Zion. That is hardly surprising; no Judaic structure beyond 70 ignored the Temple, and all Judaisms, both before and after 70, found it necessary to deal in some way with, to situate themselves in relationship to, that paramount subject. So the convergence proves systemically inert, indeed trivial.

Whether or not we classify the treatment of holy time as convergent or divergent is not equally obvious to me. Both structures point toward the end of time; but they speak of it differently. So far as the *shofar* means to refer to the coming of the Messiah, the gathering of the exiles, and the restoration of the Temple, as, in the synagogue liturgy, it does, then the iconic representation of the messianic topic and the verbal representation of the same topic diverge. For the latter, we see in our case and in much of the evidence surveyed earlier, frames the messianic topic in terms of Israel's relationship with the nations, and the principal interest is in Israel's rule over the world as the fifth and final monarchy. That theme is repeated in symbolic discourse in verbal form, and, if the *shofar* stands in synagogue iconography for what the synagogue liturgy says, then the message, if not an utterly different one, is not identical with that delivered by symbols in verbal form. So here matters are ambiguous.

The unambiguous points of divergence are equally striking. The most important comes first. Symbolic discourse in verbal form privileges the three festivals equally and utterly ignores Hanukkah. So far as the *menorah* stands for Hanukkah – and in the literary evidence, the association is firm – we may suppose that, just as the *lulab* and *etrog* mean to evoke Tabernacles, and the *shofar*, the New Year and Day of Atonement, so the *menorah* speaks of Hanukkah. Then we find a clear and striking divergence. That the *menorah* serves, also, as an astral symbol is well established, and if that is the fact, then another point of divergence is registered. In symbolic discourse in verbal form I find not one allusion to an astral ascent accessible to an Israelite, for example, through worship or Torah study. A survey of the cited passages yields not a trace of the theme of the astral ascent.

The second point of divergence seems similarly unambiguous. Critical to the symbolic vocabulary of the rabbinic Midrash compilations is study of the Torah, on the one side, and the figure of the sage and disciple, on the other. I do not find in the extant literary sources a medium for identifying the figure of the sage and the act of Torah study with the symbols of the *lulab, etrog, shofar,* or *menorah.* Quite to the contrary, the example given above from Leviticus Rabbah counterpoises the *lulab* with words of Torah. The fact that these are deemed opposites, with the former not invoking, but provoking, the latter, by itself means little. But it does not sustain the proposition that the combined symbols before us, the *lulab, etrog, shofar,* and *menorah,* somehow mean to speak of Torah study and the sage.

Thus far we see marks of convergence and also of divergence. What happens if we present a sizable repertoire of the combinations of symbols in verbal form that we find in Song of Songs Rabbah? We wonder whether a sizable sample of combinations of symbols in verbal form intersects, or even coincides, with the simple vocabulary, in combination, paramount in iconic representations of symbolic discourse in synagogues. A list drawn from combinations of symbols in verbal form found in Song of Songs Rabbah must include the following items:

Joseph, righteous men, Moses, and Solomon;

patriarchs as against princes, offerings as against merit, and Israel as against the nations; those who love the king, proselytes, martyrs, penitents;

first, Israel at Sinai; then Israel's loss of God's presence on account of the golden calf; then God's favoring Israel by treating Israel not in accord with the requirements of justice but with mercy;

Dathan and Abiram, the spies, Jeroboam, Solomon's marriage to Pharaoh's daughter, Ahab, Jezebel, Zedekiah;

Israel is feminine, the enemy (Egypt) masculine, but God the father saves Israel the daughter;

Moses and Aaron, the Sanhedrin, the teachers of Scripture and Mishnah, the rabbis;

the disciples; the relationship among disciples, public recitation of teachings of the Torah in the right order; lections of the Torah;

the spoil at the Sea = the Exodus, the Torah, the Tabernacle, the ark;

the patriarchs, Abraham, Isaac, Jacob, then Israel in Egypt, Israel's atonement and God's forgiveness;

the Temple where God and Israel are joined, the Temple is God's resting place, the Temple is the source of Israel's fecundity;

Israel in Egypt, at the Sea, at Sinai, and subjugated by the gentile kingdoms, and how the redemption will come;

Rebecca, those who came forth from Egypt, Israel at Sinai, acts of loving kindness, the kingdoms who now rule Israel, the coming redemption;

fire above, fire below, meaning heavenly and altar fires; Torah in writing, Torah in memory; fire of Abraham, Moriah, bush, Elijah, Hananiah, Mishael, and Azariah;

the Ten Commandments, show fringes and phylacteries, recitation of the *Shema* and the Prayer, the tabernacle and the cloud of the Presence of God, and the *mezuzah*;

the timing of redemption, the moral condition of those to be redeemed, and the past religious misdeeds of those to be redeemed;

Israel at the Sea, Sinai, the Ten Commandments; then the synagogues and schoolhouses; then the redeemer;

the Exodus, the conquest of the Land, the redemption and restoration of Israel to Zion after the destruction of the first Temple, and the final and ultimate salvation;

the Egyptians, Esau and his generals, and, finally, the four
kingdoms;

Moses' redemption, the first, to the second redemption in the time of
the Babylonians and Daniel;

the litter of Solomon: the priestly blessing, the priestly watches, the
Sanhedrin, and the Israelites coming out of Egypt;

Israel at the Sea and forgiveness for sins effected through their
passing through the Sea; Israel at Sinai; the war with Midian; the
crossing of the Jordan and entry into the Land; the house of the
sanctuary; the priestly watches; the offerings in the Temple; the
Sanhedrin; the Day of Atonement;

God redeemed Israel without preparation; the nations of the world
will be punished, after Israel is punished; the nations of the
world will present Israel as gifts to the royal messiah, and here
the base verse refers to Abraham, Isaac, Jacob, Sihon, Og,
Canaanites;

the return to Zion in the time of Ezra, the Exodus from Egypt in the
time of Moses;

the patriarchs and with Israel in Egypt, at the Sea, and then before
Sinai;

Abraham, Jacob, Moses;

Isaac, Jacob, Esau, Jacob, Joseph, the brothers, Jonathan, David, Saul,
man, wife, paramour;

Abraham in the fiery furnace and Shadrach, Meshach, and
Abednego, the Exile in Babylonia, now with reference to the
return to Zion.

Now let us ask ourselves some very simple questions: is there a single
combination of symbols in verbal form in this catalogue that joins the
same symbols as are combined in the symbolic vocabulary in iconic form
that we have identified? No, not a single combination coincides. Is there
a paramount role assigned to Tabernacles at all? No, in this catalogue
the principal holy day must be Passover, commemorating the Exodus,
which occurs throughout, and not Tabernacles, commemorating the life
in the wilderness, which occurs not at all. Is there a single set of symbols
in verbal form that can be served by the *shofar*? No, not one. Whatever
the sense or meaning that we assign to the *shofar*, if the *shofar* stands for
Isaac on the altar with Abraham ready to give him up, if it stands for the
New Year and Day of Atonement, or if it stands for the coming of the
Messiah and the ingathering of the exiles, makes no difference.

On the list before us, I see no point at which the *shofar* in any of these
senses will have served uniquely well or even served at all. Whatever
the sense of the *menorah*, whether invoking Hanukkah or an astral ascent,

makes no difference; it is not a useful symbol, in verbal form, for any of the combinations before us; it cannot have served in a single recombinant statement. The *lulab* and *etrog* so far as I can see can have claimed no place, in verbal form, in any of our combinations. While, therefore, at certain points the symbolic discourse in verbal form surely intersects with the same mode of discourse in iconic form, in the aggregate, symbolic discourse represented in one medium bears one set of symbols – singly or in combination! – and symbolic discourse in another medium appeals to a quite different set of symbols altogether.

V. What Is at Stake in Analyzing Symbolic Discourse?

The divergent vocabularies utilized for symbolic discourse point toward divergent symbolic structures: two Judaisms, one of them represented by the symbolic discourse in verbal form of the rabbinic Midrash compilations, the other by symbolic discourse in iconic form represented by the synagogue ornamentation. That conclusion[3] calls into question the possibility of describing, on the basis of the written and archaeological evidence, a Judaism that is attested, in one way or another, by all data equally; a Judaism to which all data point; a Judaism that is implicit in or presupposed by, all data. If there were such a uniform and encompassing Judaic structure, sufficiently commodious to make a place for diverse Judaisms, then it is at the level of symbolic discourse that we should find evidence for its description. For in the preverbal evidence of symbols should emerge messages, at least significations, that can be expressed in the diverse ways that verbal discourse makes possible (and may even require). But, as we have now seen, when we compare the symbols that reach us in two distinct forms, the verbal and the iconic, we find ourselves at an impasse. The verbal symbols serve in one way, the iconic in another, and while they occasionally converge, the points of convergence are few, those of divergence, overwhelming.

At stake in these observations is whether we can locate evidence that, beyond any text or artifact, a body of thought – a religious system, encompassing a worldview, way of life, and theory of the social group

---

[3]Goodenough's work led to precisely the same conclusion. But the proposition that "Judaism" was diverse, meaning that there was more than a single normative Judaism, has been implicit, if not entirely conventional, even from the late 1940s. The most effective and important statement of the divergence of literary and iconic evidence in general emerged in the earliest volumes of Goodenough's *Jewish Symbols in the Greco-Roman Period.* The recognition that that divergence pointed toward more than a single Judaic system or Judaism, and the specification of the meaning of that fact, derive principally from my *oeuvre.*

that held the one and realized the other – circulated. What is this "Judaism" to which my hypothesis makes reference? It is, as a matter of working hypothesis, that set of conceptions and convictions that the generality of Jews took for granted, but that no particular group of Jews made distinctively its own. It is the Judaism that all writings, all art, presupposes. And at stake in this analysis of the repertoire of symbols is, Can we claim that a single such structure served to sustain all Judaisms? Is there such a unitary, single, and harmonious "symbolic structure of Judaism" at all? That body of thought, that Judaism – perhaps formed of one Judaism out of many, perhaps identified as what is essential throughout, perhaps defined as the least common denominator among all evidence, is then alleged to be presupposed in all documents and by all artifacts. The answer to that question is simple. No evidence permits us to describe that one Judaism. So far as we are limited to the demonstration made possible by evidence – for example, sources, whether in writing or in iconic or other material form, the kind of evidence that is most general, fundamental, and susceptible of homogenization – the picture is clear and one-sided.

Now some who posit a "Judaism" of which we are informed appeal not to evidence (for example of a given period) but to an a priori: they maintain that there is one Judaism by definition and without demonstration that informs all Judaisms, or to which all Judaisms refer or give testimony. Some scholars just now claim that there is a "Judaism out there," beyond any one document, to which in some way or other all documents in various ways and proportions are supposed to attest.[4]

---

[4]One statement of the matter derives from the British medievalist, Hyam Maccoby. Writing in the symposium, "The Mishnah: Methods of Interpretation," *Midstream*, October, 1986, p. 41, he states:

> Neusner argues that since the Mishnah has its own style and program, nothing outside it is relevant to explaining it. This is an obvious fallacy. The Mishnah, as a digest, in the main, of the legal...aspect of rabbinic Judaism, necessarily has its own style and program. But to treat it as something intended to be a comprehensive compendium of the Oral Torah is simply to beg the question. Neusner does not answer the point, put to him by E. P. Sanders and myself, that the liturgy being presupposed by the Mishnah, is surely relevant to the Mishnah's exegesis. Nor does he answer the charge that he ignores the aggadic material within the Mishnah itself, for example, Abot; or explain why the copious aggadic material found in roughly contemporaneous works should be regarded as irrelevant. Instead he insists that he is right to carry out the highly artificial project of deliberately closing his eyes to all aggadic material, and trying to explain the Mishnah without it.

Maccoby exhibits a somewhat infirm grasp of the nature of the inquiry before us. If one starts with the question, "What does the authorship of this book mean to

They even know how to describe that Judaism even though no document and no artifact on its own attests to its character. And that Judaism – which I label, the "Judaism out there," that is, prior to, encompassing all documents, each with its own distinctive representation of a Judaic system, which I label a "Judaism in here" is readily defined. Indeed, that Judaism beyond, or beside, all evidences and data is such as to impose its judgment upon our reading of every sentence, every paragraph, every book.[5] Now if such evidence is to be located, then nonverbal data such

---

say, when read by itself and not in light of other, *later* writings?" then it would be improper to import into the description of the system of the Mishnah in particular (its "Judaism" – hence "Judaism: The evidence of the Mishnah") conceptions not contained within its pages. Tractate Abot, for one instance, cites a range of authorities who lived a generation beyond the closure of the (rest of the) Mishnah and so is ordinarily dated to about 250, with the Mishnah dated to about 200. On that basis how one can impute to the Mishnah's system conceptions first attaining closure half a century later I do not know. To describe the Mishnah, for example, as a part of "rabbinic Judaism" is to invoke the premise that we know, more or less on its own, just what this "rabbinic Judaism" is and says. But what we cannot show we do not know. And, as a matter of established fact, many conceptions dominant in the final statements of rabbinic Judaism to emerge from late antiquity play no material role whatsoever in the system of the Mishnah, or, for that matter, of Tosefta and Abot. No one who has looked for the conception of "the Oral Torah" in the Mishnah or in the documents that succeeded it, for the next two hundred years, will understand why Maccoby is so certain that the category of Oral Torah, or the myth of the Dual Torah, applies at all. For the mythic category of "Oral Torah" makes its appearance, so far as I can discern, only with the Yerushalmi and not in any document closed prior to that time, although a notion of a revelation over and above Scripture – not called "Oral Torah" to be sure – comes to expression in Abot. Implicitly, moreover, certain sayings of the Mishnah itself, for example, concerning rulings of the Torah and rulings of sages, may contain the notion of a secondary tradition, beyond revelation. But that tradition is not called "the Oral Torah," and I was disappointed to find that even in the Yerushalmi the mythic statement of the matter, so far as I can see, is lacking. It is only in the Bavli, for example, in the famous story of Hillel and Shammai and the convert at B. Shab. 30B-31A, that the matter is fully explicit. Now, if Maccoby maintains that the conception circulated in the form in which we know it, for instance, in the Yerushalmi in truncated form or in the Bavli in complete form, he should supply us with the evidence for his position. As I said, what we cannot show we do not know. And most secular and academic scholarship concurs that we have no historical knowledge a priori, though in writing Maccoby has indeed in so may words maintained that we do. In fact the documents of formative Judaism do yield histories of ideas, and not every idea can be shown to have taken part in the statement of each, let alone all, of the documents. But those who appeal to a Judaism out there, before and beyond all of the documents, ignore that fact.

[5]Commenting on this debate with Maccoby and Sanders, William Scott Green says, Sanders "reads rabbinic texts by peering through them for the ideas (presumably ones Jews or rabbis believed) that lie beneath them." This runs

as we have examined should have provided it, for here, by definition, in symbols, we should have been able to demonstrate that, whatever verbal explanations people attached to symbols, a fundamentally uniform symbolic structure served all Judaisms that our evidence attests.

Now to test the proposition that there was one Judaism nourishing all Judaisms, I have proposed to find out whether we may discern *the* symbolic system or structure upon which all Judaic systems relied, with which every system contended (each in its own way to be sure), and, above all, to which all Jews responded. If we had been able to show that

---

parallel to Maccoby's criticism of my "ignoring" a variety of conceptions I do not find in the Mishnah. Both Maccoby and Sanders, in my view, wish to discuss what *they* think important and therefore to ignore what the texts themselves actually talk about, as Green says, "the materials that attracted the attention and interest of the writers" (Personal letter, January 17, 1985). In my original review I pointed out that Sanders' categories ignore what the texts actually say and impose categories the Judaic-rabbinic texts do not know. Sanders, in Green's judgment, introduces a distinct premise:

> For Sanders, the religion of Mishnah lies unspoken beneath its surface; for Neusner it is manifest in Mishnah's own language and preoccupations (William Scott Green in his Introduction, *Approaches to Ancient Judaism* (Chicago, 1980: Scholars Press for Brown Judaic Studies II), p. xxi).

Generalizing on this case, Green further comments in those more general terms that bring us into a debate on the nature of religion and culture, and that larger discourse lends importance to what, in other circumstances, looks to be a mere academic argument. Green writes as follows:

> The basic attitude of mind characteristic of the study of religion holds that religion is certainly in your soul, likely in your heart, perhaps in your mind, but never in your body. That attitude encourages us to construe religion cerebrally and individually, to think in terms of beliefs and the believer, rather than in terms of behavior and community. The lens provided by this prejudice draws our attention to the intense and obsessive belief called "faith," so religion is understood as a state of mind, the object of intellectual or emotional commitment, the result of decisions to believe or to have faith. According to this model, people have religion but they do not do their religion. Thus we tend to devalue behavior and performance, to make it epiphenomenal, and of course to emphasize thinking and reflecting, the practice of theology, as a primary activity of religious people....The famous slogan that "ritual recapitulates myth" follows this model by assigning priority to the story and to peoples' believing the story, and makes behavior simply an imitation, an aping, a mere acting out.

Now as we reflect on Green's observations, we of course recognize what is at stake. It is the definition of religion, or, rather, what matters in or about religion, emerging from one reading of Protestant theology and Protestant religious experience. But in these pages, only a limited aspect of the larger debate is at issue.

a single symbolic vocabulary and a single syntax and grammar of symbolic discourse served in all extant testimonies to all Judaisms – iconic, literary evidence alike, then we should have begun to pursue the problem of defining that Judaism through the principles of symbolic discourse.

Why choose the symbolic data? Because, it seems to me, it is through the study of what is inchoate and intuitive, a matter of attitude and sentiment and emotion rather than of proposition and syllogism, therefore through the analysis of symbolic structure, that we should be able to discern and set forth the things on which everyone agreed. As a matter of hypothesis, that is the repertoire of conventions and accepted facts that made possible the characteristic disagreements, small and fundamental alike, that until now have required us in studying the formation of Judaism in the first seven centuries of the Common Era [=A.D.] to describe diverse Judaisms and not a single Judaism. All our evidence derives from Judaisms, however, which is to say, every piece of writing speaks for a particular authorship, every work of art met the specifications of a single artist and patron. True, the writings resort to conventions, for instance, the entirety of the Scriptures of ancient Israel known as the Old Testament (for Christianity) or the Written Torah (for Judaism). Admittedly, the artists and their patrons implicitly accepted whatever restrictions they recognized, made their selections, as to both themes and representational conventions, from whatever repertoire they deemed self-evident.

Why give privilege to symbolic discourse rather than the propositional kind? Consider the alternative. Were we to have compiled a list of facts we must suppose everyone knew, the truths everyone affirmed, we should still not have an answer to the question of the character of normative theological statements which all known parties affirmed. True, in the canonical literature of the Judaism of the Dual Torah, for one example, we are able to list matters of fact, bearing profound meaning, that all authorships of all documents affirm, but that serve to deliver the particular message of none of them in particular. Beyond that important, indeed paramount, corpus of literary evidence for Judaism, moreover, we may take note of beliefs and practices implicit in buildings set aside for cultic purposes – Temple and synagogue before 70, synagogue afterward – and take for granted that, whatever characterized as special one place or group, all Jews everywhere came to synagogues to do pretty much the same thing, such as say prayers and read the Torah. But our task is not only or mainly to outline the range of agreement, the consensus of practice and belief, that characterized all those Jews represented by the evidence now in our hands. For much that people affirmed was commonplace, and facts, by themselves, do not give us the outlines of a vivid religious system. We saw a case in point when we found that both symbolic vocabularies appealed to the Temple in one way or another. But that proved an inert fact, when we proceeded to see the symbolic vocabulary of Song of Songs Rabbah, which proved to have nothing in common with the symbolic vocabulary that dominated in the provenance of synagogue life.

That observation draws us to another initiative in the description of this single prior Judaism, of which we are informed a priori: What are the facts that mattered to everybody, that delivered the same message in behalf of everybody? That is a different question, since it introduces the consideration of consequence. We hardly need to demonstrate that all Jews took as fact the miraculous exodus from Egypt or the giving of the Torah by God to Moses at Sinai. But any supposition that those facts meant the same thing to everybody, that all Judaic systems through the same facts made the same statement, not only is unfounded, but also is unlikely. Facts that serve a particular system in a particular way – the revelation of the Torah at Sinai to convey the systemically emblematic myth of the Dual Torah, for instance, in the Judaism of the Dual Torah we call rabbinic – by definition do not serve any other system in that same way. So when we want to know about consequence, we inquire into facts that mattered in all systems in the same way; those are the facts that tell us about the religious and cultural system as a whole that we call Judaism, not a Judaic system or the aggregate of Judaic systems, but simply Judaism, encompassing, ubiquitous, universal, and, as a matter of fact, particular also to every circumstance and system.

A shared symbolic vocabulary can have overcome a further difficulty, namely, the very particular context to which the evidence in hand attests. The evidence we have, deriving as it does from particular synagogues or distinct books or sets of books, by its nature tells us about not the general but the specific: this place, for synagogues, that authorship, for compilers of books, that authority, for decisors of canonical composites. One authorship then makes the points important to it in its context, for its purpose – by nature, therefore, not merely informative but polemical. And another authorship will speak of what matters in its setting. Drawing two or more documents together not uncommonly yields the impression of different people talking about different things to different people. So, too, with the art of synagogues: it is by definition local and particular because a given synagogue, however it may conform to conventions of architecture and decoration that we discern throughout, still attests only to what its community – the people who paid for the building, directed its construction and decoration, and contentedly worshiped within it for centuries – desired. If we were to collect all the statements of all the books and homogenize them, we should produce a hodgepodge of contradictions and – more to the point – nonsequiturs. And if we were to combine all the representations on all the walls and floors of all the synagogues of late antiquity, what we should have would be a list of everything everywhere. In both cases, the labor of collecting and arranging everything about everything from everywhere yields uninterpretable, indeed, unintelligible facts.

Our task – to define the kind of evidence that forms the *lingua franca* of all documents and all iconic evidence alike – then demanded attention to symbolic discourse. By definition, then, documentary evidence read propositionally will not serve, because that kind of evidence excludes the mute but eloquent message of art, such as we have in abundance. The artistic evidence by itself cannot be read at all, since in its nature it communicates other than propositions and through other than syllogistic media. Arrangements of figures, to be sure, tell stories, and narrative art can be read as to its tale. But the sense and meaning the tale is meant to convey appeals to representation, and that, by definition, forms a distinctive medium for communication in other than verbal ways.

VI. The Way Forward: Symbolic Discourse and the Description of the Theology of the Dual Torah

The theology of the Judaism of the Dual Torah that took shape in late antiquity comes to expression not only in propositional but also in symbolic discourse.[6] The "another matter" construction, constitutes a play on what I have been calling theological "things" – names, places, events, actions deemed to bear theological weight and to affect attitude and action. The play is worked out by a reprise of available materials, composed in some fresh and interesting combination. When three or more such theological "things" are combined, they form a theological structure, and, viewed all together, all of the theological "things" in a given document constitute the components of the entire theological structure that the document affords. The propositions portrayed visually, through metaphors of sight, or dramatically, through metaphors of action and relationship, or in attitude and emotion, through metaphors that convey or provoke feeling and sentiment, when

---

[6]At this point I cannot claim that the principal or the preferred medium is symbolic discourse, but my instinct tells me that that is the case. However, what is required is the analysis of theological discourse in a given, important document and the comparison of what is said in propositional discourse, what in analytical, what in symbolic, and what in narrative. When we have classified and compared the media for theological expression in a given document in which theology forms a principal theme or topic, we shall be able to proceed with this discussion, which is tangential to the argument of this book.

translated into language prove familiar and commonplace. The work of the theologian in this context is not to say something new or even persuasive, for the former is unthinkable by definition, the latter unnecessary in context. It is rather to display theological "things" in a fresh and interesting way, to accomplish a fresh exegesis of the canon of theological "things."

Until now, in my judgment, we have had no method of description of theology in the canonical writings of the Judaism of the Dual Torah that is both coherent with the character of the documents and also cogent with the tasks of theological description. By theological description I mean the account of the principles and ideas concerning God's relationship with Israel (for we speak of a Judaism) that form the foundation and substrate of the thought that comes to expression in a variety of canonical writings. The problem has been the character of the documents and their mode of theological discourse. It is not that the writers speak only in concrete terms; we could readily move from their detail to our abstraction and speak in general terms about the coherence of prevailing principles of a theological order.

The problem has been much more profound. We face a set of writings that clearly mean to tell us about God and God's relationship to Israel, and Israel and Israel's relationship to God. The authorships a priori exhibit the conviction that the thoughts of the whole are cogent and coherent, since they prove deeply concerned to identify contradiction, disharmony, and incoherence, and remove it.[7] But we have not known how to find the connections between what they have written and the structure or system of thought that leads them to say, in detail, the things that they say. In working out a theory of the symbolic discourse, I hope to make possible the description of the symbolic structure set forth by that discourse, and, thereby, I further mean to open the way to the description of the theology.

The reason that I think we must begin with the elementary analysis of how discourse proceeds is simple. The kind of evidence before us offers little alternative. When we propose to describe the theological system to which a piece of well-crafted writing testifies, our task is easy when the writing to begin with discusses in syllogistic logic and within an appropriate program of propositions what we conceive to be theological themes or problems. Hence – it is generally conceded – we may legitimately translate the topically theological writings of Paul, Augustine, or Luther into the systematic and coherent theologies of those

---

[7]To prove that proposition, I need merely to point to the Talmud of Babylonia, the triumph of the Judaism of the Dual Torah and its definitive and complete statement.

three figures, respectively: finding order and structure in materials of a cogent theological character. But what about a literature that to begin with does not set forth theological propositions in philosophical form, even while using profoundly religious language for self-evidently religious purposes? And how shall we deal with a literature that conducts theological thought without engaging in analytical inquiry in the way in which the philosophers and theologians of Christianity have done, and did in that period?

Surely the canonical literature of this Judaism testifies to an orderly structure or system of thought, for the alternative is to impute to the contents of those writings the status of mere episodic and unsystematic observations about this and that. True, profound expressions of piety may exhibit the traits of intellectual chaos and disorder, and holy simplicity may mask confusion. But, as I have already stressed, such a description of the rabbinic literature of late antiquity, which I call the canon of the Judaism of the Dual Torah, defies the most definitive and indicative traits of the writings. These are order, system, cogency, coherence, proportion, fine and well-crafted thought.

To begin with, we have to justify the theological inquiry, through analysis of symbolism, into literature that self-evidently does not conform to the conventions of theological discourse to which Western civilization in its Greco-Roman heritage and Christian (and, as a matter of fact, Muslim) civilization in its philosophical formulation has made us accustomed. The Muslim and Christian theological heritage, formulated within the conventions of philosophical argument, joined by a much smaller Judaic theological corpus to be sure, does not allow us to read as a theological statement a single canonical writing of the Judaism of the Dual Torah of late antiquity. So if the literary canons of Western theology are to govern, then to begin with the literature of Judaism in its formative age by definition can present no theological order and system at all.

But that proposition on the face of it hardly proves compelling. For it is difficult for us to imagine a mental universe so lacking in structure, form, and order as to permit everything and its opposite to be said about God, to imagine a God so confused and self-contradictory as to yield a revelation lacking all cogency and truly unintelligible.[8] The very

---

[8] As a matter of fact, the great Zoroastrian theologians of the ninth century criticized Judaism (and other religions) on just this point, see my "Zoroastrian Critique of Judaism," reprinted in my *History of the Jews in Babylonia* (Leiden, 1969: E. J. Brill) 4:403-423. But not a single Judaic thinker, whether a philosopher or a theologian, whether in the Islamic philosophical tradition or the Western theological and philosophical tradition, has ever entertained the proposition that the God who gave the Torah is confused and arbitrary; and why should anyone

premises of all theology – that there is order, structure, and composition, proportion, and form, in God's mind, which in fact is intelligible to us through the medium of revelation properly construed – a priori render improbable the hypothesis that the canonical writings of the Judaism of the Dual Torah violate every rule of intelligible discourse concerning the principal and foundation of all being. If, after all, we really cannot speak intelligibly about God, the Torah, holy Israel, and what God wants of us, then why write all those books to begin with?

While theology may comprise propositions well-crafted into a cogent structure, about fundamental questions of God and revelation, the social entity that realizes that revelation, the attitudes and deeds that God, through revelation, requires of humanity, there is another way entirely. Theology – the structure and system, the perception of order and meaning of God, in God, through God – these may make themselves known otherwise than through the media of thought and expression that yield belief that theology can deliver its message to and through sentiment and emotion, heart as much as mind; it can be conviction as much as position, and conviction for its part also is orderly, proportioned, compelling of mind and intellect by reason of right attitude, rather than right proposition or position. That is to say, theology may set forth a system of thought in syllogistic arguments concerning the normative truths of the worldview, social entity, and way of life of a religious system. But theology may speak in other than dynamic and compelling argument, and theologians may accomplish their goal of speaking truth about God through other than the statements made by language and in conformity with the syntax of reasoned thought.

---

have thought so, when, after all, the entire dynamic of Judaic thought embodied within the great halakhic tradition from the Yerushalmi and Bavli forward has aimed at the systematization, harmonization and ordering of confusing, but never confused, facts of the Torah. There is, therefore, no possibility of finding in the Judaism of the Dual Torah the slightest hint of an unsystematic system, an atheological corpus of thought. True, a fixed truth of the theological system known as *die Wissenschaft des Judenthums* has maintained that "Judaism has no theology," but that system knew precisely what it meant by "Judaism," even while never explaining what it might mean by the "theology" that that "Judaism" did not have. But that is a problem of description, analysis, and interpretation for those who take an interest in the system of thought that underpins "Jewish scholarship" and Reform Judaism in particular, that is, specialists in the history of ideas in the nineteenth century, and of the nineteenth century in the twentieth century. These are not statements of fact that must be taken into account in describing, analyzing, and interpreting documents of the Judaism of the Dual Torah.

Theology may also address vision and speak in tactile ways; it may utilize a vocabulary of not proposition but opaque symbol (whether conveyed in visual or verbal media), and through portraying symbol, theology may affect attitude and emotion, speak its truth through other media than those of philosophy and proposition. From the time of Martin Buber's *Two Types of Faith*, now nearly four decades ago, people have understood that this other type of theology, the one that lives in attitude and sentiment and that evokes and demands trust, may coexist, or even compete, with the philosophical type to the discourse of which, in general, we are accustomed. Since, as a matter of fact, in the canonical writings of the Judaism of the Dual Torah we do not have a single sustained theological treatise, while we do have a monument to a faith that is choate and subject to fully accessible expression, we must teach ourselves how to describe the theology of the Judaism of the Dual Torah out of its fully exposed and complete, systemic documents, and, as we shall see, one way of doing so lies in the analysis of symbolism. Some documents utilize certain forms to make theological statements in symbolic discourse, the recombinant symbolic ones such as that which we have now examined. These documents communicate through symbolic discourse. They therefore point toward the symbolic structure that, for the Judaism of the Dual Torah, constitutes the theological statement and message.

Now that we recognize the mode of discourse that serves as one principal medium of theological speech, understanding that at stake was the portrayal of God in relationship to Israel, and Israel in relationship to God, rather than dialectical analysis of propositions concerning that relationship and the demonstration thereof, we may begin the task of the description of the theology of the Judaism of the Dual Torah – and even contemplate the further task, the theological description of the Judaism of the Dual Torah. Each thing will take place in its turn – God willing.

5

Re-presenting the Torah: Sifra's Rehabilitation of Taxonomic Logic and the Judaic Conception of How through the Torah We Enter The Mind of God

A profound exercise on the nature of Torah – God's revelation to humanity through Israel, Sifra engages in a two-pronged argument. On the one side, the authorship of Sifra calls into question the exercise of rule making through classification of like and contrast with the unlike, characteristic of the Mishnah's mode of thought. While, as a matter of fact, Sifra's authorship demonstrates that *Listenwissenschaft* is a self-evidently valid mode of demonstrating the truth of propositions the reason is that *the* source of the correct classification of things is Scripture and only Scripture. Without Scripture's intervention into the taxonomy of the world, we should have no knowledge at all of which things fall into which classifications and therefore are governed by which rules. How all of this leads us into a profound reconsideration of the nature of Torah – revelation – becomes clear only at the end.

Let us begin with a sustained example of the right way of doing things. Appropriately, what the opening composition of Sifra shows is the contrast between relying on Scripture's classification, and the traits imputed by Scripture to the taxa it identifies, and appealing to categories not defined and endowed with indicative traits by Scripture.

I. The Affirmation of *Listenwissenschaft*, Rightly Carried Out:

I:I
1.   A   "The Lord called [to Moses] and spoke [to him from the tent of
               meeting, saying, 'Speak to the Israelite people and say to them']"
               (Lev. 1:1):
         B.   He gave priority to the calling over the speaking.
         C.   That is in line with the usage of Scripture.
         D.   Here there is an act of speaking, and in connection with the
               encounter at the bush [Ex. 3:4: "God called to him out of the bush,
               'Moses, Moses'"], there is an act of speaking.
         E.   Just as in the latter occasion, the act of calling is given priority over
               the act of speaking [even though the actual word, "speaking" does
               not occur, it is implicit in the framing of the verse], so here, with
               respect to the act of speaking, the the act of calling is given priority
               over the act of speaking.
2.   A   No [you cannot generalize on the basis of that case,] for if you
               invoke the case of the act of speaking at the bush, which is the first
               in the sequence of acts of speech [on which account, there had to be
               a call prior to entry into discourse],
         B.   will you say the same of the act of speech in the tent of meeting,
               which assuredly is not the first in a sequence of acts of speech [so
               there was no need for a preliminary entry into discourse through a
               call]?
         C.   The act of speech at Mount Sinai (Ex. 19:3) will prove to the
               contrary, for it is assuredly not the first in a sequence of acts of
               speech, yet, in that case, there was an act of calling prior to the act
               of speech.
3.   A   No, [the exception proves nothing,] for if you invoke in evidence
               the act of speech at Mount Sinai, which pertained to all the
               Israelites, will you represent it as parallel to the act of speech in the
               tent of meeting, which is not pertinent to all Israel?
         B.   Lo, you may sort matters out by appeal to comparison and contrast,
               specifically:
         C.   The act of speech at the bush, which is the first of the acts of speech,
               is not of the same classification as the act of speech at Sinai, which is
               not the first act of speech.
         D.   And the act of speech at Sinai, which is addressed to all Israel, is not
               in the same classification as the act of speech at the bush, which is
               not addressed to all Israel.
4.   A   What they have in common, however, is that both of them are acts
               of speech, deriving from the mouth of the Holy One, addressed to
               Moses, in which case, the act of calling comes prior to the act of
               speech,
         B.   so that, by way of generalization, we may maintain that every act of
               speech which comes from the mouth of the Holy One to Moses will
               be preceded by an act of calling.
5.   A   Now if what the several occasions have in common is that all
               involve an act of speech, accompanied by fire, from the mouth of
               the Holy One, addressed to Moses, so that the act of calling was

given priority over the act of speaking, then in every case in which there is an act of speech, involving fire, from the mouth of the Holy One, addressed to Moses, should involve an act of calling prior to the act of speech.

B.   But then an exception is presented by the act of speech at the tent of meeting, in which there was no fire.

C.   [That is why it was necessary for Scripture on this occasion to state explicitly,] "The Lord called [to Moses and spoke to him from the tent of meeting, saying, 'Speak to the Israelite people and say to them']" (Lev. 1:1).

D.   That explicit statement shows that, on the occasion at hand, priority was given to the act of calling over the act of speaking.

I:II
1.   A.   ['"The Lord called to Moses and spoke to him from the tent of meeting, saying, 'Speak to the Israelite people and say to them'" (Lev. 1:1)]: Might one suppose that the act of calling applied only to this act of speaking alone?

B.   And how on the basis of Scripture do we know that on the occasion of all acts of speaking that are mentioned in the Torah, [there was a prior act of calling]?

C.   Scripture specifies, "from the tent of meeting,"

D.   which bears the sense that on every occasion on which it was an act of speaking from the tent of meeting, there was an act of calling prior to the act of speaking.

2.   A.   Might one suppose that there was an act of calling only prior to the acts of speech alone?

B.   How on the basis of Scripture do I know that the same practice accompanied acts of saying and also acts of commanding?

C.   Said R. Simeon, "Scripture says not only, '...spoke,...,' but '...and he spoke,' [with the inclusion of the *and*] meant to encompass also acts of telling and also acts of commanding."

The exercise of generalization addresses the character of God's meeting with Moses. The point of special interest is the comparison of the meeting at the bush and the meeting at the tent of meeting. And at stake is asking whether all acts of God's calling and talking with, or speaking to, the prophet are the same, or whether some of these acts are of a different classification from others. In point of fact, we are able to come to a generalization, worked out at I:I.5.A. And that permits us to explain why there is a different usage at Lev. 1:1 from what characterizes parallel cases. I:II.1-2 proceeds to generalize from the case at hand to other usages entirely, a very satisfying conclusion to the whole. I separate I:II from I:I because had I:I ended at 5, it could have stood complete and on its own, and therefore I see I:II as a brief appendix. The interest for my argument should not be missed. We seek generalizations, governing rules, that are supposed to emerge by the comparison and contrast of categories or of classifications. The way to do this is to follow the usage of Scripture, that alone. And the right way of doing things is illustrated.

The first lesson in Sifra's rehabilitation of taxonomic logic is then clear. Scripture provides reliable taxa and dictates the indicative characteristics of those taxa. The next step in the argument is to maintain that Scripture alone can set forth the proper names of things: classifications and their hierarchical order.

II. Scripture as the Sole Source of Valid Classification of Species

How then do we appeal to Scripture to designate the operative classifications? Here is a simple example of the alternative mode of classification, one that does not appeal to the traits of things but to the utilization of names by Scripture. What we see is how by naming things in one way, rather than in another, Scripture orders all things, classifying and, in the nature of things, also hierarchizing them.

VII:V

1.   A   "...and Aaron's sons the priests shall present the blood and throw the blood [round about against the altar that is at the door of the tent of meeting]":

     B.   Why does Scripture make use of the word "blood" twice [instead of using a pronoun]?

     C.   [It is for the following purpose:] How on the basis of Scripture do you know that if blood deriving from one burnt-offering was confused with blood deriving from another burnt-offering, blood deriving from one burnt-offering with blood deriving from a beast that has been substituted therefore, blood deriving from a burnt-offering with blood deriving from an unconsecrated beast, the mixture should nonetheless be presented?

     D.   It is because Scripture makes use of the word "blood" twice [instead of using a pronoun].

2.   A   Is it possible to suppose that while if blood deriving from beasts in the specified classifications, it is to be presented, for the simple reason that if the several beasts while alive had been confused with one another, they might be offered up,

     B.   but how do we know that even if the blood of a burnt-offering were confused with that of a beast killed as a guilt-offering, [it is to be offered up]?

     C.   I shall concede the case of the mixture of the blood of a burnt-offering confused with that of a beast killed as a guilt-offering, it is to be presented, for both this one and that one fall into the classification of Most Holy Things.

     D.   But how do I know that if the blood of a burnt-offering were confused with the blood of a beast slaughtered in the classification of peace-offerings or of a thanksgiving-offering, [it is to be presented]?

     E.   I shall concede the case of the mixture of the blood of a burnt-offering confused with that of a beast slaughtered in the classification of peace-offerings or of a thanksgiving-offering, [it is to be presented], because the beasts in both classifications produce blood that has to be sprinkled four times.

F.   But how do I know that if the blood of a burnt-offering were confused with the blood of a beast slaughtered in the classification of a firstling or a beast that was counted as tenth or of a beast designated as a passover, [it is to be presented]?

G   I shall concede the case of the mixture of the blood of a burnt-offering confused with that of a beast slaughtered in the classification of firstling or a beast that was counted as tenth or of a beast designated as a passover, [it is to be presented], because Scripture uses the word "blood" two times.

H   Then while I may make that concession, might I also suppose that if the blood of a burnt-offering was confused with the blood of beasts that had suffered an invalidation, it also may be offered up?

I.   Scripture says, "...its blood," [thus excluding such a case].

J.   Then I shall concede the case of a mixture of the blood of a valid burnt-offering with the blood of beasts that had suffered an invalidation, which blood is not valid to be presented at all.

K   But how do I know that if such blood were mixed with the blood deriving from beasts set aside as sin-offerings to be offered on the inner altar, [it is not to be offered up]?

L.   I can concede that the blood of a burnt-offering that has been mixed with the blood deriving from beasts set aside as sin-offerings to be offered on the inner altar is not to be offered up, for the one is offered on the inner altar, and the other on the outer altar [the burnt-offering brought as a freewill-offering, under discussion here, is slaughtered at the altar "...that is at the door of the tent of meeting," not at the inner altar].

M.   But how do I know that even if the blood of a burnt-offering was confused with the blood of sin-offerings that are to be slaughtered at the outer altar, it is not to be offered up?

N.   Scripture says, "...its blood," [thus excluding such a case].

In place of the rejecting of arguments resting on classifying species into a common genus, we now demonstrate how classification really is to be carried on. It is through the imposition upon data of the categories dictated by Scripture: Scripture's use of language. That is the force of this powerful exercise. No. 1 sets the stage, simply pointing out that the use of the word "blood" twice encompasses a case in which blood in two distinct classifications is somehow confused in the process of the conduct of the cult. In such a case it is quite proper to pour out the mixture of blood deriving from distinct sources, for example, beasts that have served different, but comparable purposes. We then systemically work out the limits of that rule, showing how comparability works, then pointing to cases in which comparability is set aside. Throughout the exposition, at the crucial point we invoke the formulation of Scripture, subordinating logic or in our instance the process of classification of like species to the dictation of Scripture. I cannot imagine a more successful demonstration of what the framers wish to say.

Now what about the Mishnah? In the following component of the composition, we see how the framers encompass the Mishnah's pertinent paragraph within their larger statement. This is integral to the program of the document as a whole, namely, the demonstration not merely that rules of the Mishnah derive from Scripture, which was accomplished in more than the way taken here, but also that the correct location of the Mishnah's rules is in the united Dual Torah set forth as The Torah.

VII:VIII

1.   A.   ["...and Aaron's sons the priests shall present the blood and throw the blood round about against the altar that is at the door of the tent of meeting":]

      B.   "...the blood...against the altar...":

      C.   but the one who tosses the blood is not standing against the altar, [but on the pavement]. [The rule for the disposition of the blood of a beast in the classification of a sin-offering is different. In that case the one who tosses the blood goes up to the altar to sprinkle the blood on the corners of the altar.]

2.   A.   Another rule: "...the blood...against the altar...":

      B.   **even though there is no valid meat [deriving from that offering. That is, if the meat got lost or was made unclean, nonetheless the blood is tossed on the altar. The operative criterion is the validity of the blood.]**

      C.   **How then shall interpret the verse [which equates the blood and the meat, hence if the one is invalidated, the other should also not be acceptable,] "And you shall offer your burnt-offerings, the flesh and the blood" (Deut. 12:27)?**

      D.   **Scripture joins the flesh to the blood. Just as blood is offered by being tossed on the altar, so flesh is offered by being tossed on the altar.**

      E.   **Might one think that one tosses the flesh but neatly piles up the meat on the altar?**

      F.   **Scripture says, "And the priest shall arrange them" Lev. 1:12), meaning, he tosses and arranges them, but he does not toss them and pile them up on the altar [T. Zeb. 4:2: Eliezer].**

No. 1 supplies an important clarification and also eliminates the classification of all acts of tossing the blood in a single genus, by maintaining that some acts of tossing the blood require remaining down below, others require the priests' ascending up the ramp and standing at the corner of the altar. No. 2 simply tacks on a fragment of a discussion of the base verse in another context altogether. That it hardly belongs is shown by the simple fact that the issue important at No. 2 is not raised anywhere in the present exposition. But the motive in including the passage of the Mishnah is self-evident.

III. The Reason for Scripture's Unique Power of Classification:
The Possibility of Polythetic Classification

From this simple account of the paramount position of Scripture in the labor of classification, let us turn to the specific way in which, because of Scripture's provision of taxa, we are able to undertake the science of *Listenwissenschaft*, including hierarchical classification, in the right way. What can we do because we appeal to Scripture, which we cannot do if we do not rely on Scripture? It is to establish the possibility of polythetic classification. We can appeal to shared traits of otherwise distinct taxa and so transform species into a common genus for a given purpose. Only Scripture makes that initiative feasible, so our authorship maintains. What is at stake? It is the possibility of doing precisely what the framers of the Mishnah wish to do. That is to join together masses of diverse data into a single, encompassing statement, to show the rule that inheres in diverse cases.

In what follows, we shall see an enormous, coherent, and beautifully articulated exercise in the comparison and contrast of many things of a single genus. The whole holds together, because Scripture makes possible the statement of all things within a single rule. That is, as we have noted, precisely what the framers of the Mishnah proposed to accomplish. Our authorship maintains that only by appeal to The Torah is this fete of learning possible. If, then, we wish to understand all things all together and all at once under a single encompassing rule, we had best revert to The Torah, with its account of the rightful names, positions, and order, imputed to all things.

XXII:I

1.   A.   [With reference to M. Men. 5:5:] There are those [offerings which require bringing near but do not require waving, waving but not bringing near, waving and bringing near, neither waving nor bringing near: These are offerings which require bringing near but do not require waving: the meal-offering of fine flour and the meal-offering prepared in the baking pan and the meal-offering prepared in the frying pan, and the meal-offering of cakes and the meal-offering of wafers, and the meal-offering of priests, and the meal-offering of an anointed priest, and the meal-offering of gentiles, and the meal-offering of women, and the meal-offering of a sinner. R. Simeon says, "The meal-offering of priests and of the anointed priest – bringing near does not apply to them, because the taking of a handful does not apply to them. And whatever is not subject to the taking of a handful is not subject to bringing near,"] [Scripture] says, "When you present to the Lord a meal-offering that is made in any of these ways, it shall be brought [to the priest who shall take it up to the altar]":

B. What requires bringing near is only the handful alone. How do I know that I should encompass under the rule of bringing near the meal-offering?

C. Scripture says explicitly, "meal-offering."

D. How do I know that I should encompass all meal-offerings?

E. Scripture says, using the accusative particle, "the meal-offering."

2. A. I might propose that what requires bringing near is solely the meal-offering brought as a freewill-offering.

B. How do I know that the rule encompasses an obligatory meal-offering?

C. It is a matter of logic.

D. Bringing a meal-offering as a freewill-offering and bringing a meal-offering as a matter of obligation form a single classification. Just as a meal-offering presented as a freewill-offering requires bringing near, so the same rule applies to a meal-offering of a sinner [brought as a matter of obligation], which should likewise require bringing near.

E. No, if you have stated that rule governing bringing near in the case of a freewill-offering, on which oil and frankincense have to be added. will you say the same of the meal-offering of a sinner (Lev. 5:11), which does not require oil and frankincense?

F. The meal-offering brought by a wife accused of adultery will prove to the contrary, for it does not require oil and frankincense, but it does require bringing near [as is stated explicitly at Num. 5:15].

G. No, if you have applied the requirement of bringing near to the meal-offering brought by a wife accused of adultery, which also requires waving, will you say the same of the meal-offering of a sinner, which does not have to be waved?

H. Lo, you must therefore reason by appeal to a polythetic analogy [in which not all traits pertain to all components of the category, but some traits apply to them all in common]:

I. the meal-offering brought as a freewill-offering, which requires oil and frankincense, does not in all respects conform to the traits of the meal-offering of a wife accused of adultery, which does not require oil and frank incense, and the meal-offering of the wife accused of adultery, which requires waving, does not in all respects conform to the traits of a meal-offering brought as a freewill-offering, which does not require waving.

J. But what they have in common is that they are alike in requiring the taking up of a handful and they are also alike in that they require bringing near.

K. I shall then introduce into the same classification the meal-offering of a sinner, which is equivalent to them as to the matter of the taking up of a handful, and also should be equivalent to them as to the requirement of being drawn near.

L. But might one not argue that the trait that all have in common is that all of them may be brought equally by a rich and a poor person and require drawing near, which then excludes from the common classification the meal-offering of a sinner, which does not conform to the rule that it may be brought equally by a rich and a poor person, [but may be brought only by a poor person,] and such an offering also should not require being brought near!

M   [The fact that the polythetic classification yields indeterminate results means failure once more, and, accordingly,] Scripture states, "meal-offering,"

N   with this meaning: all the same are the meal-offering brought as a freewill-offering and the meal-offering of a sinner, both this and that require being brought near.

The elegant exercise draws together the various types of meal-offerings and shows that they cannot form a classification of either a monothetic or a polythetic character. Consequently, Scripture must be invoked to supply the proof for the classification of the discrete items. The important language is at H-J: these differ from those, and those from these, but what they have in common is.... Then we demonstrate, with our appeal to Scripture, the sole valid source of polythetic classification, M. And this is constant throughout Sifra.

The power of taxonomic logic is to draw together all manner of data and to set them into relationship with one another. And, in that context, the strength of argument of our authorship is manifest: the capacity to demonstrate how diverse things relate through points in common, so long as the commonalities derive from a valid source. And that leads us to the central and fundamental premise of all: Scripture, its picture of the classifications of nature and supernature, its account of the rightful names and order of all things, is the sole source for that encompassing and generalizing principle that permits scientific inquiry into the governing laws to take place.

Does the Mishnah's authorship know the principle of polythetic taxonomy? Indeed it does, as a mere glance at the opening pericopes of Mishnah-tractate Baba Qama Chapters One and following tells us: "The distinctive feature of the ox is not the same as that of the crop-destroying beast, nor is the indicative feature of the crop-destroying beast the same as that of the ox; nor is that of either of these, which are animate, the same as that of fire, which is inanimate, nor is the indicative trait of any of these, who ordinarily go out and do damage, the same as that of the pit, which does not go out and do damage. What they have in common is that they may cause injury and you are responsible to take responsibility for them, and if one of them caused injury, whoever is responsible pays restitution by handing over land of the highest quality that he has," so M. B.Q. 1:1. Polythetic taxonomy presents no surprises to the framer of the cited passage. Not only so, but a glance at the exegesis of this passage supplied in the successor writings will reassure us that the framers of the Mishnah surely have made reference, in defining the indicative traits of the taxa under discussion, to Scripture.

Where our authorship will take issue with that of the Mishnah is in those cases, and they are exceedingly numerous, in which the Mishnah's authorship effects its taxonomy, and, consequently, its hierarchical classification, without reference to the dictates of Scripture. In our authorship's view, that is never a reliable procedure. To borrow language that originally served another debate altogether: at stake is the principle, systematically advanced by Sifra, of proof *sola Scriptura*.

IV. Sifra's Theory of Torah and Revelation: The Rehabilitation of Taxonomic Logic within the Re-presentation of The Torah

In consequence of Scripture's provision of valid taxa, we can, of course, proceed to invoke and utilize precisely that logic of hierarchical classification that the framers of the Mishnah employed. Here is a full statement of the consequence of adopting Scripture's categories. We find the appeal to comparison and contrast time and again, and at no point do we distinguish one category from another in such wise as to make comparison no longer logical. Let us now examine specific illustrations of the right way of pursuing that same taxonomic logic of hierarchical classification that the Mishnah's framers have carried out in the wrong way. Our first example allows us to see an unimpeded flow of classification: this is like that, therefore this falls under the rule of that, pure and simple.

CCIX:I
1.   A.   ["If a man lies with a beast, he shall be put to death, and you shall kill the beast. If a woman approaches any beast and lies with it, you shall kill the woman and the beast; they shall be put to death, their blood is upon them" (Lev. 20:13-16).]
       B.   "If a man":
       C.   excluding a minor.
       D.   "lies with a beast":
       E.   whether large or small.
2.   A.   "he shall be put to death":
       B.   through stoning.
       C.   You say that it is through stoning. But perhaps it is some another of the modes of execution decreed by the Torah.
       D.   Scripture says, "and you shall kill the beast."
       E.   Here we find reference to "killing," and elsewhere likewise we find the same ["If a woman approaches any beast and lies with it, you shall kill the woman and the beast; they shall be put to death, their blood is upon them"].
       F.   Just as elsewhere "killing" involves stoning [as is proven presently], so here too, "killing" involves stoning.
3.   A.   We thereby derive the penalty for one who commits sexual relations upon a beast. Whence do we find the penalty for serving as the passive partner in sexual relations with a beast?

B. Scripture says, "Whoever lies with a beast will surely die" (Ex. 22:18).

C. Since [in the context of the present verse] it cannot speak of one who commits sexual relations upon a beast, interpret it to provide an admonition against serving as the passive partner in sexual relations with a beast.

4. A. We have derived the penalty for both the active and the passive partner to sexual relations with a beast.

B. Whence then the admonition?

C. Scripture says, "And you shall not lie with any beast and defile yourself with it, [neither shall any woman give herself to a beast to lie with it; it is perversion]" (Lev. 18:23).

D. We thereby derive the admonition for the active partner. Whence the admonition for the passive partner?

E. "Scripture says, 'No Israelite man may be a cult prostitute' (Deut. 23:18).

F. "And further: 'And there were also cult prostitutes in the land' (1 Kgs. 14:24)," the words of R. Ishmael.

G. R. Aqiba says, "It is not necessary to derive proof from those passages. Lo, Scripture says, 'And you shall not lie with any beast [and defile yourself with it],' you shall not lie as passive partner."

5. A. "If a woman approaches any beast and lies with it, you shall kill the woman and the beast; they shall be put to death, [their blood is upon them]":

B. You maintain that it is through stoning, but perhaps it is through any one of the other forms of inflicting the death penalty that the Torah specifies?

C. Scripture says, "his blood is upon him,"

D. and elsewhere we find the same language, "their blood is on their head" (Lev. 20:27).

E. Just as that usage elsewhere refers to inflicting the death penalty through stoning, so the same language here involves stoning.

6. A. We thereby have derived the penalty. Whence the admonition?

B. Scripture says, "Neither shall any woman give herself to a beast to lie with it; it is perversion" (Lev. 18:23).

The predictable materials, Nos. 1-6, go through the necessary motions. What is important is the givenness of the classifications. This demonstrates beyond doubt that our authorship accepts the principles of *Listenwissenschaft*, with like following the rule of like, unlike following the opposite of that rule. Once categories are defined, no one will call into question the basic logic of comparison and contrast in a system of hierarchization.

V. Silence and the Articulated Critique of the Mishnah's Logic: When Sifra's Authorship Does and Does Not Demolish the Logic of Comparison and Contrast

While setting forth its critique of the Mishnah's utilization of the logic of comparison and contrast in hierarchical classification, the authorship of Sifra is careful not to criticize the Mishnah. Its position favors restating the Mishnah within the context of Scripture, not rejecting the conclusions of the Mishnah, let alone its authority. Consequently, when we find a critique of applied reason divorced from Scripture, we rarely uncover an explicit critique of the Mishnah, and when we find a citation of the Mishnah, we rarely uncover linkage to the ubiquitous principle that Scripture forms the source of all classification and hierarchy. In the following passage we see how our authorship treats the Mishnah when it wishes to cite passage of the Mishnah and also to set into the correct relationship categories of things that the Mishnah sets forth.

XXI:I

1.   A   "If your offering is a meal-offering on a griddle, [it shall be of choice flour with oil mixed in, unleavened. Break it into bits and pour oil on it; it is a meal-offering:]"

      B.   This teaches that the offering requires the use of a utensil [for its preparation and presentation].

2.   A   Reference is made twice to the word "your offering." ["If your offering is a meal-offering on a griddle, it shall be of choice flour with oil mixed in, unleavened. Break it into bits and pour oil on it; it is a meal-offering. If your offering is a meal-offering in a pan, it shall be made of choice flour in oil."] This serves to establish an analogy.

      B.   Here "your offering" forms the basis for a classification. Just as 'your offering" here involves adding oil and saturating the meal with oil, so "your offering," used later invokes the requirement of adding oil and saturating the meal with oil.

      C.   And, further, just as the classification of "your offering" noted below involves putting on oil in a utensil prior to the preparation of the offering, so "your offering" in the present instance also involves putting on oil in a utensil prior to the preparation of the offering.

Here the classification of two species into a single genus does succeed, so No. 2, with both species subject to the same rule. No objection is raised.

XXI:II

1.   A.   "...choice flour with oil mixed in":

      B.   This teaches that one mixes the oil into the fine flour. [M. Men. 6:3A-B: All meal-offerings prepared in a utensil (baking pan or frying pan) require three applications of oil: pouring oil into the utensil, stirring the meal into the oil, and then again putting oil into the utensil.]

      C.   Rabbi says, "And as to the loaves [baked in an oven, one stirs them with oil (M. Men. 6:3C)] ["In the case of loaves, they stir oil into them...as it is said, 'Loaves mixed with oil'" (Lev. 7:12) [T. Men. 8:7B-C]."

D. They said to him, "But in connection with the cakes that accompany the thank-offering, is it not said, 'Flour mixed with oil' (Lev. 23:13)" (T. Tos. 8:7C]?

E. "And it is possible to stir in only with flour. [B. Men. 75a: It was not possible to mingle the cakes with oil but only the flour.]

F. How does one do this? One puts oil into the flour and stirs it in, then oil into a utensil and prepares it, and stirs it, and mixes [the flour] with oil. [Tosefta's version: "How does one do this? He puts oil into the utensil and fries it. Then he puts oil into the flour and stirs it and breaks it up. And he then pours oil on it as one pours oil on pounded beans" (T. Men. 8:5C-D].

G. Rabbi says, "One puts oil into a utensil and prepares it, and stirs it, and then mixes the flour with oil, and then goes and pours oil on it."

All I see here is a reworking of the language we find, also, in the Mishnah and the Tosefta. I see no motif of critique of the Mishnah for its omission of prooftexts. Perhaps it is implicit or tacit; but, if so, in it I find no stakes at all. Our authorship knows that the Mishnah contains the Torah, and that is why, I maintain, it has undertaken the work it presents to us here.

XXI:III

1. A. "unleavened":
   B. Might one suppose that this is merely the desirable way of doing the deed [but still, optional]?
   C. Scripture says, "...it will be...,"
   D. meaning that it is a firmly-established requirement of the rite.
2. A. "Break it into bits":
   B. Might one suppose that that means into two pieces?
   C. Scripture says, "bits."
3. A. Might one suppose one should turn it into crumbs?
   B. Scripture says, "...it...."
   C. *It* is to be broken into pieces, but the pieces are not to be broken into pieces.
4. A. As to the meal-offering of an Israelite, one folds it one into two, then two into four parts, and divides it at each fold. As to the meal-offering of priests, one folds it one into two, then two into four parts, but does not divide it. As to the meal-offering of the anointed priest, one did not fold it up. R. Simeon says, "The meal-offering of priests and the meal-offering of an anointed priest are not subject to the requirement of breaking up, because they are not subject to the taking of a handful, and anything which is not subject to the taking of a handful is not subject to breaking up" [M. Men. 6:4B-G].

The systematic exegesis leads to a restatement of the Mishnah's rule in the Mishnah's language. But of course the point important to the Mishnah, which is the definition of the rule of breaking up in accord with the hierarchization of the castes, is utterly outside the frame of reference.

XXI:IV
1. A. "Break it into bits and pour oil on it; it is a meal-offering":
    B. This serves to extend the rule of breaking up to all meal-offerings.
    C. Might one suppose that that same rule extends also to the two loaves and the show bread?
    D. Scripture says, "it...."
    E. How come you encompass all meal-offerings but exclude the two loaves and the show bread?
    F. After Scripture has used inclusionary language, it has then made an exclusion.
    G. Just as these are distinguished in that part of the offering is placed on the altar fires, so excluded are the two loaves of bread and the show bread, none of which is put on the altar fire [but all of which is given to the priests to eat].
2. A. "Break it into bits and pour oil on it; it is a meal-offering":
    B. This serves to extend the rule of pouring oil on the offering to all meal-offerings.
    C. Might one suppose that that rule extends also to a meal-offering that is baked?
    D. Scripture says, "on it."
    E. I shall then exclude the loaves, but not the wafers?
    F. Scripture says, "it is [a meal-offering]," [encompassing wafers under the rule of applying oil].

The clarification introduces other forms of meal-offering and speciates them.

XXI:V
1. A. "If your offering is a meal-offering in a pan, it shall be made of choice flour in oil":
    B. **What is the difference between a baking pan and a frying pan? "The frying pan has a cover, and the baking pan has no cover,"** the words of R. Yosé the Galilean. R. Hananiah b. Gamaliel says, **"A frying pan is deep, and what is cooked in it is spongy, and a baking pan is flat, and what is cooked in it is hard"** [M. Men. 5:8C-E].
2. A. "...it shall be made of choice flour in oil":
    B. This teaches that preparing this meal-offering requires putting oil in a utensil prior to preparing the flour.

Once more we simply review the Mishnah's clarification of Scripture, now represented the Mishnah as merely a secondary amplification of what Scripture says.

The laconic passage at hands contains an important fact. When the Mishnah is cited by our authorship, it will be presented as part of the factual substrate of the Torah. When the logic operative throughout the Mishnah is subjected to criticism, the language of the Mishnah will rarely, if ever, be cited in context. The operative language in dealing with the critique of the applied logic of *Listenwissenschaft* as represented by the framers of the Mishnah ordinarily is, "is it not a matter of logic?" Then the sorts of arguments against taxonomy pursued outside of the framework of Scripture's classifications will follow. When, by contrast, the authorship of Sifra wishes to introduce into the context it has already established a verbatim passage of the Mishnah, it will ordinarily, though not always, use, *mikan amru*, which, in context, means, "in this connection [sages] have said." It is a simple fact that when the intent is to demolish improper reasoning, the Mishnah's rules in the Mishnah's language rarely, if ever, occur. When the authorship of Sifra wishes to incorporate paragraphs of the Mishnah into their re-presentation of The Torah, they will do so either without fanfare, as in the passage at hand, or by the neutral joining language "in this connection [sages] have said."

VI. *The Torah* as a Proper Noun and the Rehabilitation of Hierarchical Classification

The authorship of Sifra never called into question the self-evident validity of taxonomic logic. Its critique is addressed only to how the Mishnah's framers identify the origins of, and delineate, taxa. But that critique proves fundamental to the case that that authorship proposed to make. For, intending to demonstrate that *The Torah* was a proper noun, and that everything that was valid came to expression in the single, cogent statement of The Torah, the authorship at hand identified the fundamental issue. It is the debate over the way we know things. In insisting, in agreement with the framers of the Mishnah, that there are not only cases but also rules, not only species but also genera, the authorship of Sifra also made its case in behalf of the case for The Torah as a proper noun. This carries us to the theological foundation for Sifra's authorship's sustained critique of applied reason.

VII. Sifra's Theology of Revelation

In appealing to the principle, for taxonomy, of *sola Scriptura*, I mean to set forth what I conceive really to be at stake. It is the character of The Torah and what it is, in The Torah, the thing that we wish to discern. And the answer to that question requires theological, not merely literary and philosophical, reflection on our part. For I maintain that in their delineation of correct hierarchical logic, our authorship uncovered, within The Torah (hence by definition, written and oral components of The Torah alike) an adumbration of the working of the mind of God. That is because the premise of all discourse is that The Torah was written by God and dictated by God to Moses at Sinai. And that will in the end explain why our authorship for its part has entered into The Torah long passages of not merely clarification but active intrusion, making itself a

component of the interlocutorial process. To what end we know: it was
to unite the Dual Torah. But on what basis? To answer this question let
me start once again from the very beginning: the place of Sifra in its
canonical context.

VIII. The Singularity of Sifra

The authorship of Sifra stands all by itself in the canon of the
Judaism of the Dual Torah. Its reading of Scripture and uses of
Scripture, put together in the way in which Sifra presents its statement of
Scripture and the Mishnah within the context of Scripture, enjoy
virtually unique standing. True, in formal terms, Sifra falls into the
standard classification of verse-by-verse commentary to a book of the
Written Torah. In general, in making midrash compilations, redactors
would gather materials of Scripture exegesis and organize them in the
order of appearance of verses of Scripture or of the unfolding of a story
in Scripture. At the outset, people adhered to the exegetical and
redactional pattern already established by the Yerushalmi's verse by
verse or sentence by sentence reading set forth for the Mishnah. That is
to say, they followed the order of verses of a biblical book, just as the
framers of the Yerushalmi followed the order of Mishnah sentences of a
given tractate. They undertook to explain words or phrases, imposing
upon Scripture that set of values they regarded as self-evident and
factual, the values of sages' worldview and way of life. The same modes
of exegesis and organization – that is, the same logoi and topoi – that
determined the content of self-evident comment in self-evident order on
the Mishnah also dictated what would be done on Scripture. So the
original work of collecting and arranging the compilations of exegeses of
Scripture followed the patterns set in collecting and arranging exegeses
of the Mishnah. Just as the Talmud, which is Mishnah exegesis, treats
the Mishnah, so the earliest collections of scriptural exegesis treat
Scripture. My thesis, as is clear, may be expressed as a simple formula of
relationship:

Talmud	*Exegetical Collection*
Mishnah	Scripture

But while Genesis Rabbah on Genesis is to be compared to a Talmud
tractate devoted to a particular tractate of the Mishnah on that tractate,
Sifra on Leviticus bears slight resemblance to a Talmud tractate's
treatment of a tractate of the Mishnah.

While it is the fact that Genesis Rabbah is composed of units of
discourse as cogent, in their way, as the ones in the Talmud of the Land

of Israel, we should look in vain in the Talmud of the Land of Israel for a tractate that, instead of commenting on a Mishnah tractate, undertakes essentially to rewrite large tracts of it. For when we pass the, admittedly considerable, passages in which words or phrases are amplified, what do we find in Sifra? It is a series of discursive essays, such as we have now examined at length, in which profound reflection on the nature of probative logic is expressed in examples and cases. While the units of discourse of Genesis Rabbah fall into precisely the same taxonomical categories as those of the Talmud of the Land of Israel, the paramount classification of units of discourse in our document surely do not.

That is not to suggest we find in the two Talmuds no counterpart to the critique of applied reason that we have examined with such admiration. It is to state as mere fact that the two Talmuds, and certainly not the Bavli, in no way undertake the deconstruction and recomposition of a Mishnah tractate in the way in which our authorship has taken apart and then put back together in a different way the book of Leviticus. The Mishnah in the Bavli always retains its paramount and autonomous position, dictating the program of discourse throughout those passages in which the Mishnah is at issue; Scripture fills the rest. Neither Talmud, and certainly not the Bavli, proposes to rewrite the Mishnah tractate in the way in which our authorship restates, within the setting of Scripture, the language and propositions of the Mishnah; and none pretends to penetrate into the deep structure of probative logic in the way in which our authorship has accomplished its purpose.

To appreciate the singular position attained for themselves by our authorship, we do well to reflect on the contrary position defined for themselves by the framers of midrash compilations for Scripture, represented by Genesis Rabbah. Their work, in the main, was dictated for them by the program of Mishnah exegesis worked out in the two Talmuds, particularly in the first of the two. Let me explain. What the masters of biblical exegesis did in Genesis in the compilation, Genesis Rabbah, was what the masters of Mishnaic exegesis did in whatever Mishnah tractate they chose for study. It follows that the compiling of the first collection of biblical exegesis falls into the same intellectual framework as the Talmud of the Land of Israel, whether this was before, at the same time as, or in the aftermath of the composition of the Yerushalmi. Like the Yerushalmi, Genesis Rabbah emerges in two distinct literary stages: first, people worked out its components; second, people arranged them. These may well have been the same people at much the same time, but the literary work divides into separate and distinct stages. First came writing compositions expressive of complex ideas, framed in sophisticated ways. Second came selecting and arranging these units of discourse into the composition now before us.

As I said, the taxonomical framework suitable for all units of discourse of the Yerushalmi moves, without significant variation or revision, to encompass and categorize the materials of the earliest composition of scriptural exegesis, Genesis Rabbah. This fact I demonstrated in *Midrash in Context* (Philadelphia, 1984; second printing: Atlanta, 1988: Scholars Press for Brown Judaic Studies).

Let me make this more concrete. The framer of an exegetical unit of discourse in the Yerushalmi ordinarily would do one of two things: first, a phrase-by-phrase exegesis of the Mishnah; second, amplification of the meaning of a passage of the Mishnah. So a Talmudic sage confronting the Mishnah had the choice of explaining the meaning of a particular passage or expanding upon the meaning, or the overall theme, of a particular passage. The same was so for scriptural verses. True, in dealing with Scripture a sage might systematically interpret one thing in terms of something else, a verse of Scripture in light of an autonomous set of considerations not explicit in Scripture but (in his mind) absolutely critical to its full meaning. But that is still not much more than the exegesis of the passage at hand for a given purpose, established a priori. That is an exercise fully familiar to the framers of the units of discourse of the Talmud in their confrontation with the Mishnah.

To move on to the taxonomical categories for a scriptural book, these are four, of which the first two are closely related and the fourth of slight consequence. The first category encompasses close exegesis of Scripture, by which I mean a word-for-word or phrase-by-phrase interpretation of a passage. In such an activity, the framer of a discrete composition will wish to read and explain a verse or a few words of a verse of the Scripture at hand, pure and simple. This is a commonplace in Sifra as well. The second category, no less exegetical than the first, is made up of units of discourse in which the components of the verse are treated as part of a larger statement of meaning rather than as a set of individual phrases, stichs requiring attention one by one. Accordingly, in this taxon we deal with wide-ranging discourse about the meaning of a particular passage, hence an effort to amplify what is said in a verse. I cannot find a dozen instances of this kind of discourse in Sifra.

Nor is there a parallel in Sifra to the useful third taxon of the other midrash compilations, which encompasses units of discourse in which the theme of a particular passage defines a very wide-ranging exercise. In this discussion the cited passage itself is unimportant. It is the theme that is definitive. Accordingly, in this third type we take up a unit of discourse in which the composer of the passage wishes to expand on a particular problem, (merely) illustrated in the cited passage. The problem, rather than the cited passage, defines the limits and direction of discourse. The passage at hand falls away, having provided a mere pretext for the real point of concern. The fourth and final taxon, also deriving from the Yerushalmi, takes in units of discourse shaped around a given topic but not intended to constitute cogent and tightly framed discourse on said topic. These units of discourse then constitute topical anthologies rather than carefully composed essays. In place of these last three taxa, as we now recognize full well, comes the preoccupation with the Mishnah and the problem of the Mishnah.

The taxonomic structure just now described derives from the categories inductively discovered for the Yerushalmi, and it serves for other midrash compilations, but not for Sifra. The upshot is that types of units of discourse that we find in the Yerushalmi and the ones that comprise Genesis Rabbah fall into precisely the same categories and only into those categories. Taxonomically, all that changes from Genesis Rabbah and the compilations like it to the Yerushalmi (or vice versa) is the document subjected to exegesis (as well, of course, as what is said about it). Because the modes of thought and discourse turn out to exhibit precisely the same definitive traits and only those traits, they sustain a remarkably monothetic taxonomy. Third, that is why I propose the simple equation: The Yerushalmi is to the Mishnah as compilations of exegesis are to Scripture. But none of this is the case for Sifra.

IX. The Parsimonious Proper Noun and the Capacious Common Noun

We have concentrated upon Sifra's authorship's brilliant critique of applied reason. Its rehabilitation of the available system of reason was accomplished in such a way as to reopen the entire question of the definition of the Torah. By returning to Scripture as the source for taxa, by appealing to Scripture, and Scripture alone, as the criterion for like and unlike, and by then restating the whole of Scripture, for the book of Leviticus, to encompass words not in the original, Written Torah but only in the other, Oral Torah, that authorship exhibited remarkable imagination. Certainly, by any intellectual criterion, their solution to the problem of the Mishnah exhibited the wit and daring that merely laying things out side by side, exegesis of Scripture, exegesis of the Mishnah, such as had been done in the Bavli, scarcely adumbrated.

Two solutions to the problem of the Mishnah competed, at least in logic and intellect. A brief review at the end places into context the conclusion of the study as a whole. The one transformed the word *torah* into a common noun, denoting many things, above all, status and classification. A teaching, book, or person might enter the status of *torah* or the classification of *torah*. That left ample space for actions, persons, books, and a broad range of categories of entities, so that *torah* might serve as an adjective as much as a common noun, for example, a Torah teaching, a Torah community, and the like. While, therefore, the Torah remained the scroll that contained the Pentateuch, a variety of other meanings broadened the sense of *torah*. In consequence, from the Mishnah onward, the canon of Judaism called *torah*. or *the Torah* found ample space for endless candidates for inclusion. The other solution preserved the limited sense of the word *torah*, referring always and only to The Torah, that is to say, the Pentateuch. But then this other approach reread The Torah, the Written Torah, and found space for a variety of fresh candidates for inclusion. This was accomplished through a vast restatement of The Torah, a new and extraordinarily widened statement of what was encompassed within the Torah.

X. How the Torah Leads Us into the Mind of God

It is one thing to absorb the Torah, oral and written, into a single sustained and systematic statement, as did the authors of the Talmud of Babylonia. But it is quite another to join in the processes of thought, the right way of thinking, that sustain the Torah. The authorship of Sifra proposed to regain access to the modes of thought that guided the formation of the Torah, oral and written alike: comparison and contrast in this way, not in that, identification of categories in one manner, not in another. Since those were the modes of thought that, in our authorship's conception, dictated the structure of intellect upon which the Torah, the united Torah, rested, a simple conclusion is the sole possible one. Now to answer the question of the basis on which our authorship represented itself as participants in, and interlocutors of, The Torah, such that they were prepared to re-present, that is to say, simply rewrite (and therefore, themselves write) The Torah.

In their analysis of the deepest structures of intellect of the Torah, the authorship of Sifra supposed to enter into the mind of God, showing how God's mind worked when God formed the Torah, written and oral alike. And there, in the intellect of God, in their judgment humanity gained access to the only means of uniting the Torah, because that is where the Torah originated. But in discerning how God's mind worked, the intellectuals who created Sifra claimed for themselves a place in that very process of thought that had given birth to The Torah. Our authorship could rewrite the Torah because, knowing how The Torah originally was written, they, too, could write (though not reveal) The Torah.

Epilogue

Can Humanity Forget What It Knows?

Civilization hangs suspended, from generation to generation, by the gossamer strand of memory. If only one cohort of mothers and fathers fails to convey to its children what it has learned from its parents, then the great chain of learning and wisdom snaps. If the guardians of human knowledge stumble only one time, in their fall collapses the entire edifice of knowledge and understanding. More important, therefore, than finding new things is sifting and refining the received truths. And the generation that will go down through time bearing the burden of disgrace is not the one that has said nothing new – for not much new marks the mind of any age – but the one that has not said what is true. These self-evident truths concerning the continuity of civilization pertain not alone to wisdom, such as philosophy and religion preserve. They address much more concrete matters than the wise conduct of affairs. There are things that we know because of the hard work of people who have come before, knowledge that we have on account of other peoples' trial and error. And that is knowledge that also hangs in the balance from age to age, and that is knowledge that we can and do forget, with awful consequences for those who will come after us, to whom we for our part are answerable.

The simple fact is that we either remember or recapitulate the work of finding out – one or the other. And now, with 5,000 years of recorded science and philosophy, mathematics, history and social science, literature and music and art, if we lose it all, we probably shall never regain what is gone. It would be too much work, require resources of time and intellect not likely to come to hand. Lest my meaning be lost in abstraction, let me give a single concrete case. When the turret of the battleship Iowa blew up, people could not repair it. The reason is that the materials and technological know-how to repair the guns, available when the ship was built in World War II, were lost beyond recovery.

217

That is what I mean when I say civilization hangs suspended by fragile strands indeed. So too, when people decided to resume construction of the Cathedral of St. John the Divine in New York City, people found out that only a few stone masons were left in the world who could work the giant blocks from which a cathedral is built; they could train young apprentices, or the work would not be done. Languages, too, have come and gone; someone once told me of meeting the last person in the world who spoke Cornish as a native language, and linguists make haste to preserve what is nearly going to be lost as an example of the potentialities of intelligible speech.

I owe this point to a biologist at Rutgers University, David Ehrenfeld, writing in *Orion* (Autumn, 1989, pp. 5-7), who argues that "loss of knowledge and skills is now a big problem in our universities." That is a problem, he maintains, not in the humanities, which we know are dying, but in the natural sciences. His case in point is one that surprised me. He says, "We are on the verge of losing our ability to tell one plant or animal from another and of forgetting how the known species interact among themselves and with their environments." This is because subjects fall out of the curriculum, or are taught piecemeal by people on the periphery of the university. He says, for example, "Classification of Higher Plants," "Marine Invertebrates," "Ornithology," "Mammalogy," "Cryptograms" (ferns and mosses), "Biogeography," "Comparative Physiology" – "you may find some of them in the catalogue, but too often with the notation along side, 'not offered....'" Ehrenfeld explains: "The features that distinguish lizards from snakes from crocodilians from turtles...aren't any less accepted or valid than they were twenty-five years ago, nor are they easier than they used to be to learn on your own from books without hands-on laboratory instruction." But people do not work on those fields. Ehrenfeld further explains why the question is an urgent one. He tells the following story:

> One morning last April, at eight o'clock, my phone rang. It was a former student of mine who is now a research endocrinologist at a major teaching hospital in Houston. She had an odd question: at what point in animal evolution was the hemoglobin molecule first adopted for use specifically as an oxygen carrier? It was an essential piece of information for medical research she was planning.

The information the student wanted was in an elementary "introduction to comparative biochemistry." When Ehrenfeld asked colleagues who was working on this sort of thing, he found out, nobody. The graduate students had never even heard of the field of comparative biochemistry.

Now here we have a very concrete case of the loss of knowledge once possessed. Ehrenfeld comments: "not outdated, not superseded, not scientifically or politically controversial, not even merely frivolous: a whole continent of important human knowledge gone." It was not dead, it lived only in books, which no one read or understood or could use in the quest for knowledge. Ehrenfeld draws from this story conclusions that need not detain us. In his view the loss of comparative biochemistry is because of the flow of funds into the wrong hands, into the hands of people who are not "capable of transmitting our assembled knowledge of the natural world to the next generation." So he says, "I fear for conservation when there is no one left in our places of learning who can tell one moth from another, no one who knows the habits of hornbills, no one to puzzle over the diversity of hawthorns."

If we now take the case as exemplary, we may ask ourselves, where, in society, do we assign the task of holding on to what we know and making sure the next generation gains access to that? The stakes are too high for the answer to invoke the episodic and the anecdotal: "here am I, send me." The accident of individuals finds its match in the uncertainty of books; putting whatever is worth knowing into books, encyclopaedias for example, will not serve, since mere information does not inform, and facts without explanation of what they mean and how they fit together do not bear meaning or serve a purpose. In age succeeding age, in some few places, the mind of humanity in the past is recreated, not preserved inert but actively replicated, reenacted as a model for the mind of humanity to come. I speak of course of schools as those few places, of teachers as the actors out of knowledge in intellectually replicable form. For to preserve what we know we must repeat the processes of discovery, since the only mode of really learning is our own discovery, which permits us not merely to know things, but to understand something. All the facts in the world about moths and hornbills and hawthorns, left uninterpreted, will not yield comparative biochemistry.

As it happens, I have spent my life working on a document that composed so as to present, within a few volumes, the life and structure, the way of life and world view and social theory, of an entire world of humanity: the Jewish people. A few remarkable intellectuals undertook to write a book that would serve as not a mere source of information but as a handbook of civilization: how to form society, what society had to know to do its work, all of useful knowledge so formed as to yield meaning and order and coherence: the deep structure of a social being. To write a book to do that, they worked out not an encyclopaedia of information but a guide book for a journey of mind, of intellect: this is how to think, this is what to think, this is why to think. They made certain, therefore, that what they knew would be known by coming generations, not because the institutions would endure, nor because the politics would accord to their doctrines priority of place. Indeed, the writers of this document would have found surprising Professor Ehrenfeld's certainty that problems are to be solved by putting money in the right hands, or keeping it out of the wrong ones.

What they did was two things. First, they wrote a book that could be sung. Second, they wrote notes to the music, so that anyone could sing the song. They did not spell out everything, rather, they gave signals of how, if you wanted to spell things out, you could on your own do so: don't ask, discover. So they opened the doors of learning to make place for all to come, learning serving then as an active verb, with discovery its synonym. These notes – signals of how a moving argument would be reconstructed, how reason might be recapitulated – were few, perhaps not the eight notes of our octave, but not an infinite repertoire of replicable sounds either. But the medium – notes to the music – is only secondary. Their primary insight into how civilization as they proposed to frame it should be shaped lay in another matter altogether. It had to do with their insistence upon the urgency of clear and vigorous and rigorous thought, the priority of purpose to argument, the demand for ultimate seriousness about things to be critically examined. Through practical reasoning and applied logic, they formed the chains to link mind to mind, past to future, through a process that anyone could enter – and no one, once in, would leave.

I said they wrote a book that could be sung. I mean that both literally, in that, their writing was a document meant to be said out loud, not read silently; meant to be studied in community through debate, not meditated upon privately and personally; writing that was, in the old and classic sense, political – public, shared, subject to coercion, if in the form of reason rather than naked power to be sure. But I mean that in another sense as well. The great author, James Baldwin, said in a short story, every song begins in a cry. So when I say they wrote a book that could be sung, I meant to invoke metaphor of a piece of writing that begins not with the words and the music, but in the guts, a piece of writing that is thought before thinking, insight before application and explication, attitude and emotion prior to their reformulation in propositions formed of words. I speak of revelation, such as most of us have known and of which all of us have heard: the unearned insight, the unanticipated moment of understanding. That is what I mean by a book that could be sung, of truth in a form of such art that whoever hears will see and feel, know in a knowledge that is defining.

So if it is possible to forget what we have learned, leaving for a coming generation the task of recapitulating processes of discovery and interpretation, it also is possible to imagine and even identify the means by which, as a matter of fact, humanity has defended itself from the loss of what it already has in hand. If I use the Talmud, on which I work, as a case in point, others may well identify other appropriate cases. I think of such fields as music and mathematics, philosophy and its offspring in the social sciences, and a variety of the natural sciences as well, as fields of learning that link us to the accumulated treasures of important knowledge and sustaining truth. What they have in common is rules of right thought, a heritage of conventions to be replicated, retested, and realized from age to age, a process of testing and reevaluation, an endless openness to experiment, whether in the laboratory or in thought. Indeed, much that we in universities identify as useful and important knowledge qualifies. For as a matter of fact, so far as the sum of human knowledge is concerned, either we in universities will convey it to the coming generation, or it will be lost for all time.

It is the simple fact that nearly everything that we teach in universities comes to us from somewhere else, and most of it comes to us from generations of intellects long ago. Whether philosophy or mathematics or music, whether how we regain the past in history, or how we interpret the facts of the natural world, the treasure and storehouse of human knowledge are realized, today, in the here and now, in universities – or those treasures are lost, much as comparative biochemistry formed a threatened species of learning when people lost access to what that field had to tell them. So the task of universities, if not unique then at least distinctive among all of the institutions that preserve and hand on past to future, is to preserve civilization and afford access to civilization. Ours is the task of remembering, recapitulating, reenacting. Ours is the task of reminding, in a very odd sense of the word, that is, to regain mind. We form the links in the great chain of learning, and if we prove strong to the task, another generation will know what we do, but if we prove weak, the work of many generations past will be lost, and many generations to come will be the losers. The stakes in universities and what they do therefore are not trivial; we do more than serve, carry out a more than transient or merely useful task. We preserve, but in a very special way: we show the generation to come the how of knowledge, not merely the what; we show in our time what humanity has done over all time to make sense of the world.

Lest these observations on the nature of knowledge, the danger of forgetting what we know, appear mere commonplaces, let me point out alternative views. For I set forth a profoundly conservative theory of universities and their tasks, based on a deeply conservative premise on the character of civilization and society. I do maintain that it is more difficult to keep what we have than to add to what we know. I very much take to heart Professor Ehrenfeld's warning that, if the few old men who know how to work the giant blocks of stone die without heirs, we shall no longer know how to build cathedrals, and, in time to come, when we see them, we shall not even know what they are, the way, when we see the monstrous statues on Easter Island, we do not know what they are. Then the failure of civilization, the forgetting what we know, looms large in my mind: we can lose what we have but get nothing better. Society defines what is at stake, and risking its slender goods for the main chance threatens utter chaos: "gone, not outdated, not superseded, not even controversial, not frivolous: a whole continent of important human knowledge gone"! Indeed, so far as civilization finds nourishment in knowledge and understanding – and I cannot define civilization without knowledge and understanding – there can be no greater catastrophe than that loss of a continent of human knowledge; that clod that washes out to sea is all the ground we ever had on which to make sense of something.

What, then, we must ask ourselves, does the fact that humanity indeed can forget what it now knows dictate for public policy in the here and now? The stakes having been defined in the way I have, the upshot is not to be gainsaid.

First, our principal task in universities must be the work of rigorous teaching. At stake in our classroom is the coming generation and its capacity to know and make sense of things. Therefore, our main effort focuses upon the how of learning, by which I mean, upon how our students grasp what we wish to tell them, on the processes by which we turn information into useful knowledge, useful knowledge into understanding – all through (re)discovery, the recreation of intellect in age succeeding age.

The corollary, second, is that the creation of new knowledge is less important than the recapitulation of received knowledge. Most professors most of the time in most universities know little about what it means to create new knowledge. As a matter of fact, it is estimated that two-thirds of all professors have published scarcely a line; of those who publish books, most publish one, few more than one, which means the discovery of new knowledge in the responsible form of a statement for the criticism of others ends with the dissertation; and, so I hear, 95 percent of all scholarly books come from perhaps 5 percent of the scholars. What this means is that most professors most of the time in most universities find themselves expected to do what few of them have ever done, and few still have done more than once. We have therefore to reconsider the entire structure of higher education, and our task is to reframe our work in such a way that the work people really do – and want to do and often do supremely well – is valued, and that that work is done. Most professors should teach more than they now do; but they also should study more than they now do in order to teach what they themselves have made their own.

Third, the recapitulation of received knowledge is not the same thing as the mere repetition of things people think they know, or have heard from others assumed to know what they are talking about. Teaching is now defined in some few, conventional ways. For example, the teacher talks, the students listen. The teacher is the authority, the students inert and passive respondents thereto. Or opinions are exchanged, so that no one is authority, and there is no task but to say what one thinks. For another example, students listen to professors but not to one another, and professors listen to no one but themselves. For a third example, writing lots of things down on paper is taken to demonstrate knowledge and understanding. But what if – what if teaching is understood in other terms altogether, as engagement in a shared task of learning and understanding and explanation? What if teaching is a form of leading, specifically, of leading by example – follow me! That is, to be sure, a risk-laden mode of teaching, and it is a way of teaching that fails much more often than it succeeds. For it makes the teacher into the model – the example, rather than the authority, and models or examples are there to be examined and criticized. And that mode of teaching makes the classroom into a laboratory in which mental experiments are undertaken. Since, in this reading of the act of teaching, the professors turns out to be the guinea pig, my call is for us to play a not very inviting role. But it is an honest one, and it is one that serves.

Fourth and last, if as I claim our task is to echo the natural sounds of knowledge which are knowledge, then some sounds will resonate, others not. Today, of course, we make a cacophony of noise; most of what we teach is mere facts, about this and that, and no theory instructs us on what takes precedence, and why some facts are trivial or merely particular. For example, entire areas of learning even now turn out to be made up of an endless series of cases, this, that and the other thing, yielding no theory, generated by no theory: pointless information, or cases that yield no truth to speak of. One such field is ethics; you can study journalistic ethics, medical ethics, legal ethics, you can even raise money for professorships in all of these subjects. And you can make yourself into an expert on some field of ethics, medical ethics having attracted more than its share of failed careerists and bright-eyed opportunists than any other field of learning in the 1980s, much the counterpart of social science in the 1950s, or computer science in the 1970s. But these entrepreneurs of learning, trained in one thing so doctors of everything, make things up as they go along, for what sounds right is right; there is no theory of the thing they study, because there is no principled inquiry into the foundations of analysis and criticism. Yet we in the West have inherited a tradition of philosophical ethics that comes to us from the Greeks and a tradition of theological ethics that comes to us from ancient Israel through Christianity and Judaism; we have those theories, those principles of decision making, that have laid the foundations for coherent thinking about a cogent subject. When a field can give only examples and cases, its casuistry attests to its intellectual bankruptcy. The field of medical ethics as currently practiced exemplifies better than any other presently current why when civilization perishes, charlatans prosper. But the casuistry serves because philosophy is not learned, and, reinventing the wheel, the ethicists in the hospitals unwittingly teach a dreadful lesson indeed: what it means to lose what you've got.

So yes, humanity can forget what it knows, and that is so in biology and philosophy, and the costs are there to see at Easter Island, or in the shelves of books we no longer can read but need to read, and in the areas of learning that are true and useful but no longer accessible. The task is not new knowledge but the reconsideration of knowledge. When we succeed – and we in universities are the only one who can do the work – we shall hold on to what we have received, because we shall have made it our own. And that is what I conceive to be the principal work of any generation: to make what has come to us as a gift into something that is our own, that is, something that we, too, can use; in the case of learning, I mean, to make learning our own in such a way that we, too, can learn.

Index

South Florida Studies in the History of Judaism

DATE DUE

HIGHSMITH 45-220